TREATING
THE MENTALLY ILL
From Colonial Times to the Present

TREATING
THE MENTALLY ILL

From Colonial Times to the Present

Leland V. Bell

PRAEGER

PRAEGER SPECIAL STUDIES • PRAEGER SCIENTIFIC

Library of Congress Cataloging in Publication Data

Bell, Leland V
   Treating the mentally ill.

   Bibliography: p.
   Includes index.
   1. Mentally ill--Care and treatment--United
States--History. I. Title.
RC443.B42   362.2'0973   80-168

ISBN 0-03-055751-8

Published in 1980 by Praeger Publishers
CBS Educational and Professional Publishing
A Division of CBS, Inc.
521 Fifth Avenue, New York, New York 10017 U.S.A.

© 1980 by Praeger Publishers

0123456789   038   987654321

Printed in the United States of America

for Eric and Rachel

ACKNOWLEDGMENTS

This book is an account of the main themes of American mental health care since colonial times. It is about treating the mentally ill and what people have thought about that treatment. Above all, it is a book written for persons interested in a historical orientation to the problems connected with the delivery of psychiatric care.

In the course of my research, I have been grateful to several individuals. The librarians and the staffs of the Ohio State University Health Sciences Library, Columbus, and the University of Michigan Medical Center Library, Ann Arbor, gave prompt attention to my requests for information and materials. I received courteous assistance from the staff of the Hallie Q. Brown Library, Central State University, Wilberforce, Ohio.

In many ways I am indebted to Chester R. Burns, M.D., Ph.D., of the Institute for the Medical Humanities, University of Texas Medical Branch, Galveston, Texas. While a visiting professor at the Institute, I engaged in research at the Moody Medical Library on the UTMB campus. This is a delightful place, overlooking the Gulf of Mexico. It has a number of energetic reference librarians, a stimulating history of medicine staff, a rare book room, and a special collection of books related to psychiatric history.

My gratitude goes also to Dr. John C. Burnham, Professor of History, Ohio State University, who took time from a very busy schedule to read the entire manuscript. His valuable suggestions and sharp criticisms helped me to improve the book.

The work of Sarah McCullough of Yellow Springs contributed to the clarity of the manuscript.

Finally, my wife, Evelyn, offered helpful advice and criticism.

L.V.B.
Yellow Springs, Ohio

CONTENTS

INTRODUCTION

A historical probe into the multi-faceted field of mental health care reveals that dilemmas endure and persistent problems defy resolution. One major difficulty rests with the nature of the subject matter, in that the terms and concepts used in mental health work lack clarity and cannot be precisely defined. Historically, mental illness has received various labels. In the eighteenth century the word "lunacy" prevailed. For example, in the 1750s Benjamin Franklin, in a petition calling for the founding of a general hospital in Philadelphia, wrote of the need to provide accommodations for "lunaticks." Throughout the nineteenth century the terms "insanity" and "madness" were in vogue. While the label "mental illness" has persisted in the twentieth century, many professional and lay persons are uncomfortable with it. Today "mental health," a term of many connotations, is popular. Some professionals use it as a slogan to win political and public support for their programs and activities. For others it may represent an all-encompassing concept that embraces everything connected with the care and treatment of the mentally disturbed. Mental health is often equated with preventive psychiatry, or it may function as a euphemism for mental illness because it avoids unpleasant associations with the mentally disordered. Mental health may also relate to the American dream of health and happiness; it stands as a positive middle-class goal, a quest for the good life.

If the changing terms used for designating mental illness have lacked precision, the concept behind the terminology has broadened with time. In the eighteenth century a mentally disturbed person suffered from either mania—a condition characterized by erratic, violent behavior—or melancholia—a state of general withdrawal or depression. The nineteenth century witnessed an increase in the types of mental disorders, with such categories as monomania (paranoia) and dementia praecox (schizophrenia) becoming familiar psychiatric entities. This classification process continued unabated until recent times. An increasing number of mental disturbances have been identified, making it possible for a mentally ill person today to receive a specific label derived from one of the manuals of psychiatric disorders published by the American Psychiatric Association. The current debate over the meaning of mental illness, notably whether it falls within the domain of medicine, has retarded this terminological proliferation. Indeed, there has been a slight rollback that has seen such behavioral labels as "homosexuality" and "alcoholism," formerly identified as deviant conduct, removed from the list. In short, the terms and concepts of mental illness have remained vague. The mental illnesses of the past differ from those of the present, and will take still other forms in the future. What comes into focus here is the ever-changing fuzzy lines between the normal and the abnormal, or sanity and insanity.

An equally baffling and perplexing problem has been the etiology of mental illness. The root causes of insanity remain elusive, and have included an array of factors ranging from immorality to social stress. In early America, for example, people equated madness with sinful behavior, insisting that mental derangement sprang naturally from a life-style of debauchery, sexual excesses, and criminal activity. Throughout the nineteenth century many accepted a hereditarian assumption and believed that a person's insanity originated with a mad relative or ancestor. An influential segment of psychiatry has always maintained a somatic orientation, holding to the conviction that mental illness has a concrete biological basis related to genetics, to a physical defect, or to a chemical or hormonal imbalance. Under the impact of Freudian theory, the critical events of childhood became a major focus of twentieth-century etiological studies. It was assumed that a series of traumas occurring early in life established patterns of behavior that produced a damaged adult personality. In recent years much research has delved into the "social causes" of mental illness. Here, evidence has been sought to demonstrate a relationship between mental disorder and such variables as culture, economic position, social alienation, rural-urban residence, and family life. While this interest and research have produced etiological insights, the quest for sound knowledge persists. The multitudinous and multifaceted experiences of life that undermine or sustain an individual's well-being may defy synthesis. Mental illness may be ubiquitous, a given of biology, sociology, or fate. One fact has not changed—the social rejection of the mentally ill. While the term, concept, and causes of mental illness have remained obscure, society has consistently scorned, pitied, and quarantined the insane. No group of persons since the lepers has been more loathed and feared than the mad, and their enforced isolation and ostracism from the community has rested ultimately upon a deep contempt for them. Some of this disdain is conveyed in the labels popularly assigned to a mentally disturbed person: "batty," "nuts," "cracked," "looney," and "out of his mind"; has "lost his marbles" or "flipped-out." These labels represent jeers that spurn, humiliate, and stigmatize an individual. The mentally ill person has been viewed as subhuman, a maniac capable of committing despicable crimes.

This image has been sustained in American literature. An example is the late eighteenth-century Gothic novel, *Wieland, or the Transformation*, by Charles Brockden Brown, in which insane behavior is clearly identified. A mad person succumbs to uncontrollable passions; he groans and screams and is prone to violence and crime. The protagonist of *Wieland* kills his wife and children. The self-destructive person who turns inward and inflicts violence upon himself or herself is still another form of the literary and popular image of the mentally ill. The continually rising suicide rate has given credence to this view, and it has been dramatized and romanticized by the suicides of notable poets and writers, including John Berryman and Sylvia Plath.

This image of the mad person is inaccurate and distorted. Most of the mentally ill do not exhibit violent behavior. They are helpless individuals who remain psychologically disoriented and incapable of making sound, rational judgments, a condition that elicits scorn from normal people. Society values the resourceful and self-reliant person, and ranks dependency next to cowardice as one of the undesirable human qualities. There can be no sympathy for persons who seem bereft of reason and incapable of either fending or fighting for themselves. Relatives or friends of the mentally ill share these attitudes and values, and when confronted with an insane family member, they are overwehelmed with feelings of shame and guilt. With little solace or help coming from those closest to them, the mentally ill are often left, lonely and loveless, to the care of strangers at specially designated places that are psychologically and physically removed from society. This has been the historical reality for the mentally disturbed: confinement over a long period of time in an institution, in a communal setting with other mentally troubled and tortured persons.

The mental institution, the central fact in the history of American mental health care, has been given such derisive labels as "madhouse," "nuthouse," "looney bin," "snake pit," and "funny farm." Each carries a negative connotation, signifying an undesirable place separate from the wider society. The labels reflect the continuing popular condemnation of the mental hospital, an institution that has been subjected to more maligning attacks than any other public facility. In many instances where places became custodial warehouses, the criticism has been justified. But a blanket censure of all mental institutions distorts reality. Many selfless individuals have worked for institutional change. Most prominent were the eighteenth-century Quaker, William Tuke; the nineteenth-century reformer Dorothea Dix; and the twentieth-century founder of the mental hygiene movement, Clifford Beers. Each fought to better the conditions of the mentally ill and to overcome community inertia, scorn, and hostility toward the insane. While humanitarians have sought change, societal and professional pressures for reform and experimentation have forced mental institutions to make basic alterations, a development reflected in the changing institutional names and ideologies since the early nineteenth century. The public asylum movement gathered momentum in the 1830s, a time that saw antislavery agitation, the building of utopian communities, and movements for improving prisons and public education. The asylum concept signified a retreat to a peaceful, rural setting where a person could find rest, receive guidance, and engage in therapeutic recreational and occupational activities designed to facilitate recovery and return to normal life.

Around 1900 the hospital ideal gained prominence, stressing a scientific, clinical approach to treatment and marking a closer identification of psychiatric care with the field of medicine. This trend was accompanied by the growing professional interest in psychotherapy and the emergence of the mental hygiene movement. Both developments coincided with Progressive reform efforts to make governments more responsive to the popular will and to curb huge concentrations of economic power. After the mid-twentieth century the hospital ideal was supplanted by the mental health center, which sought community involvement with the mentally ill. Long-term institutionalization was avoided, and the participation of professionals and lay persons of many persuasions was encouraged in a drive to treat patients in the community. Mental health centers were launched in the 1960s during the Kennedy-Johnson era, a period that witnessed intense civil rights activity and interest in participatory democracy. In short, mental health care has been revitalized by pressures from the community and the mental health professions.

Awareness of historical trends can be useful in several ways. The patterns of the past can help to clarify contemporary issues and to suggest options for the future. How the mental hospital evolved through time has a vital bearing on present dilemmas of institutional psychiatry. Today a major controversy deals with the feasibility of closing mental hospitals, an issue illuminated by a knowledge of the heavy, crippling burdens carried by the state mental institution. The future, too, relates to the past. Historical experiences suggest directions and prospects, notably in the ares of therapy and the delivery of mental health care. An understanding of the historical settings in which the mentally ill have received the best care and treatment is important for developing future mental policies.

Historical knowledge can also be useful in countering the popular assumption of progress found in contemporary mental health circles. Reflected in professional journals and administrative reports, this view regards the past as an era of unsophisticated practices and mistaken therapeutics, and identifies the present as an enlightened age that has produced humane treatments based on scientific principles. Not only does this perspective ignore the diversity, complexity, and irony of history; it also diminishes the important contributions of previous mental health workers. A sensitivity to their accomplishments and failures can link the present with the past and emphasize the roots of contemporary practices.

TREATING
THE MENTALLY ILL

From Colonial Times to the Present

1
FROM DEMONOLOGY
TO MORAL TREATMENT

In seventeenth-century America the mentally ill received scant attention. The raw frontier life in the thin line of settlements stretching along the Atlantic coast gave colonists little time or opportunity to cope with the problems of society's unfortunates. Preoccupied with the basic issues of subsistence, people remained indifferent to irregular behavior unless it posed a threat to public order. Indeed, colonists equated insanity with disruptive, violent, and deviant conduct, and assumed that it was caused by either demonological possession or moral turpitude. Religious authorities prompted the view that erratic behavior signified a person's compact with diabolical, supernatural forces by arguing that a possessed individual acted wildly, had unusual strength, made animal noises, and often spoke a language that had not been learned. Cotton Mather, the controversial Puritan clergyman and author who saw the mentally ill as agents of Satan, commented that the possessed had "melancholy and spirtual delusions" and were "taken with very strange fits." His publications, *Memorable Providences Relating to Witchcraft* and *Possessions and Wonders of the Invisible World*, elaborated on satanic possession. He and others deemed madness God's punishment for moral corruption. In his unpublished medicoreligious study, *The Angel of Bethesda*, Mather combined religious concepts with medicine and identified sin with "a sickness of the mind."

The connection between sin and insanity became a potent belief in colonial America, much stronger and more widespread than the assumption of the devil's power to influence human behavior. Colonists took religion seriously and adhered to a strict moral code. Ministers extolled their congregations to pursue virtuous lives; they warned that God avenged the practice of immorality; He brought "frightful diseases" and an early death. Although presumably "distem-

1

pered in the head," the deviant—a damnable sinner—was a wicked, inferior subhuman who had lost all rights and privileges. Sinful behavior naturally demanded retribution, and colonists meted out harsh punishments to the transgressor. Cruel treatment, including whippings and beatings, was believed necessary to purge the afflicted of sin and terrorize him or her back to sanity.

The link that colonists made between insanity and immorality set a pattern for identifying the mentally ill in America. Members of any society have always found it easy to mark its outcasts as mentally deranged. Seventeenth-century Americans placed the morally deviant in this category. Social and intellectual nonconformists, the aged, the poor, and minorities have, in like manner, felt not only the pain of ostracism but also the brunt of false charges regarding their sanity.

Equally fundamental to the American efforts to look after the insane has been the differing qualities of care given to the mentally ill of different socioeconomic classes. The affluent patient received the best treatment, often on an individualized basis and with refined techniques; the poorer patient received custodial care combined with frequently violent treatment. The relationship between therapy and a person's position in society developed most sharply in the early nineteenth century, when a system known as moral treatment was introduced in American mental institutions. But in the seventeenth century the distinction was blurred by the prevailing negative attitudes toward insanity and the crude, exotic remedies applied to cure it. The upper- and middle-class sick found relief within the family. Here the afflicted individual may have received solace from relatives and a family physician. The existing moral condemnation of the mentally ill may have encouraged some affluent households, sensitive to community ridicule, to hide the disturbed family member in the cellar or in the attic, chained to a bed or a post. If the family milieu itself contributed to a person's disorder, home care became a private hell.

A typical physician attending the insane in seventeenth-century America administered an assortment of concoctions made from such ingredients as human saliva and perspiration, earthworms, powdered dog lice, or crab eyes. Special importance was attributed to an herb called Saint-John's-wort, which was blessed, wrapped in paper, and inhaled to ward off attacks from the devil. Astrological lore found expression in prescriptions: one physician instructed that bloodletting and blistering be timed with phases of the moon; another called for boiling live toads in March and then pulverizing them into powder, a delicacy credited with preventing and curing all kinds of diseases. From his medical treatises a doctor might prescribe ancient and medieval remedies. Hellebore, an herb used by the ancient Greeks to cure mental disorders, was specified as being "good for mad and furious men." A preparation known as "spirit of skull" involved mixing wine with moss taken from the skull of an unburied man who had met a violent death. Hot human blood, as well as pulverized human hearts or brains, presumably helped to control "fits." While these prescriptions represented the best known "cures," the nauseating quality of the mixtures suggests that the remedy rather than the illness was the more formidable obstacle to recovery. Vomiting may actually have been helpful, and certainly had powerful psychological effects. In any event, the "cures" reflect the state of medical knowledge in colonial America, a time when physicians and laymen read and used the same medical recipe books. Most doctors remained preoccupied with common maladies and epidemics.

The care of the indigent insane was covered by informal local arrangements, a custom derived from the Elizabethan Poor Law of 1601, which made each town responsible for its needy. A typical colonial New England statute might be entitled "An Act for the Relief of Idiots and Distracted Persons," and it would identify the community as the legal and responsible guardian of the mentally disturbed individual. The insane were accepted as community wards because of their inability to sustain themselves rather than because of their disordered mental state. Occasionally a village shirked this duty. Under the cover of night, officials eager to rid themselves of a community burden would kidnap and transport a homeless victim to another village. At other times these harmless individuals, half-naked and ill-fed, were permitted to drift from place to place, subject to the taunts and abuse of local thugs. Strangers suspected of becoming public charges were ostracized and "warned out" of town, a harsh practice mercilessly applied to pregnant women and the sick as well as to the mentally disturbed. The physically able insane were often auctioned, like slaves, to persons who would use their labor in return for caring for them. The object of this custom was to dispose of public wards at nominal cost to the community. Considered a danger or a nuisance to public order, violent cases were sometimes placed in cages, kennels, or blockhouses, where they were chained and whipped. In providing relief, colonial towns made no distinction among the mentally ill, criminals, orphans, the sick, the aged, the physically maimed, and the unemployed. These undifferentiated dependents were thrown together in jails and workhouses. Here they remained in dingy cells, attics, or cellars, treated with scorn and indifference, and allowed to vegetate and suffer alone. This condition persisted throughout the eighteenth century and well into the nineteenth century. No medical treatment was involved or available; care was strictly custodial. The pauper insane were particularly unfortunate, lacking both family and friends.

While this general condition of indigent groups demonstrated the inhumanity and the insensitivity of the wider society toward the poor, the situation was not unique to colonial America. The practice today of discharging mental patients, who have no social nor financial means, into the community, where they must reside in dismal slum hotels, can hardly be viewed as an enlightened policy. The history of mental health care is not a success story or a story of progress; it does not follow a straight-line development from grim, torture-like activities of early times to benign, enlightened practices of the present. Indeed, the harsh realities of colonial life dictated a harsh policy toward indigent groups. Colonists were subject to Indian attacks, and they faced such natural calamities as famine and epidemics. Idleness and vagrancy were viewed with disdain. Cooperative group effort sustained a community, and any form of dependency became a burden, an obstacle that threatened community survival. Social dependents thus were not only morally reprehensible, but also required controls and restrictions so that they could not undermine the cohesive fabric of society.

By the mid-eighteenth century the confinement of mentally disordered persons in a general welfare institution, the almshouse, was well-established in the larger towns and urban centers. This development was largely a response to a major demographic change: the increase of population accompanied by a concurrent increase in the numbers of dependent persons. The informal arrangements for care in the rural village were not easily applicable to such new and growing cities as Boston, New York, and Philadelphia. The size of the dependent population necessitated the creation of some rational system. In 1800 the almshouse was a familiar urban institution intended for all kinds of dependents, including the insane, a fact that hampered its administration. Contemporary observers, commenting on the difficulty of controlling its heterogeneous clientele, noted that daily life in an almshouse was always punctuated with great noise and violence.

The hospitalization of the mentally disturbed individual, another mid-eighteenth-century development, was more portentous for the future of mental health care than the almshouse movement. In the early 1750s the first general hospital in British America, the Pennsylvania Hospital in Philadelphia, the largest colonial city, initiated a policy of accepting mental patients. Its founding father was a Quaker, Dr. Thomas Bond; and its prime mover, Benjamin Franklin, insisted that it make provisions for the care and treatment of the mentally ill as well as for the physically sick poor. This concern over problems associated with disease and poverty, a matter of social welfare, was the primary reason for the establishment of early American hospitals.

Franklin drafted a petition to the Colonial Assembly of Pennsylvania regarding the founding of the Pennsylvania Hospital, in which he clearly identified mental illness as a major social problem. He stressed issues related to the insane: their numbers were increasing; some of the mentally disturbed appeared to be violent and became "a Terror to their Neighbors"; others wasted their physical and material resources and became victims of predators who took advantage of their disordered condition. However, Franklin drew attention to the apparent success at Bethlehelm Hospital in England, where many of the "Mad People" were restored to health. He hoped that similar success could be achieved in Philadelphia. Early in 1752 the Pennsylvania Hospital admitted its first mental patient, placing him in one of the cells in the basement. Physical facilities eventually were enlarged and improved, yet the number of mental patients was small. The institution remained a general hospital serving patients of all classes, including slaves.

New York Hospital in New York City was another general hospital established in the eighteenth century that admitted the mentally disordered, reserving cells for them in the basement of its north wing. One of its founders, Dr. Samuel Bard, a distinguished physician, took notice of the treatment of the insane at the Pennsylvania Hospital and wanted to provide similar care in New York. A 1794 institutional publication, *Address to the Citizens of New York*, noted that New York Hospital provided asylum for "the poor sick" who suffered from "diseases of body and mind," and it identified insanity as the most lamentable of all maladies.

The first institution in America devoted entirely to the treatment of the mentally ill opened in October 1773 at Williamsburg, Virginia. From the beginning it functioned as a hospital, and was later named Eastern Lunatic Asylum. Dominated by laymen, a "keeper" rather than a physician administered it. The institution had selective admissions policy, excluding the transient, the aged, and the alcoholic. The Galt family managed the asylum's affairs for 89 years, with Dr. John M. Galt II becoming its most distinguished medical superteindent in the mid-nineteenth century. This institution failed to stimulate interest in other areas of the country. Local leadership had inspired its founding, and kept its work and policies confined to the surrounding area. The asylum's physical plant remained small, and the political and military turmoil of revolution kept it closed in the mid-1780s. It was not until the 1830s, an era of optimism, experimentation, and reform, that the proliferation of special state institutions for the mentally ill began.

The kinds of treatment given individuals at the Pennsylvania and New York hospitals, as well as the Williamsburg institution, were assumed to be humane and therapeutically effective. Cell keepers armed with whips enforced a strict discipline, and varied forms of physical restraint, including chains, leg irons, and iron rings, governed the care of patients. The "madd shirt" was widely applied at the Pennsylvania Hospital. It was a tightly fitted canvas garment that stretched from the head to below the knees, carefully restricting the wearer's movement. Since physicians assumed that a calm, subdued patient was saner than a violent one, good therapy involved the beating and terrorizing of individuals into submission. Cold showers, bloodletting, blistering, and the use of emetics, cathartics, and sedatives complemented the harsher techniques. Contemporary accounts of the physical conditions of patients depict them as half-naked, sleeping, on dirty straw, and chained to unpainted walls in unheated basement cells. These conditions stemmed from the prevailing belief that the insane were not affected by extreme temperature and were indifferent to their physical existence. At the Pennsylvania Hospital a small admission fee entitled sightseers to watch the patients. This common practice provided entertainment to the callous, who goaded the inmates into acts of extravagant behavior. The treatment of the mentally ill in eighteenth-century hospitals represented little improvement over their conditions in jails and almshouses.

During the latter part of the eighteenth century, new ideas stirred Western thought, countering the earlier pessimism and antipathy associated with caring for the mentally ill. The general intellectual movement known as the Enlightenment espoused an ideal of infinite progress toward the perfectibility of mankind. A belief in the essential goodness of man, a faith in reason and science, and a conviction that man could reshape society's institutions into more efficient and humane patterns became dogmas to eighteenth-century philosophers. These ideals not only contributed to setting the direction of the French and American revolutions but also released a widespread humanitarian movement aimed at improving the conditions of human life. The intellectuals asserting this fresh outlook formed a varied and heterogeneous group. Included were university professors such as Adam Smith, Cesare Beccara, and Immanuel Kant; doctors like John Locke; administrators such as Charles Montesquieu and Robert Jacques Turgot; and writers like Voltaire, Denis Diderot, and Jean-Jacques Rousseau.

A dramatic example of the impact of the new altruism upon the field of mental health occurred in 1793 when Philippe Pinel, physician at the Bicêtre, an asylum in Paris, ordered the chains struck from 53 patients, an act symbolizing the inauguration of a new era in the treatment of the mentally ill. He published his famous *Traité médicophilosophique sur l'aliénation mentale, ou la manie* in 1801; it was translated into English five years later as *A Treatise on Insanity*. The study expressed the hope of the Enlightenment. "The insane," he wrote, "far from being delinquents to be punished, are sick people whose distressing state deserves all the care and consideration due to suffering humanity." Pinel was an empiricist concerned with the concrete results of therapy, not a theoretician devoted to abstract speculations about the nature of madness. He held that the traditional methods of treating the insane, including vomiting and physical punishment, hindered recovery. On the contrary, he believed that a humane style emphasizing compassion won the patient's confidence and ultimately restored health.

The attitude of the person attending the insane was significant. "A coarse and unenlightened mind," Pinel argued, might interpret the behavior of mental patients "as malicious and intentional insults," but "a man of better feeling and consideration" would guide his wards back to reason with soothing coolness and kindness. Pinel's altruism had limitations. He related compassionate treatment to a patient's social status, commenting that a "well-bred" Frenchman would be governed by more humane principles than a peasant or a slave. While opposing the use of chains to restrain patients, he favored rigid methods of control, such as the cold shower or spray and the straitjacket. Above all, the French physician praised the quiet and orderly management of the mentally ill, a situation achieved by creating an atmosphere of intimidation. Accordingly, when patients became violent or incorrigible, they were pacified best with stern attitudes or at most with threats of physical punishment. In short, Pinel effected a revolution in the care and treatment of the mentally ill: the substitution of psychological coercion for the application of random force.

Pinel's American contemporary, Benjamin Rush, a signer of the Declaration of Independence and a physician at the Pennsylvania Hospital, exerted a powerful influence upon parts of the American medical profession through his practice, lectures, and writings, particularly *Medical Inquiries and Observations upon the Diseases of the Mind*. It stands as the first important American book on mental disorder. Between 1812 and 1835 it went through five editions. A native of Philadelphia who received medical training at Edinburgh, London, and Paris in the 1760s, Rush held a chair of medicine and chemistry at the University of Pennsylvania. Students flocked to hear his lectures. As a popular professor and well-trained physician, Rush stood in a commanding position to dominate the medical profession. At this time he was uniquely qualified—out of approximately 3,500 persons practicing medicine in America, only about 200 had professional medical degrees. His prominence in medical circles was complemented by his active participation in public affairs. Immersed in politics and committed to American independence, Rush achieved fame during the Revolution. He served as a member of the Continental Congress, became the surgeon general of the Continental Army, and was a member of the Pennsylvania convention to ratify the Constitution. He was recognized in his time as one of America's foremost doctors, and his book later earned him the title "Father of American Psychiatry."

Rush stressed a somatic approach to mental illness, assuming that it stemmed from a bodily malfunction: hypertension in the brain's blood vessels. From this premise it followed that the strain could best be relieved by extensive bloodletting; and Rush remained, throughout his medical career, a dedicated adherent of this remedy as the most effective way of treating insanity and all other diseases. In *Medical Inquiries* he made constant references to "copious bleeding" as the necessary first step toward improving a patient's mental condition. Other remedies Rush prescribed to affect the circulation of the blood included purges, emetics, a meager diet, and two therapeutic mechanisms, the tranquilizer and the gyrator. The former was a chair with straps that bound the patient's wrists and feet. A boxlike wooden hat that lowered over the head and attached to the chair back prevented head movement. Through firm restraint the tranquilizer presumably reduced the pulse. The gyrator had the opposite effect. The patient was strapped to a revolving board with the head farthest from the center. Rush reasoned that the rapid rotation helped to force blood toward the head, thereby restoring the blood vessels to normalcy. Both instruments evoke images of Inquisition chambers, but in his concept of mental illness, the tranquilizer and the gyrator were logical devices for treating capillary diseases of the brain.

One of Rush's case histories illustrates the basic methods he used in treating the mentally ill. The patient was a middle-aged man of moderate means and social standing who became mentally distraught after experiencing a series of political disappointments. At Pennsylvania Hospital he displayed unusually violent behavior, tearing apart clothes, sheets, and blankets. He was credited with destroying 40 blankets, and the bed and the furniture in his room were broken. Bloodletting was prescribed as treatment. The hospital record book indicated that he was given 47 bleedings, "by which he lost between 400 and 500 ounces of blood," and the tranquilizer was employed. Upon discharge this man wrote to Rush, expressing gratitude for the care he received at the hospital Unfortunately, a few months later he suffered a relapse and hanged himself.

In addition to vigorously defending the efficacy of venesection, Rush, like Pinel, regarded fear and authority as essential therapeutic tools. He once noted that the insane were comparable to untamed animals, and a physician, like an animal trainer, broke his patient by employing all the necessary shock and coercive techniques required to achieve submission. These included dousing the patient with cold water, keeping the patient awake for 24 hours in a standing, erect position, applying ice to the shaven head, and instilling a feeling of terror with threats of corporal punishment and death. Rush cited a case of a woman whose loud, abrasive, obscene language disturbed the entire hospital. After efforts to calm her with light punishment and threats failed, she was placed before a large bathtub and told to prepare for death. The attendant then threatened to drown her. The experience apparently had the desired effect; Rush records, "From that time no profane or indecent language, nor noises of any kind, were heard in her cell."

Deception was fundamental to Rush's therapeutics, a curious method for a man who believed that lying was a disease. According to the Pennsylvania doctor, a cure for a patient who suspected that a mouse resided in his or her body was to conceal a mouse in the feces. This would help to persuade the patient that the cause of the illness was no longer within him or her. An adolescent prankster's trick was apparently the best treatment for an individual convinced that he or she was made of glass: pull the patient's chair out, causing a fall, and then produce pieces of glass to suggest the broken parts of the body. Rush approved of a cure, learned from a colleague, for an inmate who assumed that he had been transformed into a plant. The doctor attending this patient persuaded him that a plant needed water; but instead of giving him water, the doctor urinated on his head. However ludicrous these examples may seem, Rush upheld the use of fraud in dealing with the mentally ill. Taking an ends-justifies-means position, he maintained that a doctor could use any technique so long as it enhanced the patient's well-being.

Rush was most outspoken on the question of what constituted mental illness. The dividing line between madness and sanity has always been a perplexing problem, and the interpretations have varied from society to society and from one historical epoch to another. Rush made the distinction without flinching, equating insanity with nonconformity. Sanity meant following regular habits, accepting a conventional life-style; madness represented social deviance, a departure from the norm. Alcoholism and crime became mental disorders, and

Rush even ranked the mental health of political opinions. The Loyalists, those who supported England during the American Revolution, suffered from a disturbance Rush termed "Revolutiana." It was a fear for the safety and protection of themselves and their property. In sharp contrast with the mental breakdown of the Loyalists was the excellent mental health of the revolutionaries. They cheerfully accepted deprivations and optimistically looked forward to the new order. The anxieties engendered by the success of their revolution, however, made them susceptible to illness. Independence brought an open, free society; and, unprepared for this situation, many Americans succumbed to what Rush labeled "Anarchia," a disorder caused by an excess of liberty. Here Rush provides some insight into a possible relationship between political order and mental health. This does not change the fact that he interpreted insanity in the narrowest of terms, matching it with social variance.

Rush remains a significant figure in the history of American mental health. An intimate of the founding fathers, his articulate, magnetic, aggressive personality and his concrete role in training doctors at Pennsylvania Hospital enabled him to wield enormous influence over a budding medical profession. Like Pinel, he struck off the chains of the insane at a time when popular opinion felt only dread and repulsion toward the mentally ill, and insanity itself represented a disorder without remedy. Still, Rush's stringent measures for controlling the mentally ill, coupled with his rigid classifications of insanity, set precedents for the future practice of psychiatry.

While Benjamin Rush exerted a marked impact upon the medical profession, the example of William Tuke's Retreat at York, England, provided the inspiration for the institutional care of the mentally ill in American private establishments. Operated by the Society of Friends, the Retreat was founded in 1792. A religious-humanitarian atmosphere permeated the institution. Tuke insisted that a patient should be encouraged to continue "paying homage to his Maker" and believed that religious services, even a short reading of the Bible, had a quieting effect on disordered minds. The most important quality at York was its emphasis on "moral management," a term implying the control of inmates by means of an implicit reward-punishment system. If they behaved well and accepted institutional discipline, the patients received rewards: visits from friends and relatives, permission to walk about the grounds, opportunity to engage in useful work and healthful recreation, and above all, approval from the superintendent. Counterbalancing these rewards were punishments designed to coerce proper behavior. The recalcitrant, violent patient was bound to a bed and released only after the attendant secured promises of agreeable conduct. To cope with an unusual case, the administration promptly isolated and restrained the patient.

The threat of punishment remained a constant factor in the management of the Retreat. While the institution employed such methods of intimidation, it also favored milder forms of control. Indeed, the Quakers, who prided themselves on their humanitarianism, believed that even the insane possessed an element of the divine and merited humane care. The primary aim of their reward-punishment system was to cultivate in the patient an acute sense of right and wrong. In encouraging patients to recognize that self-restrained, orderly behavior was "right" and that erratic, disruptive conduct was "wrong," they displayed kindness, understanding, and sympathy toward their wards. It was this humanitarian aspect that William Tuke's grandson, Samuel Tuke, emphasized in his book *Descriptions of the Retreat*, published in 1813. The close link between English and American Friends assured that it received immediate attention in America, where it provided guidelines for the establishment of institutions patterned after the York asylum. Four private mental hospitals owe their existence directly to Tuke's Retreat: the Friends' Asylum at Frankford, Pennsylvania; Bloomingdale Asylum in New York City; the McLean Asylum in Massachusetts; and the Hartford Retreat in Connecticut. In these institutions moral treatment, denoting the application of moderate persuasion techniques to cure mental disorder, was inaugurated.

Founded in 1813, the Friends' Asylum at Frankford had several unique qualities that contributed to its success. Isolated in a pleasant rural environment a few miles from Philadelphia, the asylum, a four-story building surrounded by 52 acres of land, provided a quiet, restful sanctuary far removed from curiosity seekers. The superintendent lived in the building with the patients. Inmates were grouped according to sex and behavior: each had a private room, with men housed in one wing and women in the other. The sexes mingled freely only in the two recreation rooms. Unsettled patients were quartered in dark rooms on the fourth floor. The administration believed that the boisterous needed seclusion to regain their composure, and at the same time their segregation left the quiet and the convalescent free from annoying harassments. The number of inmates averaged from 15 to 30 per year, and only Quakers deemed curable were admitted. This small, homogeneous patient population and the restrictive admission policy that excluded the extremely violent and the very poor facilitated the practice of moral treatment. A warm family atmosphere was created in which the superintendent, his wife, and the attendants developed an intimate relationship with each inmate, giving exclusive attention to individual problems. Patients were allowed to leave the asylum to visit friends and to attend religious services in Frankford. They worked outside under a minimum of supervision, and without fences and guards. This liberal policy tempted a few to escape, but the asylum's personnel believed that it encouraged the patients' self-confidence.

Assuming that work provided good exercise, instilled habits of order, and diverted attention from the patients' disturbances, the institution specialized in what was later called occupational therapy. A snag in the program came from many upper-class men who felt that manual labor was beneath their station in life. For those willing, carpentry, broom making, and farming offered men useful activity, while women busied themselves with needlework and varied household tasks. A typical patient's day included a few hours of manual labor, outdoor games, carriage rides, and long walks, Eventually the asylum created intellectual and educational activities. It established a library and set up a lecture program; the staff urged patients to pursue their intellectual interests.

Although Frankford stressed kind, permissive means of restoring mental health, disruptive, defiant patients were controlled by the traditional medical treatments and restraining devices. An inmate oblivious to persuasion or threats of punishment was bled and blistered; if this had no effect, the patient was confined to bed, placed in a straitjacket, or restrained by Rush's tranquilizer chair. The small number of violent patients at the asylum made harsh restraint an atypical procedure.

Bloomingdale Asylum, an affiliated institution of New York Hospital, first admitted patients in 1821. An administrator of the hospital, Thomas Eddy, a Quaker merchant, humanitarian, and philanthropist, became its prime mover. Involved in numerous reform movements and associations, including the Free School Society, the Manumission Society, the Society for the Reformation of Juvenile Delinquents, and the Humane Society, Eddy was impressed by the system of treating mental illness at York, England. He commented that Samuel Tuke's *Description of the Retreat* had "extended" and "enlightened" his views, and he outlined a set of rules taken from Tuke's book to govern the management of Bloomingdale Asylum.

Eddy's main concerns were assuring the patient's comfort and restoring a sense of order and discipline to the patient's life. He demanded the abolition of chains and urged that patients be kept clean and properly employed. To ensure that each inmate received adequate care, he advised doctors to keep a written record of each patient, noting the affliction. its progress, and the types of treatment used to facilitate a cure. In view of the prevailing indifference to keeping records on mental patients, this call for maintaining case histories represented a unique proposal. A weekly reading from the Bible was considered essential for encouraging proper patient behavior.

Eddy was not above advocating the fear of physical punishment as a means of control. He conceded that confinement and restraining devices were needed for dealing with the noisy and the violent, but urged attendants to strive to influence patients by acts of kindness rather than by coercive punishments. His proposals drew a favorable response from the hospital administrators, who later specified that Bloomingdale aimed at effecting a system of moral management. They stressed that medical remedies, notably moderate bloodletting and blistering, would continue—but as a complement to the essentials of moral treatment outlined by Eddy.

The McLean Asylum opened in 1818 and, like Bloomingdale, evolved from a general hospital. A humanitarian interest in the conditions of insane persons in the Bay State led several benefactors of the Massachusetts General Hospital to specify that their funds be channeled into building an "insane hospital." One contributor, John McLean, a Boston merchant, allotted a gift of over $100,000, and in gratitude the institution took his name. This first New England mental hospital had an aggressive physician-superintendent, Dr. Rufus Wyman, who proclaimed that McLean would inaugurate "a revolution in treatment."

Knowledgeable about the current trends in his profession, Wyman was well qualified to begin the experiment. His inspirations were Pinel and Tuke. While he often quoted from the French doctor's writings, Tuke's influence was more direct. Wyman had read the English Quaker's works; he visited Frankford Asylum, the American counterpart of the York Retreat; and he knew Thomas Eddy, the staunch advocate of Tuke's system of moral management. Wyman was completely committed to the moral treatment of the insane. The traditional medical methods of bleeding, purging, and a meager diet, he argued, were rarely helpful, often injurious, and occasionally fatal. Convinced that the physical coercion of patients yielded equally negative results, the McLean superintendent wanted an atmosphere of nonviolence to pervade the asylum: punitive restraining devices were never used, inmates were cautioned to avoid violence, and attendants were forbidden to strike patients.

Wyman was careful to choose attendants who were mature, patient, moral individuals dedicated to his therapy and capable of sustaining abuse without resort to retaliation. In the asylum's early years he employed former schoolteachers recommended by clergymen. They had demanding duties and stayed with patients the entire day, keeping alert to their needs and tidying their rooms.

The maintenance of neat appearances was part of a general asylum policy of carefully regulating the inmates' lives. Enforcing consistent habits by setting aside specific hours for rising, retiring, eating, working, and exercising, Wyman held, pacified the mind and distracted the patients from their mental states. The main elements of therapy at McLean were work and recreation. Men were kept busy at woodworking and gardening, women at sewing and embroidering. Every patient had time for reading and walking about the grounds. Leisure hours were filled with playing chess or ninepins and listening to music. The asylum overlooked the Charles River, and in the summer patients enjoyed picnics and boating excursions.

To further the fulfillment of moral treatment, Wyman organized patients by sex, and by type and degree of illness, into groups called families. Each was under the direction of a supervisor and occupied a specific area of the asylum. Later in the institution's history, difficult individuals incapable of living with others were segregated in a separate building called the Lodge. It housed the retarded, the epileptic, and those subject to fits of raving and violence.

The Hartford Retreat sprang from the humanitarianism of clergymen and physicians who were disturbed by the lack of proper facilities for the mentally ill in Connecticut. The culmination of their intense campaign to establish an asylum came in 1824, when the Retreat accepted its first patients. Seeing the institution as a unique experiment, the founders announced that it represented "the reverse of everything which usually enters into our conception of a mad house." In fact, they made a deliberate effort to pattern the asylum after the York Retreat. Like McLean, the future of Hartford became tied to one man, Dr. Eli Todd, a follower of Pinel and Tuke. During its formative years he administered the Retreat and devoted himself to shaping it into a humane institution offering individualized patient care.

Like many progressive physicians of the 1820s, Todd scorned the medical methods proposed by Benjamin Rush, particularly extensive bloodletting, and he vigorously attacked the use of arbitrary force to control patients. He saw a need for stern authority over a patient exhibiting quarrelsome, aggressive behavior. The measures used to restrain such a person, however, were explained to the patient with the understanding that as soon as there was proper behavior, the restraint would be lifted. In most cases Todd favored a positive, gentle approach to caring for the mentally ill. To treat each inmate with "the tenderness of genuine sympathy," he insisted, gave comfort and security, and enhanced the chances of recovery. A patient brooding over problems was diverted to recreational activities; a lethargic, bored inmate was encouraged to pursue intellectual interests. Todd's concern for individuals found expression even in small matters, such as his insistence that every patient's hands be washed before meals. This personal touch expressed the main aim of the Retreat: to make a patient's stay a peaceful and a rejuvenative experience.

The Frankford, Bloomingdale, McLean, and Hartford institutions have a special significance in the history of mental health care in America. Their contribution rests with initiating moral treatment, a compassionate approach to the care of the mentally ill. The physicians in charge of these asylums were domineering men who kept all authority in their hands. Every aspect of asylum life felt the force of their personalities. As practical, hard-working individuals who theorized little about the nature and etiology of insanity, they sought to mitigate the harsh, crude practices of their contemporaries. Under their guidance moral treatment became a distinct method of therapy. It entailed instilling in the patient a sense of right and wrong. It involved the removal of the patient from family and friends to an institution in a peaceful environment, individualized care by a sympathetic physician, occupational therapy, recreation, and the general avoidance of physical restraints or drastic medical treatments. In short, moral treatment placed the patient in a total therapeutic community that accommodated individual psychological conditions. This method of therapy had its greatest impact on the next generation of asylum superintendents, who introduced moral treatment into the state institutions of the 1830s and 1840s.

The fact that the new treatment was applied almost exclusively to middle-class patients marked an equally portentous development for the future. Although Bloomingdale admitted some poor people as patients, the general policy of these institutions, especially McLean and Hartford, aimed at excluding the insane poor, who were viewed as physically and behaviorally offensive and were assumed to be less curable than the well-to-do. Asylum administrators were upper middle-class, and preferred patients from the same social stratum. An influx of insane paupers, they argued, stigmatized an institution and drove away middle-class patients, who refused to associate with their social inferiors. Within each institution the quality of care varied with the socioeconomic position of the patient. The most affluent received special treatment; they enjoyed the best living quarters and food, and often dined and conversed with the superintendent. In short, moral treatment carried a badge of social approval and brought optimism and hope to the "best people," the well-bred and socially prominent.

The concept of moral treatment itself had a class bias. In attempting to mold patient behavior, physicians working within the framework of this system accepted middle-class values as the norm. Their emphasis on order, moderation, and self-control related to a middle-class life-style and naturally applied best to patients from this class. Such a situation facilitated the introduction and success of moral treatment in private mental hospitals, where doctors and patients came from similar social backgrounds. Doctors easily established rapport with their patients; patients readily grasped the therapeutic techniques of their physicians. Later, when poor people having different values formed the majority of patient populations in mental institutions, moral treatment ran into difficulties.

The treatment introduced at Frankford, Bloomingdale, McLean, and Hartford touched only a small minority of the mentally ill in America. In the 1820s the overwhelming majority of the insane still lived in almshouses and jails. Most laymen remained indifferent to this condition, and were oblivious to the new psychiatric ideas. The lag in opinion, however, was not peculiar to the early nineteenth century. The public has never been stirred by the plight of the mentally ill, a potent factor in explaining why physicians and mental health specialists have been given virtually unrestricted powers in caring for their patients.

In the early 1800s a popular medical handbook, William Buchan's *Domestic Medicine*, a mid-eighteenth-century publication, remained the public's frame of reference. A chapter entitled "Affections of the Mind" indicated how the "passions" of anger, grief, and love affected bodily health, each acting as a major factor in causing and curing a disease. While asserting that mental disorders remained inscrutable and complex, and almost defied cure, Buchan outlined a regimen for alleviating melancholy, "a degree of insanity" that, if unchecked, terminated in "absolute madness." This regimen included a diet consisting of vegetables, fruits, honey, and water. Onions, garlic, salted fish, and meat generated "thick blood" and should be avoided. Exercise was important, mainly to promote perspiration and "all the other secretions." A sea voyage, or a long journey to a warmer climate with agreeable companions produced happy effects. Soothing music and entertaining stories facilitated recovery. Beneficial results also followed bloodletting, purging, and induced vomiting. In short, Buchan recommended traditional folk medicines, common sense, and customary medicinal methods for treating the insane.

2
THE ASYLUM MOVEMENT

The decades between 1830 and 1850 saw the movement for the establishment of state institutions for the insane gather momentum. Two factors account for this development. First, the example of the effectiveness of moral treatment in private asylums gave support to a growing belief among physicians that insanity was curable. An 1828 annual report from the Hartford Retreat, for instance, announced that 90 percent of the patients recently admitted had recovered. Here apparently was concrete evidence that helped to dispel the pessimism associated with caring for the insane. The achievements of private hospitals generated an optimism necessary to promote the asylum idea. Second, the obviously inadequate and limited facilities for housing the insane aroused a reform impulse directed at securing government provision for them. This was largely a humanitarian drive of middle-class reformers who felt a paternalistic responsibility for the less fortunate members of society. Their ranks included many Protestant clergymen and professional people as well as physicians.

The effort to better the conditions of the insane formed part of a widespread reform movement that permeated American life in the 1830s and 1840s. Imbued with an optimistic sense of mission, many reformers worked to improve the lot of the blind, the deaf, the slave, the convict, the alcoholic, and the insane. Others called for the abolition of war, agitated for women's rights, and demanded the extension of the system of public education. A few experimented with the establishment of model utopian communities. During this great reform era the insane asylum came of age. Physicians and reformers identified it as the most beneficial and practical solution for the care and treatment of the mentally ill. The pre-Civil War asylum movement culminated in the work of Dorothea Dix. Her encouragement, determination, and eloquent appeals led state after state to construct asylums, making these formidable structures a familiar part of the American landscape.

An example of the humanitarian impulse to effect better conditions for the insane occurred in Massachusetts. In 1825 the Boston Prison Discipline Society, under the direction of Rev. Louis Dwight, began an investigation of local jails. Dwight discovered that prisons housed a surprising number of insane persons who lived under appalling conditions. Confined in cold, dark, unventilated cells where they slept on straw litters, their isolation was broken only when food was passed through a small iron door. Upon seeing a man in this condition, Dwight commented: "The first question was, is that a human being? The hair was gone from one side of the head, and his eyes were like balls of fire." Stirred by such descriptions, which were widely circulated in the Society's annual reports, influential Bostonians urged the state legislature to form a committee to investigate prisons.

This project received a stimulus when Horace Mann, a new member of the Massachusetts House of Representatives at the start of his remarkable career as a social and humanitarian reformer, took the initiative and directed attention to the need for a separate state institution for the mentally ill. Mann's vigorous prosecution of the project and his effective speeches before the legislature describing the positive effects of moral treatment at private asylums reached fruition with the establishment in 1833 of Worcester State Lunatic Hospital. This marked Mann's first important achievement and the beginning of a state mental institution devoted to the therapeutic treatment of the insane.

Worcester began under the dedicated leadership of Dr. Samuel B. Woodward, a distinguished physician who sustained a paternalistic humanitarianism and a deep faith in science throughout his career. Guided into a medical career by his physician father, he received a diploma from the Connecticut Medical Society and became a general practitioner. Later he was secretary of the Connecticut Medical Society, served as the physician of the penitentiary at Wethersfield, Connecticut, became an examiner at the Yale Medical School, and was elected to the Connecticut Senate. He participated in the planning and the establishment of the Hartford Retreat, where he became a colleague and close friend of Dr. Eli Todd, who later recommended Woodward to Massachusetts authorities for the superintendent's post at Worcester.

Woodward directed Worcester for 13 years, and under his leadership it achieved national recognition and became a model for other state asylums. His personality accounted for this success. Vigorous, dedicated, optimistic, he accepted the idea that an individual has a moral duty to work for a better society. This commitment led him into humanitarian movements ranging from temperance to penal reform, and he never lost a deeply felt obligation to aid distressed persons. Such idealism prevented Woodward from remaining oblivious to society's maltreatment of the mentally ill; his optimism convinced him that insanity was curable and open to rational investigation and understanding.

The Worcester superintendent did not offer any new theory about the nature of mental disturbance. Like other physicians of his day, he saw it as a somatic disease, the result of an impaired brain. He acknowledged psychological causation, but in vague, imprecise terms, arguing that insanity developed when an individual violated the natural and immutable laws governing human behavior. In short, in theory and practice he was not an abstractionist concerned with experimentation, but an empiricist, an administrator attentative to the concrete results of therapy and the daily tasks of operating an institution. This utilitarian approach and optimism contributed to his success in treating the insane.

Woodward was devoted to moral treatment, but relied also on medical therapies in order to pacify violent patients. This he accomplished through the administration of laxatives, morphine, and opium, which quieted the intractables and made them responsive to other therapeutic procedures. In his view opium was the most effective agent and was given until a patient had "contracted pupils and began to rub his nose." The thrust of Woodward's moral treatment focused on regular routines, individualized care, occupational therapy, and religious training. At Worcester the hospital routine began with the rising of patients at 4:30 A.M. in the summer and 6 A.M. in the winter. At 8 A.M., after the patients had breakfasted and cleaned their quarters, Woodward commenced his daily visits. He checked the orderliness of their rooms, examined each inmate, listened to patients' needs and complaints, and prescribed medication, work, or recreation. In the afternoon he fulfilled his administrative duties while the attendants and the assistant physician supervised the inmates activities. The patients retired in the early evening soon after supper.

During the early years of the institution, the small inmate population permitted Woodward to give each patient his close attention. He stressed the positive therapeutic value of a respectful relationship between patient and physician, which, he believed, helped to win the patient's confidence and restore the ability to develop normal human ties. In governing the mentally ill it was important to "give them your confidence, and they will rightly appreciate it, and rarely abuse it." Woodward saw himself as the kind, generous, sensitive father who affectionately provided for the wants and needs of his "children." He emphasized the utility of occupational therapy. To keep inmates active, he assigned varied tasks and constructive leisure activities, such as reading in the hospital library and attendance at religious services. He considered religion an important curative tool: it helped the mentally ill to gain an awareness of proper conduct and an appreciation for the moral laws controlling society. Occasionally the goodwill of local townspeople provided a pleasant diversion. During one summer a local fire department brought its engine every week to the asylum to be hosed and cleaned by patients.

Woodward's therapeutics produced a significant recovery rate. The majority of "cured" patients were middle-class inmates, which demonstrates that methods of treatment ran along class lines. Worcester accepted three types of patients:

the criminally insane, the insane poor, and the "harmless." The latter category represented the middle classes, and they reaped the benefits of Woodward's system. They received such privileges as having charge of their personal belongings in their own rooms; they lived and worked with each other and apart from other groups of inmates. Woodward promoted this policy because he insisted that interactions among a homogeneous group of patients from similar social and educational backgrounds enhanced recovery. Furthermore, the staff devoted more time and attention to them. Many lower-class patients arrived at Worcester from jails and almshouses. Upon entry they often exhibited extreme behavior. Treatment for these persons consisted of their being subdued by the staff, who then left them alone. In Woodward's words they were "vulgar" and "abusive." This situation forecast attitudes and policies that dominated asylums during the 1860s and 1870s, and contributed to the transfer of the insane poor to custodial institutions.

Woodward popularized the notion that insanity was most curable if the afflicted received early hospitalization and proper treatment. He compiled figures on the number of patients cured at Worcester, showing incredible recovery rates. Although later generations of physicians questioned the accuracy of his statistics, he never lost a confident belief that the mentally ill could be restored to perfect health. It was easier to cure the insane than those stricken with pneumonia or rheumatism. This optimistic message was carried in his annual reports, which circulated nationwide.

The 1830s and 1840s were portentous decades in the history of mental health. New facilities for the insane were erected throughout the country. The reports from Worcester stirred an interest in mental illness and offered guidelines for other physicians concerned with improving the lot of the insane. Among the institutions opening at this time were the Utica State Lunatic Asylum in New York, the Tennesse Hospital for the Insane at Nashville, the Maine Insane Hospital at Augusta, the Vermont Asylum for the Insane at Brattleboro, the Ohio Lunatic Asylum at Columbus, the Georgia State Lunatic Asylum at Milledgeville, the New Hampshire Asylum for the Insane at Concord, and the Pennsylvania Hospital for the Insane at West Philadelphia. Two municipal mental hospitals also opened: the New York City Lunatic Asylum at Blackwell's Island and the Boston Lunatic Asylum.

In the decades preceding the Civil War, the study of mental illness achieved the status of a speciality. Its practitioners directed asylums as superintendents, assistant superintendents, and visiting physicians, and formed a small, elite group of the medical profession, numbering fewer than 200 out of an estimated total of 20,000 physicians in the United States. Essentially administrators and organizers, most had little interest in theory, especially psychological theory. They were eclectics who borrowed notions from various sources and made little effort to crystallize their ideas into a coherent intellectual system.

Most of their concepts came from John Locke's sensationalist psychology, phrenology, and the Scottish common sense school of philosophy. Locke contributed the assumption that knowledge was acquired through the sense organs. From this they concluded that if the senses were defective or damaged, the mind would receive false impressions that would cause faulty thinking and unusual behavior. The theory of sensationalism justified placing a violent patient in solitary confinement. Since the body responded to external stimuli, withdrawal to a darkened room without sound or human contact would pacify the inmate by eliminating disturbing influences. Associationism warranted the removal of a patient to an asylum. In an institution the patient broke with past ties, which contributed to mental distress, and learned new routines and relationships.

Some asylum superintendents accepted the basic tenets of phrenology, a European theory that captured a respectable medical following in the middle decades of the nineteenth century. According to the phrenologists the brain was divided into many segments, each having a different intellectual, behavioral, or emotional trait or faculty. Insanity resulted when these areas became unbalanced. Other superintendents found the Scottish common sense school appealing. Among its notions was the conviction that at birth humans instinctively had personal capacities for duty, perception, self-interest, and moral taste, through which was gained a knowledge of correct ethical awareness. They knew the difference between good and evil, and their innate moral faculty made them responsible for their actions. This faculty psychology gave support to a rationalistic view of mental illness, the idea that insanity meant the loss of a person's reason.

All the vagueness and contradictions implicit in these theories did not perplex asylum administrators. They were pragmatists who often labeled theories as curiosities, and preferred observing their patients to reading books about insanity.

While these early physicians scrambled theories and placed little credence on their clinical value, they did agree that mental illness was a somatic disease. It was a disease of the brain, and supposedly an autopsy on an insane person would reveal evidence of physical damage. This view was not supported by their scientific research, nor did it encourage neurological or anatomical investigation. Instead, most physicians assumed that the brain's surface was exceedingly malleable and that its convolutions revealed an individual's life experience. All of a person's emotions, habits, and thoughts were engraved on the contours of the brain. And if such stimuli had this direct physical effect, then presumably an individual's behavior could be changed in a corrective environment. Here was a very optimistic belief: the great malleability of the brain's tissue made it susceptible and sensitive to changing situations. An environment that instilled proper health habits and training in almost any disturbed person would stimulate the formulation of new tissue and erase the contours caused by an erratic, unstable life-style. Armed with this assumption, a physician could be very hopeful about treating the mentally ill. The asylum obviously would provide the corrective milieu in which the insane would be effectively manipulated, controlled, and eventually cured.

The view that environmental factors were major determinants in shaping the brain's surface, and thus in affecting behavior, also encouraged a vigorous analysis of the social etiology of mental illness. Eager to prevent and cure insanity, asylum superintendents examined and criticized almost every aspect of the American social environment. Few habits, institutions, or movements escaped their scrutiny as they theorized that defects in the social order were key elements responsible for insanity.

Their analysis began on the most general level, with the assertion that insanity was linked to civilization. It was widely believed that advancing civilization produced a disproportionate increase in the numbers of insane persons. The term "civilization" was loosely defined as an urban industrial society with a sophisticated intellectual and cultural life. All of the frivolities, pressures, tensions, and stresses of living in such a complex social order overtaxed the brain and fostered mental illness. It followed, then, that simple agrarian societies knew little of mental disturbance. This view was accepted on the basis of hearsay evidence and the popular writings of travelers and adventurers.

The United States, however, was not a primitive culture. In the eyes of numerous Americans, it was the most civilized nation, and it produced one of the highest rates of insanity in the Western world. This was explained by placing the blame on the loss of stability and order in American life, a problem attributed to the fluidity and openness of a society that permitted unlimited social advancement and encouraged inflated ambition. American society had spawned the driving, zealous man eager for success in business, one who believed that any economic endeavor was within this range of competence and ability. He strove to reach an unattainable goal, and in the process encountered sleepless nights and other stresses, making him prone to mental illness. Possessed by a restless drive to better himself, he worked furiously and anxiously, and ignored the basic rules of good health. This resulted in a diminished appetite, loss of weight, and increased nervous irritability. A deteriorating pattern was thus set in motion, and it hurled him on a downward drift into insanity. Even if he achieved his mark and soared to the top of the business world, he remained susceptible to constant strains—the fear of bankruptcy or the collapse of his business brought on by unexpected economic changes.

Politics, like business, operated at a fervid pace. Amariah Brigham, superintendent of the Utica State Lunatic Asylum in New York, felt that the nation's convulsive political life contributed to the rise of insanity. In the scramble for political power, many office seekers were struck down with mental disorders, a penalty for excessive ambition. The mental health of voters was threatened by constant political agitation and ever-increasing demands to make choices on difficult public issues. The press stirred passions not only through its lurid reporting of murders, suicides, and robberies but also by carrying the speeches of demagogues, the debates of heated conventions, and the radical statements of poltical party platforms. Details of such events and activities day after day familiarized people with the sordid aspects of life and politics, blunted their moral sensibilities, and stimulated a craving for more sensations. This "morbid condition" invariably produced immoral reactions, and for many harried individuals terminated in mental disorder. The very nature of the American form of government, a system that granted liberty and encouraged citizen participation, increased the rate of insanity. In contrast, a country with a despotic government had a low frequency of insanity but produced dull, plodding minds.

Curiously, the Civil War, a very intense political struggle, allegedly fostered the mental health of the nation. Dr. George Chaote of Taunton State Lunatic Hospital at Taunton, Massachusetts, reported that the number of admissions to his institution during the war years was 20 percent less than during the year preceding the conflict. Other asylum administrators presented similar statistics, and attributed the trend to a mood of "disinterested benevolence." The war inspired noble, self-sacrificing ideals that diverted attention from personal anxieties and tribulations, an apparent fact favorable to the preservation of mental stability.

The same compulsion that Americans displayed in the quest for wealth and power characterized their intellectual life. Most medical superintendents accepted the idea that an overworked mind induced mental disorder. Sanity was maintained by striking a balance between mental and physical activities. What disturbed these men, however, was not simply the intense pursuit of abstract subjects but the changed character of the nation's intellectual life. Now it seemed that anyone could engage in philosophical speculations, and many had neither the talent not the capacity to assimilate intellectual knowledge. When ambition exceeded ability, a frustrated and distraught mental condition ensued. Another distressing trend was the careless rejection of past ideas and traditions. Isaac Ray, of the Maine Insane Hospital, nostalgically saw the time of his own youth as a settled, stable era when people respected their elders' beliefs and ideas, and accepted their station in life, content with modest holdings and the performance of domestic chores. On the other hand, Ray lamented, the younger generation knew no bounds. With scorn for logic, it delved into subjects that were once the province of learned scholars. The result of this rash intellectual activity was increased mental disturbance.

When medical superintendents examined the institutions that normally worked for stability—religion, the school, and the family—they found little that was reassuring. These institutions appeared to be weak and ineffectual, and often contributed to the unsettled conditions of the wider society. Religion was "a solemn subject of contemplation," to be calmly and dispassionately observed. This attitude colored the analysis of spirtualism, revivalism, and other forms of religious expression. Ray and Brigham viewed such popular movements as disruptive excesses that led to mental disorder. Spiritualism encouraged people to believe in communion with the dead. Dr. James Althon of the Indiana

Hospital for the Insane at Indianapolis, found this to be a delusion responsible for more outbreaks of insanity than any other factor. Revivalism startled minds and stirred anxieties about a person's salvation or punishment in the afterlife. Such unsettling reactions disoriented and perplexed people, and in their annual reports medical superintendents placed these and similar cases in a broad category termed "religious insanity."

In this critique of the social environment, some of the sharpest blows were directed at the schools and the family. The schools damaged young minds by stimulating the tensions so obvious in society. Primary educational institutions accepted children at too early an age, kept them in class too long, gave them too much information at too rapid a pace, and disregarded recreation and rest as healthy relief from the drudgery of long hours of study. Physicians frequently complained about "the pernicious practice" of forcing intellectual training while neglecting a child's physical development and strength. Furthermore, the schools instilled an overly competitive spirit by leading students to strive for goals beyond their means and talents.

This type of training set in motion habits that turned into nervous disorders later in life. While the schools miseducated the youth, the family ignored its traditional responsibilities. Accepting the common assumption that the home should shelter its members from society and provide authority and child training, asylum superintendents attested that many parents failed to discipline their children, and left them free to gratify their whims. Consequently, a pattern of irresponsible license was fixed, and children were encouraged to believe that life consisted only of opportunities for wishful pleasures. An indulgent childhood produced the immature adult who lacked self-restraint and acted on impulse. Mental disease would decrease only when family authority was restored.

In making this spirited, incisive assault on the social etiology of insanity, medical superintendents acted as guardians of the nation's mental health. They were guiding the country around the pitfalls leading to mental illness. Committed to improving society and preventing insanity, their analysis, giving social and environmental factors paramount importance in provoking insanity, became a call for action rather than a cry of despair. If the structure and nature of society caused mental illness—if, indeed, an individual was caught in an inescapable matrix of social tensions beyond control and comprehension—then society had a moral obligation to ameliorate the condition. All of society could not be reconstructed; the only solution was the creation of a unique, corrective environment for the insane: the asylum, a place screened from the anxieties of the world and structured to provide its inmates with an ordered, disciplined life geared to facilitate their recovery.

One of the strongest proponents of the concept of the asylum as the key to curing mental illness was Dr. Thomas S. Kirkbride, who was superintendent of the Pennsylvania Hospital for the Insane at West Philadelphia between 1840 and 1883. Kirkbride received his medical degree from the University of Pennsylvania.

He served as resident physician at the Friends' Asylum at Frankford and later as surgeon at the Pennsylvania Hospital. Before he became superintendent at the West Philadelphia institution, he visited several northern asylums, including Bloomingdale, McLean, Hartford, and Worcester. He was most impressed with the work of Samuel Woodward. Kirkbride gained a national reputation for his book *On the Construction, Organization, and General Arrangements of Hospitals for the Insane With Some Remarks on Insanity and Its Treatment* (1854), an important study that dealt largely with the rational planning and construction of an asylum.

Almost a practical handyman's guide, the book outlined the steps in the building of an ideal mental hospital, from the choice of a site to the construction of the roof. It specified the location of air ducts, water pipes, dumb waiters, the sewage system, and gaslight fixtures, as well as the size of rooms and the dimensions of doors and ceilings. Kirkbride listed the ingredients for making plaster and even commented on the correct procedure for scrubbing floors. While recommending durable materials ranging from slate for the roof and stone for stairways to hardwood for the floors of patients' rooms, he analyzed every aspect of construction and often supplemented his text with detailed illustrations. The exterior of the institution followed a linear design with wings extending in a step pattern from each side of the central part. The wings housed the wards; the domed center structure had offices, receiving rooms, and a private apartment for the superintendent and his family. Kirkbride set the asylum's maximum capacity at 250 patients. He advised that it be located in the country near a large town, on approximately 100 acres of land. Half of this acreage was to be set aside for the patients' gardens and recreation grounds, and should be enclosed by an inconspicuous but substantial wall. In addition to these technical and architectural matters, Kirkbride defined the duties and responsibilities of the asylum administrator and related the principles for staffing the hospital. The institution required "active," "cheerful," "kind," "educated," "trustworthy" employees and a staff large enough to maintain an attendant-patient ratio of one to ten.

In justifying the need for the mental hospital, Kirkbride stressed its social utility, arguing that it provided the atmosphere and facilities in which a person could be effectively treated, cured, and returned to the community to assume a productive role. Home or family treatment, incarceration in a jail or almshouse, and even ordinary hospital care, he cautioned, only delayed proper treatment, and in most cases diminished the patient's chances for recovery. Every state needed a special institution for its insane, he said; and curiously, for this point in the history of mental health care, he emphasized the custodial work of the asylum. The main function of the mental hospital was to cure the curable, but it had another vital task; to protect society from "irresponsible" and "dangerous" people. Raising the specter of raving madmen roaming freely in the community and threatening people with injury and death, he asserted that the injuries and the lives lost as a result of the actions of the insane were greater than those caused by railroad accidents. Here, for all his professional experience and awareness, Kirkbride gave support to the popular image of the insane as a menace to society, an unfortunate stigma that has lingered from colonial days to the present.

The principles of construction and organization presented in this book soon became known as "the Kirkbride plan," and they were utilized by other asylum administrators who were determined to mold a new environment for the insane. There were no precedents. The almshouse and the jail were obviously inadequate models; European asylums, which were frequently converted forts, castles, or monasteries, could not be imitated. Kirkbride's ideas offered guidelines for their first concrete task—the erection of a proper physical structure for their patients. His plan became the model for asylums in over 30 states. In some cases it was accepted without modification, as in the Alabama Hospital for the Insane, completed in 1860. In other instances Victorian influences and other changing architectural tastes produced structures complete with Gothic towers, heavy domes, and Tuscan roofs.

The asylum movement received an impetus from lay reformers, many of whom worked at the local or state level without national recognition. The drive and determination of one individual, Dorothea Lynde Dix, who devoted her entire life to improving conditions for the mentally ill, eventually brought her international distinction. Born in 1802 in the small rural village of Hampden, Maine, she had a difficult, unhappy childhood because of an alcoholic father and an indifferent mother. At the age of 12 she ran away to Boston, to live with her wealthy grandparents. Here she was subjected to a puritanical upbringing and received training as a teacher. She headed a private day and boarding school until 1836, when her health failed and she was ordered to rest and recuperate. Soon afterwards her grandmother died and left her a modest income for life.

Dix's decision to embark on a humanitarian career was triggered when she accepted a position as Sunday school teacher to female convicts at a jail in East Cambridge, Massachusetts, in March 1841. What she saw there fired her resolve to act for the benefit of the insane. She began her crusade in Massachusetts and took it to almost every state east of the Mississippi River, to Canada, and later to Europe. In her travels Dix investigated jails, almshouses, and private homes. The results of these studies were often cited in her memorials presented to state legislatures in which she related the horrors of maltreatment. All of the sights, sounds, and smells of callous brutality were described in detail. In jails and almshouses the mentally disturbed who could not conform to rules were prodded with iron bars and beaten into obedience with canes. In private homes reinforced closets, stalls, pens, and woodsheds kept an insane family member in painful isolation. She recorded the haunting wails, the rattle of chains on frost-covered floors, and the stench arising from human excrement, unwashed bodies, filthy clothes, and rancid food.

Her piercing observations moved legislators and publicized the need for reform. Dix's solution to the problem echoed Kirkbride and other mental hospital administrators. Insanity was curable, she claimed, for the statistics of leading authorities showed remarkable recovery rates. She urged legislatures to supply the necessary funds for the construction of asylums—the only answer to providing humane care for the mentally ill. She criticized poorly administered hospitals caught in a rut of custodial care, and her championing of better facilities for the insane poor represented a democratic reform, differing sharply from the elitist concerns that had led to the establishment of private mental institutions earlier in the nineteenth century. Familiar with the latest psychiatric theories and therapeutics, she knew the leading medical superintendents and frequently visited their asylums to observe treatment procedures. They praised her work and, like them, she advocated moral treatment.

By the mid-1840s the public asylum had become an accepted institution. Few questioned either its necessity or its validity. None felt this more than the medical superintendents. One noted that the asylum was "an indispensable part of the machinery of human society." Administrators took pride in the new institution, and through the medium of their annual reports they expounded on its virtues. In self-congratulatory terms they recounted the salutary effects of a "well-regulated asylum." Their stress on regularity became the crux of the problem of curing mental illness. The control of inmates through a precise, calm routine had the greatest rehabilitative value. Punctuality and order in the asylum counteracted the instability and tensions of society, and, combined with the kindness and compassion of the staff, invariably restored good health. For some superintendents the asylum offered more than recovery; it became a regenerative institution, a place where a prolonged residence transformed an individual into a better person. A patient received new and correct views on human nature, on how to live properly, and on the means of preserving "a sound mind in a sound body." This instruction permanently relieved the malady, and the patient left the asylum morally strengthened and uplifted, capable of assuming responsibilities and following a life-style of high ideals.

To control and to effect change in patient behavior, asylum administrators constantly resorted to innovations. Social dances, sleigh rides, the establishment of music and drama clubs and craft groups, the provision of such facilities as a greenhouse, a whittling shop, and a sewing room were often complemented with a lecture-concert program. Several asylums put out a newspaper written, edited, and printed by inmates. Patients were encouraged to write on all subjects because it was believed that this type of activity promoted self-control and diverted "the mind from its delusions." An asylum school was a popular innovation. Here some patients learned to read and write, while others attended mathematics, history, and geography classes. Gratified by "the beautiful sight" of inmates studying and listening to lectures without disruptions, asylum administrators viewed the school as a valuable, beneficial tool in moral treatment. The knowledge imparted was viewed as of secondary importance; what counted was the school's contribution to the patients' high spirits, contentment, and self-discipline. By imposing new habits and associations on inmates, these diversions helped to fulfill one of the asylum's objectives: resocializing the patient for a full and healthy life.

Exaggerated proclamations and claims about the success of the asylums received wide publicity and acceptance. There was no dissent as superintendents vied with each other in announcing the fruits of their labor. Dr. Samuel Woodward of Worcester stated that over 80 percent of his institution's patients recovered. Dr. Luther V. Bell of McLean Asylum, Dr. John Galt II of the Williamsburg, Virginia, hospital, and Dr. William Awl of the Columbus, Ohio, asylum each claimed a 100 percent cure rate. Others boasted that their cure rates greatly increased each year. The statistics supporting these bold statements were not without problems. The definition of recovery lacked precision—a "cured" patient often left the asylum only to return after suffering a relapse, and this could occur more than once. Thus a single patient could be responsible for several statistical "cures." Despite this problem and the fact that some superintendents inflated their figures to impress colleagues and legislators, their statements reflected the optimism, hope, and confidence of their time. The practice of moral therapy brought the treatment of mental illness into a new age. There was indeed convincing testimony that insanity was curable, that the asylum held the promise of a millennium for the mentally disturbed. In the history of the care and treatment of the mentally ill, the self-assurance of the 1830s and 1840s would never reappear.

Despite the glow of confidence radiating from psychiatric circles, there were difficulties. The premature discharge of patients was called "the grand evil." When friends or relatives visited an inmate and saw a relaxed, cheerful, and rational person, they assumed that the patient was well; frequently, against professional advice, they insisted upon removing the innate from the asylum. When this happened and the patient returned to the community too soon, a relapse occurred. The derangement reappeared, sometimes with a greater intensity than before the first admittance to an asylum. Misgivings were also expressed over the paucity of information on insanity available to the public and the medical profession. The subject received scant attention in educational institutions, even in medical schools.

Still, these problems were not insurmountable obstacles, and solutions seemed near at hand. The circulation of the annual asylum reports helped to disseminate information and awaken public sentiment to the need for more asylums. In this effort superintendents appreciated the assistance of the country's most prestigious medical periodical, *The American Journal of the Medical Sciences*, which in the middle decades of the nineteenth century published lengthy summaries of asylum reports. This journal's editors lauded the achievements of hospital administrators, designating their work "a noble philanthropy" without historical parallel. The reports bore evidence of their "zeal and industry" and of their contributions toward comforting and providing relief for the insane. The editors, too, were immersed in a wave of confidence and saw progress everywhere.

A powerful instrument for explaining the utility and necessity of asylums was created in October 1844, when 13 superintendents of mental hospitals met in Philadelphia and formed the Association of Medical Superintendents of American Institutions for the Insane, the first national psychiatric organization. Between 1892 and 1921 it was the American Medico-Psychological Association, and since 1921 it has been known as the American Psychiatric Association. A scholarly periodical, the *American Journal of Insanity* (now the *American Journal of Psychiatry*), became its official organ. The 13 founders, later designated the "Original Thirteen," were Samuel B. Woodward of Worcester, Isaac Ray of the Maine Insane Hospital at Augusta, Luther V. Bell of the McLean Asylum, Charles E. Stedman of the Boston Lunatic Asylum, Nehemiah Cutter of the Pepperell Private Asylum in Massachusetts, John S. Butler of the Hartford Retreat, Amariah Brigham of Utica State Lunatic Asylum, Samuel White of the Hudson Lunatic Asylum at Hudson, New York, Pliny Earle of the Bloomingdale Asylum, Thomas S. Kirkbride of the Pennsylvania Hospital for the Insane, William M. Awl of the Ohio Lunatic Asylum at Columbus, Francis T. Stribling of Virginia Western Lunatic Asylum at Staunton, and John M. Galt II of Virginia Eastern Lunatic Asylum at Williamsburg. The majority were young and had broad interests ranging from literature to public affairs. Influential in their communities, they had ties and friendships with legislators, businessmen, and reformers that enabled them to move in high social and political circles.

Of the "Original Thirteen," Woodward, Kirkbride, Ray, Brigham, and Earle exerted the deepest impact on their profession. Woodward was well-known for his work at Worcester, and Kirkbride for his devotion to asylum organization and construction. Ray's publications, notably *Treatise on the Medical Jurisprudence of Insanity, Mental Hygiene,* and *Contributions to Mental Pathology,* made him one of the world's leading authorities on insanity and its treatment. As founder and first editor of the *American Journal of Insanity*, Brigham stood in a commanding position to influence the public and his colleagues. His reports from Utica reveal an efficient and enthusiastic administrator committed to improving the status of the insane. Earle's active career included hospital administration; travel abroad, during which he became familiar with European, especially German, psychiatry; and significant contributions to the literature of mental illness. His most important work, *The Curability of Insanity*, questioned the validity of statistics claiming high rates of insanity. Disposed to practice moral therapy, all revered the asylum as a beneficent institution for housing, controlling, and treating the mentally ill.

The main concern of the Association of Medical Superintendents was the administration and organization of asylums. Discussions at annual conventions and the concerns of committees reveal an interest in the problems connected with the day-to-day management of institutions. Members heard reports on the value of different kinds of fuels for heating hospitals, the best types of reading materials for patients, and the means of employing inmates in winter. They debated the duties of night attendants, the need for chapels and chaplains, and the merits of visits with patients by their friends. While concerned with these practical matters, the Association also aimed at educating the public about mental disorders. The stated objective of the *American Journal of Insanity* was "to popularize the study of insanity." Superintendents wanted strong links established between their work and the wider society. Contacts with the lay as well as the professional world, they believed, would help to enlighten the community, remove prejudices about insanity, and improve the mental health of the nation. Articles in their journal stressed that insanity was a natural, curable disease; that mental patients were human beings and not wild beasts; that asylums were pleasant, humane establishments that could best cope with mental disease and speed patients back to normal life.

The ardor and zealousness with which such themes were stated is rare in the history of mental health care. These early psychiatrists were crusaders armed with moral righteousness and a conviction that their methods gave solace and ultimately restored health to the most hapless of patients. However self-centered, innocent, and naive they appeared to later generations, their confident optimism and dedication inspired hope and aroused public support for the construction of asylums.

3
CUSTODIAL CARE

During the third quarter of the nineteenth century, the asylum became a custodial institution, a travesty of its former self. Diverted from the original mission of rehabilitating the insane, the mental institution sank into a mire of apathy and indifference. A stale atmosphere of pessimism replaced the fresh wind of optimism that had generated the early asylum movement. This dramatic change in purpose and mood evolved with the rapid proliferation of asylums. In 1876, 58 state asylums, 10 city and county asylums, 9 charitable institutions, and 9 private asylums held 29,558 patients. The U.S. census of 1870 estimated the total number of insane at 44,932. Although more than 15,000 remained in jails, almshouses, and private homes, the dream of Dorothea Dix appeared close to fulfillment.

New facilities for treating the insane sprang up everywhere. But the dream was turning into a nightmare. The difficulties stemming from overcrowded institutions, a heterogeneous patient population, and the increasing number of chronic cases produced a professional attitude of insensitivity toward the mentally ill. Doubts about curability, acceptance of a hereditary etiology, and a rigid somaticism deepened the growing malaise and shifted the entire thrust of treating the insane. In effect, the basic problems of mental illness in a mass society emerged, and the solutions offered set patterns of care that prevailed for decades. The hope, confidence, and élan of the "Original Thirteen" generation were dissipated. The therapeutic role of the mental hospital slid into the background as more and more asylum practitioners shifted their emphasis away from moral treatment and toward providing custodial care for the swelling numbers of insane.

Fundamental to the change was the simple fact of overcrowded facilities.

By the 1850s overcrowding was the norm in mental institutions. In every part of the country this condition was documented with repetitive dullness. Annual reports from asylums recorded that wards were "overflowing with patients," "overcrowded to the extreme limit," or "occupied to the utmost capacity." In spite of the establishment of new asylums and the construction of additional wings at old ones, the situation worsened. In 1871 Dr. G. A. Shurtleff of the Insane Asylum of California complained that "227 are sleeping on beds nightly prepared for their use in the halls"; Dr. H. A. Buttolph of the New Jersey State Lunatic Asylum noted that his institution held an excess of 200 patients. And the numbers of inmates in other hospitals were between 100 and 200 above normal capacity. The surging increase in patient population can be readily explained. New state laws required that all insane persons viewed as dangerous to a community's security be sent to asylums. Also sent were many of the mentally ill who had been confined in jails and almshouses. The mere establishment of mental hospitals drew attention to deviant behavior, especially in urban areas. An individual who had formerly been tolerated as an eccentric might now be deemed insane and subject to confinement. The sharp growth in the general population produced a concurrent proportionate increase in the numbers of mentally ill. Finally, the initial planning for state mental hospitals was based on insufficient data and foresight. Ignorant about the actual incidence of insanity, reformers underestimated the potential size of the insane population and called for the establishment of relatively small institutions.

Overcrowding had a devastating effect on the asylum milieu. Problems of hygiene intensified. Epidemics of dysentery, "malarial fever," cholera, smallpox, and diarrhea struck at numerous institutions. In the crowded wards, which frequently had poor sewage, ventilation, and water systems, disease spread rapidly and resulted in the deterioration of the patients' health. A high mortality rate caused greater distress, with many asylums reporting large numbers of deaths. The cholera epidemic that raged through the New York City Lunatic Asylum in the summer and early fall of 1865 attacked 96 patients and left 71 dead. Actually, without the added factor of epidemic disease, the number of deaths occurring in mental institutions was rather alarming, in some instances decreasing an asylum's annual population by 20 percent. In yearly institutional reports administrators cited such a statistic and accepted it with apparent equanimity.

The drastic increase in the number of inmates had a negative effect on the relationship between physician and patient. A superintendent burdened with the problems of administering several hundred patients could not be attentive to the needs of each inmate. The personal care given to patients in the early nineteenth-century private and public asylums was no longer possible in the large midcentury institutions. Dr. George Chandler, Woodward's successor at Worcester, confessed that a physician in charge of more than 100 patients lost contact with them. He could not specify individual therapy, and remained ignorant of each patient's progress. Chandler favored the small hospital in which the superintendent maintained a devotion to his wards, and they expected and received treatment from him. By the mid-1860s his desire represented a wishful ideal—the typical mental hospital held over 500 patients, and this size increased with time. In short, the congested mazes in asylums prevented a regular and easy contact between doctor and patient. Respect for the individual was lost; the patient became part of an unruly mob, without personal identity, a subject to be controlled rather than treated.

The deluge of inmates forced a constriction of the patients' living area. Rooms used for leisure activities were transformed into sleeping quarters. This reduction of recreational space meant a curtailment of an essential element of therapy—the opportunity for constructive relaxation—and it demanded a tighter obedience to rules, making a patient's asylum stay a rigid and restrictive experience. Wards designated for convalescent patients were filled with persons suffering from all sorts of mental disorders. A violent, disorderly individual or one in a deep catatonic state might be quartered with those who were recuperating. Administrators complained that such difficult circumstances hampered their efforts at treatment, diminished the chances for recovery, and, in some cases, prevented it altogether.

The changing nature of the patient population aggravated the difficulties arising from congested facilities. In the early years of the asylum movement, patients shared a common middle-class cultural background. Physicians too had a similar heritage, a fact that facilitated the practice and success of moral treatment. By midcentury the influx of paupers and immigrants, along with the admission of the criminally insane, the mentally retarded, the aged, and the alcoholic, altered the asylum's class makeup and psychological character. In only one aspect did asylum populations remain constant: there were usually more men than women, and in most instances the number of males exceeded females by 10 percent. Some institutions operated on a belief that men could be cared for more easily and at less expense than women. Presumably women required more comfortable facilities and furnishings, as well as additional attendants to meet their needs.

There was general agreement that men and women became mentally ill for different reasons, with a disparity in temperament and social roles accounting for this sexual distinction. A man was governed by "the intellect"; a women, by "feelings and emotions." Thus, male mental disturbances frequently resulted from an "overworked brain"; female disorders, from a "state of excitement." More significant were the contrasting social positions that exposed the sexes to dissimilar tensions. Active in the business world, seeking wealth and status, men feared that the failure of their plans for material success might plunge them into poverty and destitution. Women, on the other hand, were devoted to the home and to intimate relationships, and consequently suffered grief and frustration over disappointed love, domestic troubles, or the loss of friends.

While these causes of male and female insanity received endorsement, disagreement arose over the comparative curability of the sexes. The most objective study on the subject, published by Dr. Edward Jarvis, concluded that men were more susceptible than women to insanity, were less curable, and had a higher mortality when mentally ill. These findings ran counter to the prevailing professional opinion that women were especially prone to nervous disorders and recovered less frequently than men. Whether this view influenced treatment of female inmates is a moot question; but in the history of mental health care, those designated less curable received inadequate attention and were relegated to the custodial wards.

The great increase in the number of chronic or incurable patients was an alarming and most unwelcome trend, and was viewed by superintendents with indignation. Many chronic cases were transferred to recently established asylums in order to relieve some of the pressures on the older ones. But this initial effort to resolve the issue failed. The numbers were too great, and administrators raised an almost universal cry: mental hospitals were "rapidly becoming filled with incurables." They blamed this condition on inert legislatures that failed to appropriate funds for the construction of additional facilities. Where allotments were provided, the time lag between the decision to build and the admittance of the first inmate stretched into years. During the interim those waiting for treatment became incurable cases. The rise of chronicity was also attributed to public ignorance regarding the treatment of the mentally ill. Lay people persistently waited too long before committing a disturbed individual, and the delay usually resulted in a life term in an asylum.

This argument had been used to win support for the building of the first state mental institutions. But by midcentury a new element—the pauper and the foreign-born—had radically changed the makeup of patient populations. As the numbers of this group swelled, superintendents held them responsible for the prevalence of widespread chronic insanity. An invidious assumption linked the poor and the immigrant to hopeless mental illness. This connection was made in one of the most influential and important nineteenth-century studies of mental illness, Jarvis' *Report on Insanity and Idiocy in Massachusetts* (1855). Jarvis, a prolific writer, published numerous studies on mental illness in which he always based the conclusions on a statistical analysis of the data. Born and educated in Concord, Massachusetts, he was working in a textile factory at the age of 16 and seemed an unlikely candidate for a professional career. His interest in attending college and his obvious scholarly talent, however, encouraged his father to send him to Harvard, where he received a degree in 1826. He initially hoped to enter the ministry, but a speech impediment led him to abandon the plan; he chose medicine because he believed that it would give him an opportunity to serve humanity.

After receiving his medical degree Jarvis practiced in his home town, later in Louisville, Kentucky, and eventually settled in Dorchester, Massachusetts. There

he took a special interest in treating persons afflicted with mild emotional distur-
bances. Active in community life, he served as a trustee of the Massachusetts
School for the Idiotic and Feeble Minded Youth and of the Worcester State
Lunatic Asylum, and was a physician at the Massachusetts School for the Blind.
Pursuing his interest in statistics, Jarvis worked on the federal censuses of 1850,
1860, and 1870, and for 30 years remained an active member of the American
Statistical Association. His main concerns were research and writing, with the
aim of educating the public about physical and mental health. His 1855 *Report*
represented one of his most important studies and had wide social implications.

The analysis of insanity in terms of ethnic and class distinctions was of
special significance. According to Jarvis' *Report* most patients in the Massachusetts mental institutions were incurables, and paupers and immigrants—notably
the Irish—had a special propensity for insanity. Implied in this assertion was a
notion that soon won general acceptance in mental health circles: poverty and
mental illness were related to inherited characteristics rather than to external
conditions. In short, inferior biological stock caused both pauperism and
insanity. Jarvis' findings reflected his class bias, which favored native Americans.
He held a patronizing attitude toward aliens and the lower class, viewing them as
threats to the traditional New England life-style. With obvious displeasure he
observed that insane foreigners reaped the benefits of state hospitals. These
"lunatic strangers" without permanent residence received accommodations at
the expense of the natives of Massachusetts.

Jarvis' attitudes were shared by many superintendents who held a stereotyped image of the impoverished and the foreign-born. Accordingly, the poor
were thought to be listless, without goals, incapable of controlling passions, and
indifferent to comfort and good health habits. Possessing such traits, they
inevitably drifted toward a life pattern of alcoholism, debauchery, idleness,
vagrancy, crime, or mental illness. This condition resulted from an inadequate
environment. It also stemmed from "innate characteristics," from "low mental
and often feeble physical organizations." A weak constitution meant a lack of
vitality, poor health, and a short life expectancy, the basic ingredients of poverty
and insanity. While allegedly having these same tendencies, immigrants—a
significant segment of the insane poor—were stigmatized as being irritable,
incompetent, and insensitive. They floundered in a strange land without hope,
friends, or money, and became despondent and anxious, disposed to mental
disorders.

The characterization of the poor and the alien in such derogatory terms
compounded the difficulties of governing an overcrowded asylum. In their
dislike for patients thought to be unpleasant and inferior, superintendents lost
those qualities most important and necessary in treating the mentally ill: sympathy and understanding. Deterioration in care and treatment followed.

The hostile attitude of physicians toward the poverty-stricken alien formed
part of an anti-immigrant public sentiment that prevailed in American society

throughout the 1850s. This surge of nativism represented a reaction to the wave of Irish immigrants who settled in eastern and midwestern urban centers. Many people were revolted by the Irish, whom they saw as a threat and danger to American institutions. They found a political outlet in the Know-Nothing movement, which based its program on anti-Irish and anti-Catholic appeals. The popular slogan "No Irish Need Apply" expressed the discriminatory practices directed against them. In the mental health field this nativism not only had a detrimental effect on the treatment of alien patients but also cast an unfavorable image of the mental hospital. As administrators bewailed the disproportionate number of aliens in their midst, the asylum gained a reputation as a depository for incurable alien paupers. In the public view it was an undesirable place dominated by the outlandish customs and ways of foreigners and poor people.

The criminally insane posed a difficult problem for asylum administrators. Increasing numbers were admitted to mental institutions, and this fact focused attention on the question of the legal responsibility of the insane, a perplexing issue that demanded a definition of mental illness. The problem of defining insanity was complicated by a recognition that an insane person could exhibit irregular behavior yet suffer no intellectual disorientation. An English physician and anthropologist, James C. Prichard, called this condition "moral insanity," and this term precipitated a hot debate in American psychiatric circles. Prichard explained moral insanity as an affliction in which the person displayed antisocial behavior without sensing moral responsibility, even though the rational or intellectual abilities remained intact. A case in point would be a murder without a motive or any senseless crime committed by an apparently rational person.

During the 1830s and 1840s, when moral treatment reached its height, influential and prominent superintendents accepted the concept of moral insanity. Among them was Amariah Brigham, who believed that the intellect was powerless against the force of an irresistible impulse. Another was Isaac Ray, who argued that the emotions could subvert an individual's reason and compel him or her along a path of wayward ethical behavior. After 1850 there was opposition to moral insanity among the younger generation of superintendents. They argued that the idea fostered a loose morality by engendering an irresponsible, fuzzy attitude that linked insanity with licentious behavior. Relating criminal actions to mental illness posed a threat to the social order, but it also damaged the image of their profession. Sensitive to public criticism, they were fearful of being accused of coddling criminals or excusing crime in the name of insanity.

Support for the concept of moral insanity diminished, and the issue narrowed to the role of the expert psychiatric witness in criminal cases. Here the profession was kept informed, with nearly every issue of the *American Journal of Insanity* containing an article on a criminal proceeding in which the plea of insanity was a central factor in the trial. Debates at the annual meetings of the association of Medical Superintendents of American Institutions for the Insane reviewed the many ramifications of the subject, ranging from the fee to be charged by a witness to the problem of conflicting testimony among physicians. A dramatic example of the confusion occurred at the trial of Charles J. Guiteau, who shot President James A. Garfield on July 2, 1881. Eight medical witnesses testified that he was insane; fifteen deemed him sane and responsible before the law. The court agreed with the majority, Guiteau went to trial, and was eventually convicted and executed. To avoid such public scenes of battling physicians, the Association demanded the creation of an impartial, court-appointed expert.

While the chronically and the criminally insane aroused the gravest concern, there were other types of patients—the mentally retarded, the aged, and the alcoholic—who presented special problems. Few provisions were made or institutions set aside for the mentally retarded, usually called "the idiotic" or "the imbeciles," and some found their way into asylums. At all times there was a blurred distinction between the mentally deficient and the mentally ill; but whenever superintendents could, they excluded the former. They felt unprepared to cope with this luckless group, who were often a burden to their families or among the downtrodden confined in almshouses or jails. There was little public sentiment calling attention to their plight.

The aged senile, too, had no spokesman, and suffered accordingly. Asylum officials deplored the weak and helpless condition of the elderly, and urged that they be removed to a familial setting. This, however, was not an unanimous opinion. Many assumed that the aged could not recover under any circumstances, and others argued that "old demented people" were insensitive to their surroundings. An 1859 report from the Hamilton County Lunatic Asylum in Ohio noted that the insane aged were pent up day and night in small rooms without ventilation, and seemingly remained oblivious to this condition. Their mental state made them invulnerable to hardship. Here is an example of rationalized indifference.

The alcoholic were not viewed with such coldness. Moral indignation became the dominant attitude toward the intemperate. Although there was doubt that alcoholism represented a mental disorder, superintendents held a contemptuous view of the drunkard. Repeatedly they complained about the disruptive nature of alcoholic inmates who annoyed attendants, teased patients, and disregarded institutional rules and regulations. A nativist note rang through this depiction: such behavior deviated from that of the sober, upright, true Americans and was identified with lower-class aliens, among whom indulgence was supposedly rampant.

A general psychiatric characteristic of the rapidly growing and diverse mental patient community was the high proportion of severe cases. These were persons admitted in a "state of raving madness, attended with excessive excitement and violence." Today they would be labeled psychotics. Asylum reports abound with descriptions of violent, and in many instances suicidal, patient behavior. At some institutions a virtual suicide epidemic prevailed, with attendants on the alert to prevent inmates from taking their own lives. The high proportion of severely ill patients was the result of several factors: persons sent to institutions were usually social problems; asylums operated on a selective admissions policy that required accepting significant numbers of the "violent and furious"; jailkeepers eager to be rid of troublesome inmates sent them to mental hospitals. The condition in which people were brought to asylums suggests an intractable mental state and is a reflection of the methods employed to control mentally disordered people. Many came handcuffed or tied with ropes or confined in a wooden box or chained to a log. Some of these were hopeless cases who were quickly placed among the ever-expanding numbers of the chronic insane.

To cope with the problems stemming from overcrowded facilities and heterogeneous patient populations, several solutions were recommended. The demand for new asylums remained constant. While this effort aimed at easing the pressures on existing institutions, there remained some concern for the insane still incarcerated in jails and almshouses. They continued to exist under the deplorable conditions so vividly described by Dorothea Dix.

More significant than the calls for additional institutions was the new initiative taken by state legislatures. The beginning of mental health bureaucracies dates from the 1860s and 1870s, when a number of states established control boards to streamline and centralize the work of public charities. This agency, usually called the Board of State Charities or the Board of Public Charities, dictated policy to welfare and penal establishments; and the fact that mental hospitals came under its authority marked a decided setback for the asylum and the treatment of the mentally ill. State policy regarding the insane soon fell into a rut; the mental hospital became another charity, a welfare institution similar to others that provided for the control and care of indigent groups. Boards reinforced the growing welfare role of the asylum by constantly reiterating the reputed link between pauperism and insanity. The effect of policy makers, preoccupied with the apparent negative ramifications of poverty, on mental institutions became a foregone conclusion. A self-fulfilling prophecy was realized, With an uninspired state leadership devoid of concern for therapeutics and absorbed with the question of poor relief, asylums became dumping grounds for lower-class "undesirables."

While state boards were setting policy destined to transform the mental hospital into a welfare institution, superintendents moved to resolve the immediate problems associated with caring for a heterogeneous patient community. Their actions also helped to weaken the therapeutic function of the asylum. The most perplexing issue dealt with providing accommodations for the chronically insane. The subject sparked a heated debate, and battle lines were drawn over the question of separate facilities for incurables. Those favoring segregation of the chronically ill argued that their presence only "crippled the curative influences" on patients in asylums. Although this represented a minority view, the segregation principle was applied at the institution at Tewksbury, Massachusetts, and at Willard Asylum for the Insane, in Willard, New York. Both hospitals accepted only chronic cases. Tewksbury opened in 1866 as an almshouse for harmless and incurable paupers. Later it was renamed the Tewksbury Asylum for the Chronic Insane, and acquired additional stigmas. Not only did it become a substandard institution, but it operated on a policy of accepting alien patients exclusively. Authorized by the state legislature in 1864, Willard Asylum became a receptacle for paupers and by the mid-1870s held over 1,100 patients.

The majority of administrators and the Association of Medical Superintendents of American Institutions for the Insane approved of an integrated mental hospital that cared for both curables and incurables. Their protests against segregation followed several avenues of thought: an establishment for the chronic would deteriorate into a poorhouse; it would drain funds needed to support and enlarge the existing asylum system; it would become an institution enveloped with a mood of hopelessness and despair in which inmates dragged through a torpid, miserable existence waiting for the end of life. In fact, these sincere concerns had no relation to the actual patient population in many asylums. The experiments at Tewksbury and Willard were unique only because they received legal sanction. At numerous establishments from New Hampshire to Kentucky to California, the chronically ill dominated. Here the debate over segregation was academic. Superintendents were administering separate facilities composed largely of incurable cases. By the 1870s acquiescence to this condition was apparent, with annual institutional reports justifying the function of welfare. Providing seclusion, comfort, and shelter to incurables became the asylum's noblest goal. Such a state of affairs reveals a painful irony. A few decades earlier the asylum stressed its curative, therapeutic value; now it extolled the virtue of custodial care.

An added factor placed the chronically insane in an awkward, humiliating position. In several areas, notably Massachusetts and Ohio, state laws or institutional policy required that chronic patients be sent to county asylums or almshouses to make room for the recent and potentially curable insane. This was a most unfortunate situation. While Wisconsin had some success with county asylums, most local institutions were underfunded and badly supervised. Confinement in them meant little more than removal to a living grave. Economy justified the policy. Disturbed by the rising costs of welfare, state legislators moved to cut back expenditures marked for burdensome institutions, and assumed that the transfer of the chronic to almshouses would effect a sizable reduction in the state budget. Their action received support from asylum physicians, who argued that incurable paupers who were moping about mental institutions would find greater satisfaction engaged in the simple tasks provided at poorhouses. In effect this rationalized the approval for separate facilities, and it signified a return to policies and attitudes reminiscent of those before the public asylum, earlier in the century.

Segregation was also seen as a practical solution to handling the other types of "undesirables"—the alien, the criminally insane, and the alcoholic. There was an occasional cry for a separate institution for the foreign-born, but other than the Tewksbury establishment it did not elicit a significant response. Instead, aliens were kept apart either psychologically or physically within institutions. The criminally insane and the alcoholic were viewed as burdensome embarassments to asylums. For the former, totally separate provision was demanded. Unanimous opinion among superintendents appealed for the establishment of "criminal asylums" for those who had criminal tendencies, whether actual convicts or the unconvicted. New York state took the lead with the State Asylum for Insane Criminals at Auburn, authorized in 1859, and the other populous states eventually followed suit. The inebriate also needed isolation out of asylums. In most instances they were referred to county establishments.

Simplistic thinking accompanied the calls for removing patients who were not viewed as "the ordinary insane." If this one step was taken, if they were sent away, then the asylum could concentrate on its main function—providing treatment to cure the mentally ill. Relieved of the major sources of danger, injury, irritability, and anxiety, supervision would be simplified and opportunity for affording care, comfort, and hope to patients, the proper work of a mental institution, would be enhanced. This attitude represented wishful thinking. The difficulties of asylums could not be evaded with the transfer of troublesome patients. The demand itself pointed to the problem rather than to the solution. It revealed a subtle change in professional attitudes toward the insane. Faced with overcrowded wards filled with the chronic, the immigrant, the pauper, the criminally insane, and the alcoholic, superintendents became increasingly insensitive to their patients and saw them as inferior and threatening persons. The old negative stereotypes of the insane as subhuman and vulgar beings were revived.

Indicative of the shifting attitude toward the mentally ill was a declining belief in the curability of insanity. In 1857, Dr. Luther V. Bell, one of the "Original Thirteen" who earlier in his career had proclaimed 90 percent curability, purportedly remarked, "I have come to the conclusion that when a man once becomes insane, he is about used up for this world." This was an extreme statement for the 1850s; but after the Civil War, as chronic cases multiplied, Bell's disillusionment was widespread. Concrete evidence seemed to support it. A few administrators cited 50 percent recovery rate, but most avoided a percentage analysis and simply pointed to the accumulation of patients in a "hopeless state of disease."

The curability ethos received a severe blow from one of its early advocates, Dr. Pliny Earle, another member of the "Original Thirteen." The results of his years of statistical research were compiled in a book, *The Curability of Insanity*. The title is misleading. Earle noted that his findings "practically disproved" the notion that mental disorders were largely curable if properly treated. He deflated the exaggerated claims of curability made by superintendents, particularly in the pre-Civil War generation. He attacked their practice of reporting cured cases rather than cured persons. An individual admitted several times became several cases. Such a patient's history then furnished the statistics with several cured cases but not a single cured person. More important than debunking excessively curability claims was the general pessimistic tone of Earle's work. Throughout the study two related points were reiterated: recoveries were constantly decreasing, and the expansion of mental hospitals brought an increase in chronic patients. Superintendents were not to blame for this condition. Earle maintained that they had exhausted all possible remedies for treating the insane, including pacifying patients with chloroform and hashish, but to little avail. He curtly pronounced: "Very clearly, if insanity is to be diminished it must be by prevention and not by cure." Such a prognosis from so professionally prominent an individual helped to reinforce the emerging negativism associated with caring for the mentally ill.

In the years immediately after the Civil War, a time of great change in mental health care, both etiological and psychiatric theory underwent basic modifications. A new emphasis on the hereditary foundation of mental illness crept into psychiatric literature. Recognized as an important etiological factor, this notion, which superintendents frequently labeled "a hereditary predisposition," fomented debate and concern. Many of the pronouncements of asylum administrators carried a clear homiletic message. Dr. George Chaote of Taunton State Lunatic Hospital in Massachusetts warned that "debilitating indulgences" could be transmitted from one generation to the next. In strong moralistic terms he and other superintendents condemned the person whose debauchery led to insanity, arguing that such a person's children would follow the same path and a hereditary family trait would be established. There were repeated warnings against marrying a person with a family history of insanity. Dr. Joseph Workman of the Toronto Asylum in Canada declared that insanity would "die out" only when the "sane avoided intermarrying with insane stock." Rooted in the Lamarckian tradition, these statements did not convey the stark determinism of early twentieth-century hereditarian thought.

Some administrators could not accept hereditarian explanations of insanity. Dr. John P. Gray argued that "undue importance" was attached to hereditary as a major etiological factor. Gray was superintendent of Utica State Lunatic Asylum and editor of the *American Journal of Insanity*, posts he held for over 30 years. He proclaimed: "No person ever became insane simply because his father or mother, or both, or his grand-parents were insane." His stand on heredity related to his rigid somatic view of insanity. He was influenced by the work of German psychiatrists, particularly by Wilhelm Griesinger's textbook, *Mental Pathology and Therapeutics*, which stressed the maxim "Mental diseases are brain diseases." Accordingly, Gray maintained that insanity was a disorder of the brain. He reasoned that the exhaustion or the weakening of the body's "vital forces" caused brain damage that in turn produced insanity.

For Gray this interpretation represented a leap forward in the study and understanding of mental disorders. It banished the mystery, the dread, and the superstition associated with insanity. The mentally ill person was simply a sick individual suffering from a diseased brain and nervous system. The experience and observations of medical science could cure such a person. Gray established a pathology department at the Utica Asylum, and in his search for physical lesions utilized the microscope in postmorten examinations of the insane. He forecast that the microscope would reveal changes in the cerebral tissue in all types of insanity, a prediction his research never realized.

The physiological view of mental illness relegated the environmental and the moral or psychological factors in the etiology and treatment of insanity to a secondary status. Gray consistently held this position. He published statistical reports in the *American Journal of Insanity* that purportedly proved that the physical causes of insanity greatly outnumbered the moral. In his view, mental disturbance could not spring solely from such external factors as religious excesses, political stresses, or economic troubles. He related the case of a person who went mad after participating in a religious revival. The experience itself had not caused the disorder, Gray contended; it was coincidental, for the individual was already "on the verge of becoming insane." A careful examination of the patient would reveal a physical cause. While downgrading environmental factors as precipitators of mental illness, Gray struck at moral treatment, calling it a philosophy "nourished in the library," an unscientific doctrine separated from the field of medicine. Its basic methods of therapy, notably the psychological manipulation of the patient's social milieu, had little curative influence. Insanity should be treated like any other physical disease.

Gray's commanding position and his forceful personality enabled him to exert a strong impact on the profession. He contributed immensely to shifting psychiatric theory away from moral treatment and to a strict somaticism. This change of emphasis lent additional support to the growing professional ambivalence toward the insane. On the positive side, the stress on somatic methods of care helped patients who arrived at asylums in a poor physical condition. Some suffered from a nutritional deficiency such as pellegra; others were debilitated by alcoholism; a few were victims of accidental brain injuries. The administration of drugs, proper diet, rest, a comfortable room temperature, and adequate ventilation facilitated their physical well-being. On the other hand, the repudiation of moral treatment and the linking of insanity to cerebral pathology created a new scientific mythology that placed physicians in a therapeutic vacuum.

The drift to somaticism reflected the new trends in medical science. The emerging techniques of microscopy and chemical analysis permitted physicians to examine physiological disorders with greater sophistication and awareness. Gray and other superintendents embraced these developments. Science was elevating the study of insanity, they believed, to an objective discipline, transferring it out of the realm of metaphysics and into the mainstream of medicine.

For years physicians to the insane held a defensive attitude about the vagueness and obscurity surrounding their specialty. They appeared to be isolated from the medical world. Now, armed with the power of science, which seemingly affirmed insanity as a recognized physical disease, they gained a new sense of security and achievement in their vocation. Like other practitioners, they could point to the physical evidence of disease.

In fact, however, their devotion to science lacked a firm substantive quality. Although committed to objectivity, to scientific truth, to viewing medical science as the means for understanding and treating mental illness, they produced little evidence to support the new faith. The meager scientific research conducted at mental hospitals remained on a low, superficial plane. The fact that no concrete connection between brain lesions and insanity was found left physicians without a theory to justify any kind of therapy. Many resolved the dilemma with a declaration of faith, a belief that future discoveries would provide the physical evidence.

The emphasis on physiology altered the relationship between the psychiatric world and the lay community. In the past, particularly during the 1840s, strong philosophical and moral links held physicians and lay reformers together. They were united in an altruistic effort to ameliorate the conditions of the mentally ill, and they shared a common humanistic language. By the 1860s the reform impulse had ebbed, and a new medical terminology had evolved that put a wall between professionals and outsiders. Medical language perplexed laymen and alienated them from the world of the insane. Superintendents lost interest in informing the public about their work. Annual asylum reports no longer had any general educational value. These terse documents, in a bland style without interpretation or fervor, recorded building improvements and repairs and cited statistics on admissions, discharges, and deaths. This contrasted with the institutional reports of the 1840s, which expounded on the issues involved in caring for the insane, often analyzed individual case histories, and generally aimed at enlightening the public about the central problems facing the profession.

The growing professional coolness toward outsiders was further revealed at the annual meetings of the Association of Medical Superintendents. Here the discussions concentrated on medical and technical matters, and remained devoid of subjects that might attract lay interest and support. The widening gap between laymen and professionals had dire consequences. Superintendents withdrew into a shell of professionalism; they developed a self-centered attitude that hardened them against positive outside criticism. This professional isolation encouraged a negative public image of the asylum.

By the end of the third quarter of the nineteenth century, the state mental hospital had acquired an unsavory reputation. No longer a small place devoted to each patient's well-being and recovery, it more often resembled a large jail. The enthusiasm and optimism, as well as the commitment to rehabilitation and moral regeneration, associated with its founders had waned. In fact, the asylum and the penitentiary had traveled the same course. Initially, in the 1830s, the ethos of both institutions related to the communitarian experiments of Brook Farm and New Harmony. Four decades later they shared a different common denominator. Like the penitentiary, the asylum was rent with internal tensions and housed persons the public viewed as deviant and troublesome, notably the poor and alien. Furthermore, the asylum's existence was justified in the same manner as the penitentiary's. It kept the community's bothersome element isolated in a controlled environment, safely removed from society.

In short, institutionalizing the insane or the criminal neutralized a basic menace. Contributing also to the asylum's odious image was its expanding welfare function. Though ostensibly a retreat for the mentally ill, it assumed responsibility for many types of persons who lacked the ability to sustain themselves or who needed public aid. The mentally deficient, the alcoholic, the aged, and the poverty-stricken were part of its clientele. By providing custody for these dependents, the asylum became a charity. In the public eye the state mental institution quarantined the socially dependent and offensive as well as the potentially violent and dangerous.

4
A DECEPTIVE AND VICIOUS SYSTEM

A massive assault on mental institutions accompanied the transformation of the asylum into a custodial charity. The critics included newspaper reporters, state legislators, social workers, former patients, former asylum attendants, foreign physicians, physicians from the budding field of neurology, and a few superintendents. Their protests and allegations appeared in the popular press and in professional journals, and sketched a stark portrait of asylum life in the late nineteenth century. While their efforts lacked consistent direction and coordination, their focus on such issues as the use of restraining devices to control patients, the false commitment of sane persons to mental institutions, and the abuse of patients by attendants had the effect of further diminishing the stature of the asylum in the public mind. At the same time their exposés and persistent agitation marked the beginning of a reform movement that culminated in the opening decades of the twentieth century.

A paramount feature of the management of the insane in the late nineteenth-century asylums was the widespread acceptance and application of mechanical restraints. Criticism of their use always provoked superintendents. They were exceedingly irked when a prominent English physician, John C. Bucknill, condemned the practice. In 1876 the *American Journal of Insanity* reprinted Bucknill's study, *Notes on Asylums for the Insane in America*. The English doctor visited and analyzed a select group of institutions, including the Pennsylvania Hospital for the Insane, Bloomingdale Asylum, McLean Asylum, Utica State Lunatic Asylum, Boston Lunatic Asylum, Asylum for Insane Criminals in Auburn, New York, New York City Asylum for the Insane, Wards' Island, Government Hospital for the Insane in Washington D.C., and the Blockley Almshouse in Philadelphia.

Bucknill noted that the quality of care varied from place to place and identified the city asylums as substandard institutions where the insane poor were housed in hot, dirty, noisy structures "unfit for habitation" and received little attention. He urged the medical press to censure these asylums. At every institution he saw patients in poor physical health, and he attributed their "sallow and sickly" appearance to a lack of exercise and fresh air. Crowded together indoors, they breathed an overdried and overheated atmosphere; even on warm, sunny days few patients were seen outdoors in the courtyards and on paths around asylums. The English commentator's most piercing observations dealt with mechanical restraint. Shocked by the application and the visibility of restraining devices, he argued that the reliance on such apparatus largely accounted for the public's distrust of mental institutions.

Bucknill's devotion to nonrestraint was based on a well-established English tradition. The individual most responsible for charting this course was John Conolly, physician at Middlesex County Asylum at Hanwell, the largest mental institution in mid-nineteenth-century England. As early as 1830, in his study *An Inquiry Concerning the Indications of Insanity; with Suggestions for the Better Protection and Cure of the Insane*, Conolly demanded the total abolition of all restraining mechanisms. He argued that an institution operating on the principle of nonrestraint could devote full attention to moral therapy and permit all personnel to treat patients with respect. Conolly began his duties at Hanwell in 1839, and within a decade had firmly established the nonrestraint system. He once said: "The great and only real substitution for restraint is invariable kindness." His writings, especially *The Treatment of the Insane Without Mechanical Restraint*, extended his influence beyond Middlesex. Published in 1856, it was widely read and well-received, and it contributed to effecting a more humane treatment of the mentally ill in England. The English, of course, did utilize devices and the padded room, a place for restraining and isolating violent patients.

The English nonrestraint movement was known in the United States and encouraged such superintendents as Bell, Brigham, Earle, Kirkbride, and Ray to modify and reduce restraining practices at their institutions. This represented a very modest impact; neither they nor their colleagues at other asylums accepted the principle of nonrestraint. They depended on mechanical controls and claimed an absolute right to employ them when needed. A wide assortment of contrivances was readily available: steel wristlets, iron handcuffs, muffs, chair and bed straps, and the camisole or straitjacket, the most popular and most extensively used restraining device. On occasion ordinary sheets wrapped tautly over the shoulders and around the ankles tied a patient to the bed. Several asylums had "restraining" rooms. At Utica a ward was set aside for "disturbed men," who were strapped to large chairs so that only their feet could move.

Besides mechanical devices, superintendents sometimes employed other methods of restraint. Every asylum had rooms designed to isolate inmates in solitary confinement. This technique, it was argued, permitted a person to engage in "solitary vice and filthy practices." The strong arms of an attendant, as well as the administration of anesthetics and sedatives such as ether and chloroform, constrained an individual. Physical force, however, often aroused a patient's resistance, which in turn taxed the attendant's tolerance, leading him to retaliate with additional violence. While drugs provided a temporary solution, they had long-range damaging effects, and their easy and potentially secret administration made them liable to abuse. In short, the use of mechanical devices seemed the most efficient and humane technique for resolving the difficult problem of controlling "vicious" patients. Superintendents insisted that an implement such as the straitjacket was easily applied, and actually provided comfort and protection for the constrained person.

The subject of mechanical restraint was constantly debated at the annual meetings of the Association of Medical Superintendents. The arguments used to justify and affirm the practice stemmed from one basic assumption: every asylum had "a class of patients" who could not be treated in any other way. These inmates might indulge in masturbation, tear off clothing, refuse to eat and require constraint while being force-fed, or were violent and excitable, and had to be bound in order to sleep and rest. While categorizing a group of patients fit only for mechanical controls, superintendents struck at the principle of non-restraint. For them it represented an unattainable ideal because some form of restraint existed in any asylum. The very act of incarcerating a person in a mental institution frequently required coercion. Moreover, the abandonment of restraints necessitated the hiring of additional personnel, which increased institutional expenses.

It was further charged that, when tried, the experiment of nonrestraint failed; and mechanical devices inevitably were reintroduced. A most capricious and spurious argument identified nonrestraint as an alien, un-American principle suited for foreign, but not American, patients. American physicians visiting British mental institutions observed the orderly, neat, and quiet characteristics of the inmates. They were amazed at this discovery, and attributed the success of the nonrestraint system to the docility of English patients. The majority of inmates were "quiet incurables" from the lower classes who accepted the rigid class traditions and distinctions that kept them in a subservient position. They remained timid and acquiesced to the demands and instructions of their social superiors, the asylum personnel. In contrast, the open democratic society of America produced freedom-loving, boisterous, restless, and violent patients who would never accept a nonrestraint system. Dr. Clement Walker of Boston Lunatic Asylum commented that by temperament the "universal Yankees" refused submission to anyone, and could be subdued only by mechanical methods.

The deep American commitment to restraint made superintendents hypersensitive to any criticism of their coercive practices. Accordingly, Bucknill's attack produced an angry rebuttal and generated a trans-Atlantic debate lasting many years. This became a dreary and unproductive controversy because a fraction of the American administrators refused to consider the merits of the nonrestraint principle. Instead, they presented an acid denigration of it and arrogantly reaffirmed the importance and utility of restraints. For example, Dr. Jamin Strong of Cleveland Asylum for the Insane proudly remarked in his 1881 annual report: "It is well known that we have in this asylum the boldness to practice and the audacity to advocate restraint." Along with such testimonials some administrative physicians predicted that mechanical devices would never be eliminated from asylums. This narrow, inflexible position reflected an obvious and growing need for restraints in the large, overcrowded institutions of the 1870s and 1880s. Under those unfortunate conditions repression was inevitable, and mechanical apparatus simplified the burdens of managing violent patients. Its use became another manifestation of the custodial nature of asylum care. The straitjacket symbolized this period in the history of mental health care, in which restraint replaced therapy as the means for maintaining order.

Bucknill's criticisms formed only a small part of the wave of attacks on mental institutions in the last quarter of the nineteenth century. Although significant and penetrating, the British commentaries could be dismissed as the work of unsympathetic foreigners who hypocritically struck at American institutions but ignored the faults of their own. Superintendents found it more difficult to disclaim the assaults and exposés of the popular press. Throughout the country newspapers published pungent accounts depicting asylum life and abuses. Between 1869 and 1876, for instance, the *New York Tribune* carried a number of sensational articles of Bloomingdale Asylum. Under such captions as "An Infernal Institution," "Dirt and Filth Abundant," and "Devilish Treatment for the Insane," the stories condemned the inadequate and poorly prepared food served at the institution and the mistreatment of inmates by attendants.

The most serious allegations charged the asylum with holding a number of sane persons against their will. A notable case was a nun forcibly removed from a convent and confined "as a lunatic" at Bloomingdale. An enterprising reporter carried the exposé further by feigning insanity and gaining admittance to the asylum. His two weeks of experiences provided more sensational stories for the public with reports of "A Night of Horror Among Raving Patients," "Sleep Disturbed by Agonized Cries of the Dangerous Idiots," "Scanty and Foul Food," "Filthy Baths and Rude and Vulgar Attendants." The reporter also voiced his belief that some of the patients were perfectly sane.

The issue of a sane person in an asylum, popularly termed "false commitment," aroused concern among the public, and newspapers fed the interest with incessant publicity—frequently received from former mental patients. Editorials under the banner "A Sane Man Confined as a Lunatic" typified this kind of reportage. The reading public was attentive to the subject. *Hard Cash*, a novel by Charles Reade, an English author who exposed social abuses, became a best seller. Published in 1863, it dealt with the false commitment of the main character, a wealthy young man, by his business colleagues, who wanted his fortune.

The ordeal, pain, and humiliation of an individual involuntarily placed in a mental institution was dramatized in the mid-1860s in the case of Mrs. Elizabeth Packard, who upon the recommendation of her husband, Rev. Theophilus Packard, spent three years at the State Insane Asylum in Jacksonville, Illinois. The case originated with differences of opinion between the Packards on religious matters. Packard, a strict conservative Calvinist, charged that his wife's beliefs represented the ravings of a madwoman and the work of the devil. She repudiated the Calvinist doctrine of the total depravity of mankind, believed that good always triumphed over evil, and was convinced that the oppressed would be freed from their oppressors. On occasion Mrs. Packard believed that she was the Holy Ghost. The reverend found these views most reprehensible, and kept his wife isolated at home. Later he had her committed to the Jacksonville asylum. An Illinois law of 1851 gave him the legal right to place her in an institution with the concurrence of the medical superintendent.

Undaunted, Elizabeth Packard secured legal counsel and brought suit against her husband and the superintendent of the asylum, Dr. Andrew McFarland. The subsequent trial revealed most pointedly the absurdity of the criteria used in declaring Mrs. Packard insane. Three physicians had pronounced her mad; the reasons given ranged from "her aversion to being called insane" to "her feelings toward her husband." The strongest evidence of mental illness was apparently her religious opinions. A physician's statement that she viewed religion "from the osteric standpoint of Christian exegetical analysis, and agglutinating the polysythetical ectoblasts of homogeneous asceticism" brought laughter from the courtroom. It took the jury seven minutes to declare Mrs. Packard sane.

The matter did not end with her freedom. After destroying McFarland, an excellent and kindly physician, she began a crusade for tightening laws to prevent the unjust incarceration of a person in an asylum. The climate of opinion favored reform. Her own trial had dramatized the issue, and newspapers had been circulating stories of illegal commitment cases for years.

In the mid-nineteenth century, commitment procedures were very vague and informal. An order from a public official with police authority could place an indigent insane person in an institution, or an asylum superintendent could detain a member of a family at the father's or husband's request. The informality of the proceedings led to abuses; and as complaints mounted, the Association of Medical Superintendents demanded more stringent legislation. At a minimum it favored the Massachusetts system, which required a certificate signed by two physicians designating a person's mental illness and an affidavit by an asylum trustee. This concern was motivated by the superintendents' fear of legal prosecution rather than by an interest in the civil rights of patients. As Dr. S. Van Nostrand of the State Hospital for the Insane at Madison, Wisconsin, commented: "We all have a class of patients who are ready to make trouble for us." To avoid legal suits, superintendents advocated strict adherence to existing commitment laws and required detailed accounts of the health and progress of each patient.

They also opposed voluntary admissions, believing that patients freely entering an institution would be too independent and would undermine the authority of asylum officials. Equally important was a concern for keeping out poor persons without a home or means of livelihood, who might enter an asylum solely for the purpose of securing food and shelter. Voluntary hospitalization in state mental institutions was illegal until 1881, when Massachusetts enacted the first voluntary admissions law but restricted its application to paying patients.

Beginning in the late 1860s, a few states passed "personal liberty laws." Illinois took the lead in 1867 with the popularly termed "Packard Law," which made a jury responsible for committing anyone to a mental institution. This marked the introduction of due process into the commitment procedure and helped to protect patients while securing asylum officials from charges of false detention. From another perspective, it made sick people defendants in an adversary proceeding, accused of being guilty of insanity. Many superintendents found the new laws offensive, and declared that a jury and a judge were incapable of identifying insanity. A judge should make the decision on the recommendation of "qualified medical examiners." In New York, where this became common practice, a doctor qualified as a medical examiner if he was a permanent state resident, at least 24 years old, and of "reputable character," had studied medicine for three years, and had passed the state medical examinations.

The identification of a qualified medical examiner did not make the task of determining an individual's sanity or insanity any less difficult. The examining physician was urged to follow certain guidelines. First, he should not succumb to pressures to commit without an examination. Frequently the subject's relatives and friends had settled the matter among themselves, and simply wanted a doctor to concur on their decision to commit. On the other hand, they could provide the physician with useful information regarding the subject's occupation, physical health, family history, and probable causes of illness. After completing the inquiry with the family, the physician should be introduced to the person as a medical examiner, without deceit, disguise, or any false pretense. The subject's insanity might be revealed by disordered clothing or room, or a discussion on varied topics might disclose delusions. Once these were established, the physician should probe all their ramifications until convinced of the person's mental state. Finally, the certificate designating insanity should be signed with the awareness that the physician might have to defend his decision in court.

While generating interest in commitment procedures, the late nineteenth-century newspaper exposés frequently aroused legislators to investigate charges of abuse and neglect in mental institutions. One important investigation occurred in Michigan in 1879, when a joint Senate-House committee conducted an inquiry of the Asylum for the Insane at Kalamazoo. The committee uncovered examples of maltreatment so crude and callous that they were quite properly labeled "shocking and brutal crimes." A few attendants perpetrated the majority of the offenses. The most lamentable and scandalizing feature of their acts was the apparent sadistic glee they took in molesting and teasing patients. A chronicle of their pernicious mischief includes forcing an inmate to "bite off the toe nails of another," standing "an old gray haired man" on his head in a toilet, strapping patients to trees while the attendants played crocquet or rested in the shade, and constant kicking of a patient in one part of his body "to keep it sore." An atmosphere of terror pervaded the institution. One attendant testified that it was customary "to choke, kick, and pound patients who are unruly." Physicians transferred any difficult inmate to a ward where they knew the attendants would "whip him." The force-feeding of a patient refusing to eat was a brutal exercise accomplished with the aid of a wooden wedge.

Attendants and doctors occasionally worked in collusion to cover up ugly incidents. An elderly patient left alone in a running hot bath was scalded so badly that he died. This carelessness was concealed by a method "used in such cases." The markings were covered with "cotton batting" and the body was wrapped and then sewed in a sheet to conceal "his ghastly wounds." When an attendant broke the jaw of a patient by kicking him in the face, he and two other attendants who witnessed the incident formed a conspiracy to deceive the superintendent. Until the investigating committee discovered the truth, the matter was recorded as an accident resulting from a struggle to restrain the patient. An unfortunate fact of these revelations was that the guilty went unpunished. The rapid turnover of attendants meant that most had left before the investigation, and those remaining were simply discharged.

The repulsive character and acts of the offending attendants at Kalamazoo illustrated a universal and perennial problem in mental health care, the general inadequacy and inferior quality of institutional personnel. This accounted in part for a large proportion of the problems in nineteenth-century asylums. To cope successfully with their daily tasks, attendants needed patience, tolerance, and idealism, the very qualities most lacked. The undesirable working conditions turned competent and motivated people away. Early in the 1800s attendants remained on duty 24 hours by living and sleeping in the patients' quarters. On occasion they took a holiday by buckling patients in bed over a weekend. Later, night watchmen were introduced to permit uninterrupted sleep for day attendants. Nevertheless, low salaries, long working hours—normally a fourteen-hour-day and a six-and-a-half-day week—and an emotionally charged atmosphere attracted persons ill-equipped to handle problems of mental patients with sympathy and understanding. At the New York City Lunatic Asylum on Blackwell's Island, convicts cared for the insane.

Staffs remained in a constant state of flux; it was common for a third of an asylum's personnel to leave each year. Throughout the major part of the nineteenth century, no formal training for mental health workers existed. In 1882, McLean Asylum in Massachusetts established a school for nurses, and Buffalo State Asylum graduated its first class of psychiatric nurses in 1888. But more often asylum staffs were composed of transient, inexperienced persons without idealism or altruism.

Attendants carried the day-to-day burdens of late nineteenth-century asylum routine. Their main task was to keep the wards quiet and orderly, an objective in line with the custodial ideal. This function was expedited with methods that often offended and alienated patients. Putting inmates to bed early, frequently at four in the afternoon, kept them under control but posed difficulties for the incontinent patient. Even with the introduction of horsehair mattresses and canvas sheets, those who wet beds had to be changed every two or three hours. With patients spending so much time in bed, it was inevitable that the bed itself became a popular restraining device. The Utica crib, named for the New York asylum where it was first introduced in the 1840s, had a widespread application by the late nineteenth century. At one large institution over 50 were occupied. Constructed like a baby crib, it had a padded interior and a hinged lid that fastened over a person, firmly restricting movement.

Since attendants applied the restraining devices, patients viewed them with suspicion and fear, and devices did function to punish uncontrolled behavior. Their identification with disagreeable treatment contributed further to their odious image. Attendants also administered the cold wet pack to calm excited individuals. The technique varied from place to place, but generally consisted of pouring pails of cold water over the patient, followed by wrapping him in a cold, damp sheet, and ending in a rubdown with a cold, wet cloth. Attendants gave inmates warm baths in which the patient's body was immersed in water while the head was held tightly in a tub cover made out of metal or canvas. One of the cruelest tasks of attendants involved what was euphemistically called "forced aliementation" or force-feeding. A patient's refusal to eat was taken as evidence of a stubborn and resistant attitude that had to be broken. Blunt and crude methods were employed, including the use of an iron bit or a wedge to open the mouth. One attendant applied this device while another held the patient's head between his knees and two others restrained the patient's legs, feet, and arms. Later, tube-feeding became popular.

In short, the attendant's job of maintaining discipline and order, chiefly by means of restraining mechanisms and abhorrent treatment, had an adverse effect on patients. Inmates received little comfort or confidence from anyone. Preoccupied with administrative duties, the superintendent rarely saw them. The attendants' acceptance of repression as the best means of asserting authority raised an insurmountable barrier to meaningful contacts. Patients were isolated, caught in a web of neglect and degradation.

The disclosures and revelations of the 1870s and 1880s further maligned the asylum in the public eye. The public could only be dismayed and repelled by the evidences of abuse. This left a legacy of distrust and suspicion that proved difficult to dispel even when mental hospitals introduced more innovative and progressive methods of care. The image of the mental institution as a "snake pit" became firmly implanted in the public mind.

The ultimate responsibility for correcting abuse rested with the asylum superintendent. But in facing the mounting crescendo of criticism from the popular press with regard to attendant maltreatment, false commitments, and mechanical restraints, superintendents struck a defiant pose and rarely admitted any improprieties. Their defense turned outward rather then inward. They contradicted charges of abuse, calling them "unjust accusations" or "malicious falsehoods." With calculated disdain, they labeled critics insane or stupid or naive. To Dr. John H. Callender, superintendent of the Tennessee Hospital for the Insane at Nashville, and one-time president of the Association of Medical Superintendents, lay critics were "mountebanks" or charlatans who knew nothing about asylum management, who accepted as fact the "fantastic foolery" that came from "the disturbed brains of half-recovered patients." This was the basic thrust of the professional counterattack against laymen: outsiders lacked the competence and knowledge necessary for evaluating mental institutions. Such arrogance turned into bitter indignation when members of their own profession, notably physicians specializing in the new field of neurology, issued sharp protests.

Most neurologists were private physicians; some were attached to medical schools, and many were dedicated to research. In 1872 neurology gained organizational status with the founding of the New York Neurological Society. Two years later the field acquired a scholarly organ with the establishment of the *Journal of Nervous and Mental Disease*. Neurologists soon became involved in a long, acrimonious battle with asylum administrators. One of the most outspoken pioneers in neurophysiology, Dr. Edward C. Spitzka, castigated medical superintendents for their indifference to any kind of scientific research and their shallow understanding of mental illness. To support this charge, he contended that they had not produced any contribution to the fields of pathology and clinical observation. While they had ample opportunity to collect systematic data on autopsies, few were made; and usually those performing the autopsy had little knowledge of cerebral anatomy. The absence of scientific equipment was shocking; most asylums lacked a microscope.

The general state of American psychiatric literature, Spitzka maintained, revealed the superficial interests of superintendents. Their articles had little originality and dealt mainly with ephemeral topics, eulogies of deceased physicians, and elaborate justifications for mechanical restraints. Their asylum reports dwelt on subjects that had no important bearing on the study of mental illness. Tidbits on gardening, tin roofing, and the condition of drain pipes, rather than information about the prognosis and treatment of insanity, filled these documents. Throughout his writings Spitzka consistently used the term "psychiatry" to designate his field, and he demanded that the study of insanity be "considered a subdivision of neurology." He speculated that an asylum staff composed mostly of neurologists would upgrade mental institutions, spark interest in research, and improve the general care of patients. Above all, he wanted psychiatry broadened out of its institutional setting to include all physicians interested in treating mental illness.

Spitzka also outlined several reform objectives. The more important ones included restricting the use of mechanical restraints to a bare minimum and outlawing all cruel devices; curtailing the routine administeration of drugs without considering their therapeutic effects on each patient; providing suitable institutional work for patients; keeping accurate and reliable asylum records on the types of insanity, causation, admissions, use of restraints and seclusion rooms, accidents, and death rates; introducing a compulsory autopsy system for the purpose of gathering scientific data; and broadening government supervision of public mental institutions.

Spitzka's criticism of superintendents and his reform proposals typified the neurologists' assault on asylum psychiatry. The New York Neurological Society, which he used as a forum, shared his views and spearheaded a movement to investigate the Empire State's mental hospitals. In 1878 and 1879 it petitioned the legislature to examine the state's asylum system. Responding to this pressure, a committee on public health held hearings, only to exonerate the institutions. This defeat spurred the reformers to intensified organizational activity. Social workers with the National Conference of Charities and Correction, an organization consisting of members from state boards of charities, joined the campaign; and in July 1880 they and the neurologists established the National Association for the Protection of the Insane and the Prevention of Insanity (NAPIPI). Like the neurologists, social workers expressed indignation over asylum abuses, distrusted superintendents, and demanded stricter government control over mental hospitals. Their main concern was administrative reform; they sought to centralize and rationalize the system of public welfare.

One of the founders of NAPIPI, Dr. George M. Beard, a noted neurologist, gave the organization noble objectives: safeguarding the interests of the insane through the creation of state supervisory boards; encouraging research in the etiology, cure, and prevention of insanity; and broadening the public's understanding of mental disorders through the dissemination of enlightened information. The organization would succeed, he believed, if it merely made more people aware that "It is no disgrace to be crazy." Unlike the Association of Medical Superintendents, NAPIPI had an open membership.

NAPIPI received the editorial backing of the *Journal of Nervous and Mental Disease* as well as the support of the American Neurological Association, a national organization established in 1875. The intense fervor and righteousness of this reform group was expressed in an influential article, "Despotism in Lunatic Asylums," by Dorman B. Eaton, a founder of NAPIPI and active civil service reformer. Published in the *North American Review*, a popular magazine, Eaton's study denounced the authoritarian character of asylum management. To him "palatial asylums," elaborately constructed at great public expense, had failed to check the increasing rate of insanity in American society. Furthermore, by European, especially English, standards, the care of the insane was shockingly primitive and brutal, as the reports of state investigations and newspapers so painfully revealed. Eaton gave two reasons for this depressing situation. First, neither the public interest nor the medical profession had been sufficiently aroused about the treatment of the insane. Second, and more important, mental institutions were cut off from the community by a narrow circle of despotic administrators who ignored positive outside criticism, and tolerated and fostered abuses within their asylums.

This was "a deceptive and vicious system," which Eaton emphasized by analyzing the method of governing the Utica asylum. There nine trustees controlled the institution without significant checks to prevent "extravagance, favoritism, and neglect," and the superintendent ruled with "unparalleled despotism." He dominated and managed the asylum with all of the authority and powers of a divine right monarch. Since no restraints were placed on him, any effort at reform was easily thwarted. The authoritarian management of asylums, Eaton charged, was complemented by the dictatorial practices of the Association of Medical Superintendents. The organization absolutely dominated the profession by determining asylum policies nationwide, limiting its membership, and severely censuring those who questioned its affairs. In contrast, the English system of governing the insane, Eaton argued, had built-in checks that helped prevent abuses, corruption, extravagance, and the "despotism" of any special interest group. The National Board of Commissioners of Lunacy, composed of members from the medical, legal, and business professions, acted as a disinterested guardian of the country's mental institutions. It had powers of regulation and inspection, and remained receptive to public opinion. The American system, abounding in secrecy, tyranny, and restraint, presented a doleful contrast. Eaton believed that the creation of an independent board, modeled after the English one, would mark a giant positive step toward reform.

Eaton's sharp denunciation received wide publicity in popular and medical journals, and represented the main activity of NAPIPI: mobilizing support for asylum reform. It encouraged dissident neurologists, social workers, and physicians to revolt against established superintendents. It continually passed resolutions in favor of state inquiries into mental hospitals, and even demanded a congressional investigation of the nation's asylums. The organization also moved to advance the study of psychiatry in medical colleges. Only a few schools offered formal psychiatric courses, and American textbooks in the field did not increase until the publication in 1883 of Edward C. Spitzka's *Insanity: Its Classification, Diagnosis, and Treatment* and William A. Hammond's *A Treatise on Insanity in Its Medical Relations.* In an effort to remedy the neglect and meager knowledge of psychiatry in medical schools, NAPIPI called upon every college of medicine to establish a lectureship in psychiatry and a psychiatric clinic. General practitioners receiving psychiatric training would be well-equipped to detect insanity and to prescribe treatment before a person became a chronic case.

In its campaign to improve the plight of the mentally ill, NAPIPI exposed instances of unsavory politics in asylum management. The 1870s and 1880s represented an era of great corruption at all levels of government. The immorality of city machine politics complemented the irregularities in state legislatures and the scandals of national administrations. Political favoritism permeated government hierarchies, and appointments went to party regulars who frequently lacked the experience or qualifications for public office. This political jobbery often extended to state and county mental institutions, where superintendencies became political plums awarded in accordance with the principles of patronage. Two notorious cases of the 1870s, occurring in North Carolina and New York, illustrate this practice. The Insane Asylum of North Carolina at Raleigh was administered by a man who had no experience in caring for the mentally ill nor any knowledge of insanity. He was a politician who had been a clerk, a lawyer, a Confederate Army captain, a physician (for three years), and a member of the state legislature. His ability to please all of the major political factions won him the position at Raleigh. In New York City, a disappointed office seeker was pacified after receiving the superintendency of the New York City Lunatic Asylum on Blackwell's Island.

A superintendent appointed solely on the basis of political loyalty remained under constant pressure to advance his party's interests. He was expected to contribute to campaign funds, to hire party members as employees, and to buy supplies from party dealers. The insecurities and political intrigues involved in this method of hiring asylum officials turned many practitioners out of the profession. Some acquiesced, and plundered an institution before the next election left them unemployed. Ample opportunities for graft existed with a superintendent controlling the spending of appropriations, the bids on construction projects, and the provisioning of the institution. In four New York asylums in the 1870s, $4 million earmarked for maintenance and improvements was misappropriated by public officials. Although only a few superintendents were corrupt, enough scandals became public to cast an unfavorable light on the entire profession. Reformers quickly seized upon any incident of extravagance or misuse of public money, demanding investigations and the elimination of politics from all appointments to state mental institutions.

The dissatisfaction with asylums stimulated an interest in the noninstitutional care of the mentally ill, an approach NAPIPI sanctioned. This alternative received the support of many former mental patients, who, in relating their asylum experiences, presented sharp insights into the deleterious effects of asylum life. Janet Ruvtz-Rees, a former patient, called the state asylum "a mistake." In her experience a depressing atmosphere of sickness and disease saturated a mental institution. This mood affected everyone, attendants and patients alike, and overpowered any cheerful or healthy influences. Rather than institutionalizing an insane person, Ruvtz-Rees advocated the boarding of a mentally disturbed individual with a responsible family.

Some neurologists advanced the case for nonasylum treatment by rejecting the assumption of most superintendents that quick removal to an institution offered the best hope for the insane. They argued that confinement was usually unnecessary, and was detrimental to an individual's mental and physical health. The combined effects of inadequate medical care, the abrupt severing of social and family ties, and the forced and close contact with people suffering from all kinds of mental disturbances could only cause a patient's condition to deteriorate. The abuses and negligence rampant in improperly supervised and inspected asylums worsened the situation. Some neurologists in private practice believed that asylums had no curative influence and that mental patients suffering from psychoneurotic disorders were best treated at home.

Neither the support of this innovative approach nor the constant agitation for more enlightened asylum management practices was enough to keep NAPIPI alive. It represented an abortive reform movement. In 1883 it established the *American Psychological Journal*, which recorded the organization's activities and published occasional papers on the prevention of insanity. The editor, Dr. Joseph Parrish, had an interest in alcoholism, and the journal devoted most of its attention to the relationship between inebriety and mental disorder. The last issue appeared in October 1884, and soon afterward the organization fell apart.

The demise of NAPIPI may be attributed to a basic internal conflict of interests between neurologist and social worker members. Neurologists remained devoted to scientific research; social workers, to asylum reform. As the organization exposed abuses, concentrated on a drive to improve institutions, and gave little attention to promoting a scientific study of mental illness, neurologists drifted away. But in spite of its brief existence, NAPIPI achieved significance in advocating reforms and alerting the public to abuses in mental institutions. It stood as the forerunner of the twentieth-century mental hygiene movement.

The assaults of neurologists and NAPIPI jolted superintendents into a vigorous and intolerant defense of their position and institutions. They felt slighted and even betrayed by the criticism of physicians, and charged them with improper professional behavior. It was customary for medical men to extend courtesy and respect to one another and not to seek outside support in their judgments of "professional brethren." Yet the tone and language of the superintendents' counterattack were often bereft of professional niceties. Critics were called "agitators" who lived "upon the borderland of insanity" or "flippant neurospasts of the medical profession." Dr. Eugene Grisson, superintendent of the Insane Asylum of North Carolina, depicted the reforming neurologist Dr. William A. Hammond as "a Bombastes Furioso," "a Cagliostro," "a moral monster whose baleful eyes gleam with delusive light."

NAPIPI's accusation of "despotism" stung superintendents, and at the 1881 annual meeting of their association, Dr. Orpheus Everts of the Cincinnati Sanitarium retaliated with a simple statement that there was no other way of successfully managing the insane. The unique position of an asylum head required great authority and freedom to exercise wide discretionary powers. Any check or limitation placed on him would produce dissension, inefficiency, and antagonism within the institutional hierarchy. Any delay in decision making would work adversely on patients, for "insane men can not await cabinet consultations." Everts and others could answer the charge of despotism only with a rigid defense of their authoritarian methods of ruling asylums.

Reformers had leveled some of their sharpest blows at the Association of Medical Superintendents, the very heart of established psychiatry. It was assailed for depotism, exclusiveness, rigidity, for ignoring and even discouraging scientific research while fostering petty administrative and political concerns. Reformers saw it as a symbol of the status quo, a stagnant body that had retarded the growth and development of American psychiatry. The reformers' view came close to reality. The organization was an exclusive club admitting asylum superintendents only. Although it represented a powerful lobby capable of exerting significant influence on mental health matters, it remained isolated from both the community and the medical profession. This isolation was largely self-imposed. As the outcry against it mounted, the Association became exceedingly egocentric, smug, and complacent. It deliberately curtailed information to the public, assuming that silence was a good means of coping with hostile critics. It maintained a self-centered policy that its members alone were qualified to understand, treat, and manage the insane, a policy that led the organization to oppose merger with the American Medical Association. Its annual meetings were marked by the usual rhetorical self-glorification, with speakers identifying their organization with "the noblest incentives," "the loftiest ambitions," or "the most philanthropic purposes."

Superintendents resisted change, but as a result of the agitation of reformers and continued pressures of neurologists, their association slowly evolved into a more open organization. An incident at the 1881 annual meeting gave a forecast of the future. A few younger psychiatrists and an older member, Dr. Richard Gundry of the Maryland Hospital for the Insane at Catonsville, stated that many of the charges against asylums were justified and, in fact, true. The Association, they argued, should turn from self-congratulation to a serious consideration of the reformers' proposals. These remarks were refuted by the most prominent of the superintendents, Dr. John Gray; yet a crack of disunity had opened in the organization's wall of internal solidarity. It widened further in 1885, when the organization extended membership to assistant asylum physicians. In 1892 superintendents took a radical departure by changing the name of their organization to the American Medico-Psychological Association and admitting noninstitutional psychiatrists.

The persistent criticisms of reformers and the lingering dissatisfaction with the asylum system contributed to the enactment of new laws relating to the management of the mentally ill. New York, which experienced intense agitation, provides a good example. Inaugurated in the 1890s, the legislation became a model for other states. One of the new provisions placed employment in public mental institutions under the state civil service system. Vacancies would be filled by candidates selected on the basis of competitive examinations. This presumably would curb excessive political influence and insure the maintenance of minimum standards for every staff position.

To check irregularities and inefficiency, the newly established Commission of Lunacy received broad powers of regulation and inspection. It approved expenditures, assigned appropriations, and scrutinized financial records; it inspected asylums to determine the condition of physical facilities and the quality of food and services; it heard complaints from staff and patients. The Commission was composed of a physician, a lawyer, and a layman, each appointed by the governor.

The new laws also tightened controls at the asylum level. Each institution received a board of managers authorized to conduct studies and report its findings to the Commission. The superintendent was required to meet regularly with the Commission. He was obligated to visit all wards frequently and to examine new patients within five days of their arrival. He was to provide training for his staff. When necessary, institutional personnel were to consult with such specialists as dentists and ophthalmologists. Patients also benefited from the new legislation. All inmates were removed from county to state asylums. They were given greater freedom in corresponding with the outside world. New commitment laws provided for easier appeal procedures and permitted patient furloughs.

A minor but symbolic provision of the New York laws apparently aimed at emphasizing the curative, rather than the custodial, role of mental institutions. Hereafter all state asylums would be called "hospitals." In terms of the institutional care of the insane, this legislation marked a decided advance. It promised higher standards of responsibility in the administration of mental institutions, and it marked the final demise of the asylum "despot." The era of all-powerful superintendent acting like an authoritarian father dominating his household was ended. Superintendents were no longer alone in formulating policy regarding the mentally ill. This function was passing to a central state agency specifically organized to cope with the problems of mental health care. The agency, a Commission of Lunacy (or Board of Insanity) removed the mental institution from the jurisdiction of a general welfare office that had lumped the insane with such dependents as criminals and paupers. While the establishment of the new agency held out expectations of innovation and reform in the care of the mentally ill, in practice it focused largely on bureaucratic matters, devoting its energies to eliminating waste and inefficiency in mental hospital administrations.

5
BLACKS AND IMMIGRANTS

In the closing decades of the nineteenth century, two great social movements rocked American society. The nation's large black population, recently transformed from slave to free status, searched for a place in the social order. Blacks experienced anguish and humiliation in the struggle to adopt a new life-style and cope with discrimination. Their newly won freedoms were exploited, cynically manipulated, and eventually curtailed. An equally significant social alteration was generated by the waves of European immigrants who poured into the cities, industrial towns, and mining communities of the East and Midwest. Arriving from eastern and southern Europe, their customs, languages, and religion set them apart from "native" Americans who were predominantly Protestant and of English or west European origin. The rapid influx of these "new immigrants" in tremendous numbers aroused prejudices and provoked cries of alarm. Many Americans succumbed to xenophobia: Was the country being overrun by hordes of degenerate foreigners who were polluting society with disease, crime, and political radicalism?

The explosive force of racism affected both blacks and the new immigrants, adding another dimension to their plight. By the turn of the century, the categorization of Americans along racial lines was well established, with almost every minority stigmatized as inferior to the majority Anglo-Saxon population. For minorites this meant economic deprivation, social isolation, and political impotence as well as subjection to violent intimidation. While the belief that the United States represented a melting pot of nations remained popular, racial segregation and restrictive immigration laws demonstrated a careful, selective application of the assimilation ideal.

Psychiatrists generally shared the prevailing racial views. Their ethnic and racial biases were buttressed by Social Darwinian concepts of society, hereditarian notions about insanity, degenerative theories of individual development, and an influential eugenics movement. These intellectual and social trends reached a crest in the years before World War I. In consequence, when psychiatrists examined the questions and issues concerning the relationships of race, immigration, and insanity, they supplied data and opinion to support public hostility and propaganda directed against blacks and the new immigrants. The pessimistic prognosis of the mental health of these groups contributed to the segregation and immigration restriction movements that many psychiatrists supported.

Before the Civil War mentally ill blacks received little institutional care. Most were placed in almshouses and jails. Since local attitudes and practices determined accommodations, they were either excluded from asylums or segregated within an institution. Superintendents generally agreed that blacks and whites in the same wards represented "an unnatural association." Integration violated the fundamental practice of moral treatment: placing patients from similar social backgrounds in the same quarters. Accommodating patients of different social classes and races in the same wards created an atmosphere of distress, and retarded recovery.

The image of blacks held by psychiatrists in pre-Civil War America stemmed largely from their analysis of the causes of insanity. In their writings on etiology, they consistently argued that insanity accompanied civilization. Civilization brought about a high standard of living but, they argued, the pressures and tensions involved in the drive for material success caused frequent outbreaks of madness. This condition was apparent only in advanced, sophisticated societies; primitive cultures were free of debilitating mental disorders. Psychiatrists placed African and American Indian societies in the second category, designating them as savage cultures without intellectual or material attainment. Blacks in America, being only a few generations removed from a presumably uncivilized African culture, were also immune from serious mental disturbances. In 1840 over 380,000 free blacks and almost 2.5 million slaves resided in the United States. It was generally assumed by psychiatrists that slaves experienced few mental illnesses but that free blacks, in their new contact with civilization, would show more signs of mental disorder.

With the publication of the *United States Census Report* of 1840, these assumed differences in the mental health of free blacks and slaves received unexpected support. This document, the sixth decennial census, included statistical tables illustrating the distribution of the insane by race and state as well as general information about mental illness in America. One startling fact emerged from the figures. The incidence of insanity among free blacks was 11 times greater than among slaves. A breakdown of the figures made the comparison even more dramatic. According to the statistics, in the free state of Maine, one in 14 blacks was mentally ill; in the slave state of Louisiana, the figure was only one in every 4,310. It appeared that the Mason-Dixon Line marked more than a boundary between North and South. It determined a black person's mental health.

The statistics had obvious political implications. Proslavery propagandists grasped the new information and used it to argue that their "peculiar institution" fostered and preserved the mental health of blacks. This message was widely publicized in political speeches and in periodicals. At the same time, one of the nation's leading statisticians, Dr. Edward Jarvis, a Massachusetts physician, reexamined the census and found gross errors and contradictions in it. He argued that it represented a mass of falsehoods biased against northern blacks. Jarvis found that many northern towns listing insane blacks in fact had no black residents; in other places the number of disturbed blacks was higher than the number of black inhabitants. According to the census, the city of Worcester, Massachusetts, had 133 insane blacks. Jarvis discovered that the figure represented all of the white patients in Worcester State Asylum. After pointing to many other inaccuracies, he concluded that the 1840 census did nothing but "confuse and mislead." Many years would pass, he lamented, before its impressions would be removed.

Jarvis' prediction was accurate. Although his findings were published in several professional journals and he continually demanded a census correction, his pleas went largely unnoticed. The 1840 statistics helped to confirm the belief that slavery protected the mental health of blacks by freeing them from all of the cares, anxieties, intemperance, and other excesses of civilization.

In fact, there were slaveowners who observed that bondmen were burdened with nervous and behavioral disorders. They described these slaves as "demented," "sullen," "easily excited," or "mentally unsound." For economic reasons owners refused to commit an afflicted slave to an institution. Instead, the unfortunate was either whipped or assigned a less demanding task. Southern doctors believed that blacks were susceptible to unique physical and mental disorders. A Louisiana physician, Dr. Samuel W. Cartwright, recorded that bondmen were prone to two mental disorders that he labeled *Dysaethesia Ethiopica* and *Drapetomania*. The slave suffering from *Dysaethesia Ethiopica*, Cartwright claimed, broke tools, damaged crops, and injured livestock. *Drapetomania* was more serious. The doctor noted that its first symptom was a "dissatisfied" attitude; and if the condition went unchecked, it caused the slave to run away. Obviously, what Cartwright interpreted as mental illness represented the bondmen's resistance to slavery. This southern physician equated the mental health of blacks with contentment with a subservient position in society, and identified protest as a mark of mental derangement.

After the Civil War, with slaves emancipated, states recognized a responsibility for housing mentally ill blacks and admitted them to asylums. In all parts of the country segregation remained the norm within every institution. Northern and western states provided accommodations for black inmates in separate rooms or a small ward. Since most blacks resided below the Mason-

Dixon Line, the South faced the difficult situation of finding facilities for large numbers of insane former bondmen. Southern social traditions and racial antipathies remained strong, and necessitated the complete separation of black and white patients. Black patients were placed in a special wing of the main building or in an entirely separate structure. Georgia State Sanitarium at Mill-edgeville provided typical accommodations: the building for blacks was erected one-quarter mile behind the main building. A widespread movement for separate institutions was prevented by building and maintenance expenses. In 1912 only four states—Alabama, Maryland, North Carolina, and Virginia—had mental hospitals specifically designated for blacks.

Asylum administrators accepted the institutional pattern of segregation without question. To have challenged the policy would have been exceedingly incongruous. Racial views and assumptions stigmatizing blacks with inferior attributes permeated all areas of American professional and public life. More antiblack literature was published and read at the close of the nineteenth century than at any other time in American history. A significant element in antiblack polemics was Social Darwinism, an ideology derived from Charles Darwin's concepts of natural selection and the survival of the fittest. Social Darwinists justified the existing social and racial inequalities with the assertion that the black, the poor, and the immigrant were unfit, the refuse of an unsuccessful struggle to survive.

Within psychiatric circles the phylogenetic concept of higher and lower races, a tenet of Social Darwinism, had an enduring influence. According to this theory, the higher race had a long, complex, and refined evolutionary history, while the lower race had a retarded development, progressing just beyond the prehistoric past. The higher race had a larger brain than the lower race, and differences in brain size produced dissimilar behavioral patterns. The higher race acted with mature responsibility; the lower race showed a lack of discipline and exhibited childlike behavior. Needless to say, Caucasians represented the higher race; blacks, the lower.

In a lengthy article appearing in the July 1901 issue of *American Journal of Insanity*, Dr. Charles E. Woodruff specified that "the negro" had no capacity for civilization. As a member of the lower race, the black's struggle to survive produced only "crime, consumption, and insanity." Woodruff was an Army surgeon who had spent many years in the Philippines, where he developed an interest in the effects of tropical climate on black and white servicemen. From his observations he wrote a book, *The Effects of Tropical Light on White Men*, which postulated a relationship between race and climate. His basic premise narrowed to a correlation between skin color and racial habitat: "darker races" thrived and belonged close to the Equator; lighter ones remained vigorous and prospered in the temperate zones. If a race moved out of its natural habitat, it would become enfeebled and, eventually, extinct. On this assumption Woodruff predicted that blacks would die out in America. In addition to developing these ideas, he sanctioned lynch law, arguing that it represented an expression of democracy, a right of Southerners "to make and execute their own laws." The fact that Woodruff's writing appeared in *American Journal of Insanity*, the leading journal of institutional psychiatry, revealed the wide diffusion of racial thought in one of its more curious and distasteful forms.

When psychiatrists analyzed the issues involved in the relationship between mental illness and former slaves, one question excited great interest and speculation: the increased rate of insanity among blacks since emancipation. The allegation was supported with statistics. In Virginia the number of insane blacks purportedly increased 100 percent every decade. In Georgia the 1880 census revealed that one of every 1,764 blacks was insane; in 1890 the figure was one in 943. Alarmed by this development, psychiatrists offered several explanations. The number of commitments increased because blacks as well as whites accepted the mental institution as the best place to care for and treat insane persons. The swelling accumulation of chronic cases in asylums included many black patients. The unsanitary living conditions of blacks undermined their health and made them susceptible to mental disorders.

Here the old myth that slavery enhanced the well-being of blacks was resurrected. Before emancipation mental breakdowns were avoided by the regular, easygoing, simple life on the plantation, which provided healthy outdoor employment, nourishing food, comfortable clothing, and freedom from dissipation, care, and responsibility. With emancipation, however, blacks lost this idyllic life, and the results were catastrophic. They deteriorated both physically and mentally, and in most instances their rising incidence of turberculosis, syphilis, and alcoholism paralleled their increased rate of insanity. Former slaves ignored the laws of hygiene, lost control over their passions, and plunged into excesses and vice. After relating this apparent situation, one psychiatrist commented: "No wonder we have in our asylums an increasing number of idiots, imbeciles, and all types of dementias from the colored race."

The phylogenetic concept easily related to this discussion on the negative effects that freedom had on blacks. It was frequently expressed in curt, repetitive phrases or generalizations. Former slaves could not meet the demands of freedom because they represented "a subordinate race" without a history. G. Stanley Hall, the influential psychologist who brought the concepts of Sigmund Freud to the United States, believed that blacks suffered from a "tropical imagination," and others maintained that before arriving in America, blacks had been content with living in "the depths of savagery."

Dr. Arrah B. Evarts of the Government Hospital for the Insane at Washington, D.C., asserted that the mental condition of blacks was determined by their racial history. Theodore Roosevelt's *African Game Trails*, an account of his safaris, provided the source for Evarts' understanding of black history. Roosevelt typed blacks as "childlike savages" still living in the early Paleolithic Age. Accordingly, they had no religion, ethics, culture, nor mythology; they simply wandered, fought against each other, and eventually were sold into slavery. To Evarts these "years of savagery," when "the race learned no lessons in emotional control," absolutely conditioned black behavioral patterns. The time spent in slavery constituted only an era of reprieve. With freedom blacks retrogressed to their natural primitive state. The demands of a higher civilization were beyond their level of understanding or capacity for adjustment.

A composite psychological portrait of blacks emerges from the psychiatric literature of the early 1900s. Perhaps more than anything else, the terms used to depict black behavioral patterns illustrate the pervasiveness of the "Sambo" image and the popular racial stereotypes found in the "Uncle Remus" stories of the southern journalist and author Joel Chandler Harris. The terms include "overindulgent," "carefree," "irresponsible," "impulsive," "easily amused," "careless," "unthinking," and "jolly." These traits purportedly proved that blacks remained at the childhood stage of human development.

There were other elements in this psychological picture. Blacks feared darkness and rarely went out at night "unless on mischief bent." This fear represented one of "the superstitions of the race." Blacks were fascinated with any fraternal order that held ceremonies and rituals, and displayed colorful regalia and uniform. In their religious services the "sounds, motions, and residual forms and ceremonies" left "by their African forefathers" climaxed in a wild emotional melee of hysteria and exaltation. Such behavior was interpreted as being "only a step from the manic phase of manic-depressive psychosis." The most distinctive and prominent trait of the black psyche was a belief in superstition, a "peculiarity" that demonstrated the influence of "primitive African life and customs." The common superstitions included belief in spirits, ghosts, witchcraft, palmistry, and voodoo. An exotic faith held that animal teeth and snakeskin had magical powers of protection. A full moon "to the colored man" was "a reminder of death," a foreboding time when any dangerous task should be postponed. Indeed, blacks even interpreted a break in the daily routine as an evil omen and sign of bad luck.

This psychological portrait could not be complete without a reference to sexual behavior. In this area blacks showed no modesty nor sense of morality, and all sexual desires were "fully satisfied." Promiscuity was rampant, and began at an early age. After studying a small southern black community, one psychiatrist commented that its only virgin was a newly born baby.

From this psychological portrait it was concluded that blacks were prone to specific types of mental disorders. Their obsessive fears and superstitions promoted dementia praecox; their emotional and restless nature produced manic forms of psychoses. Although their loose morality and poor hygiene encouraged the spread of syphilitic disorders, psychiatrists agreed that they had few sexual perversions. Their open, shameless sexual abandon checked the development of deviations arising from repressed or unfulfilled urges. Also, blacks seldom experienced depression or involutional melancholia because they lived a superficial life concerned with concrete, everyday happenings, and had no consciousness of sin or the graver emotions of grief and remorse.

Some psychiatrists distinguished between black and white psychoses, and rated the former on a lower level. They assumed that blacks had not reached the "evolutionary advancement" of Caucasians, and therefore rarely plunged into the depths of insanity. Suited for routine tasks and submission to others, mentally ill blacks could even continue to function in the work world. When their daily work was impaired, they had reached the stage of absolute incurability; and for these persons the mental institution was the last resort, a place without hope. This prognosis was verified in numerous statistical studies showing that few black inmates improved, and a high percentage died, in asylums.

Whether submerged in slavery or free after emancipation, blacks were regarded as inferior beings, and this view determined the direction of any psychiatric theorizing about them. Too simple to suffer from insanity as slaves, too unstable to maintain sanity as free persons, they experienced the brunt of society's double racial standard. Whatever the explanation for their mental disorders, the conclusions pointed to deficiencies, notably a limited capacity for growth and a pathological personality and life pattern. Obviously, then, blacks functioned best when controlled and kept within the bounds of their shortcomings.

At the turn of the century, when America erected the social, legal, and political barriers of segregation, psychiatrists took the cues of the wider society. In an argument distinguishable from the rhetoric of red-neck politicians only by the grace of the language, Dr. J. Allison Hodges, professor of nervous and mental disease at the University College of Medicine in Richmond, Virginia, demanded the total segregation of blacks from white society. Speaking before the 1900 annual convention of the American Medico-Psychological Association, he told the delegates that blacks had been given too much freedom, that they needed restrictions, and that the protective shield of segregation would help to restore their mental health. Here is a logic similar to the antebellum justification of slavery.

Racist thought always presents a dichotomy, attributing inferiority to some and superiority to others. While blacks were characterized in the most negative terms, a cult of Anglo-Saxon superiority flourished. Academicians such as sociologist Edward A. Ross and economist Francis Walker, leading journalists including Thomas Bailey Aldrich, editor of the *Atlantic Monthly*, notable intellectuals like Brooks Adams, and powerful politicians such as Henry Cabot Lodge and Theodore Roosevelt glorified Anglo-Saxon institutions and culture. A host of less-known individuals in the scholarly, intellectual, and political worlds echoed their praise.

Psychiatrists, too, joined the chorus. A remarkable example was a paper, "Is the Anglo-Saxon Race Degenerating?," by Dr. James Russell, superintendent of the Asylum for the Insane at Hamilton, Ontario, delivered at the 1900 annual meeting of the American Medico-Psychological Association. Russell argued that Anglo-Saxons had produced the greatest civilization the world had ever known. It represented "an expression of brain power and intellectual activity unrivaled in recorded history." Its future seemed uncertain. It could progress to greater heights or decay and decline, in the historical pattern of such great societies as Rome.

But, argued Russell, contemporary Anglo-Saxon civilization had a unique quality lacking in previous cultures. It had "the living, vitalizing power of Christianity," which inspired noble acts of humanity and provided a force of vigor for the future. Identifying his colleagues as "the mind healers of the races," he urged them to broaden their perspective beyond the routine, mundane tasks of caring for the insane and to be alert to any sign of racial decay. The most corrupting influence on the race, in his view, was the "mad struggle for wealth." This acquisitive drive diverted attention from the more enduring elements of civilization, notably its artistic, intellectual, and spiritual values.

But the Anglo-Saxon race had "immense virility" and would continue advancing peace, prosperity, and liberty throughout the world. In this statement Russell articulated an idea, deeply ingrained in American thought, that exerted a powerful influence over American foreign policy: Anglo-Saxons had a special mission to carry their institutions and culture throughout the world. His article also bore a striking resemblance to the ideas of Anglo-Saxon destiny expressed in a late nineteenth-century best seller, *Our Country: Its Possible Future and Its Present Crisis*, by Josiah Strong, a well-known and influential Congregational minister.

The doctrine of Anglo-Saxon superiority helped to form attitudes toward the new immigrants who began arriving from eastern and southern Europe in significant numbers in the 1880s. Within mental institutions sharp antiforeign sentiment had existed since the midcentury, when Irish patients entered public asylums. Psychiatrists viewed them with disdain, as repulsive persons who overcrowded mental hospitals with chronic cases. Beginning in the mid-1880s, asylum administrators took a new position on the immigrant question. They demanded the enactment of tighter immigration restriction laws. This proposal echoed the cries of a widespread anti-immigration movement.

Out of the 1880s emerged a host of antiforeign organizations urging the passage of stricter laws to curb immigration. Extremist groups such as the American League and the American Protective Association were joined by labor, industrial, and commercial organizations, including the National Board of Trade. The old idea of America as a refuge for the poor and the oppressed was disavowed. The immigrant became the scapegoat for the problems and tensions confronting a society engaged in rapid industrialization: labor conflict, violence, crime, political corruption, vice, and perpetual change.

In the psychiatric community the issue of restrictive immigration legislation first surfaced at the 1884 annual meeting of the Association of Medical Superintendents. Foster Pratt of Kalamazoo introduced a series of resolutions urging Congress to prevent the "defective classes" of Europe and Asia from entering the country. Pratt's concern focused on the cost of maintaining dependent aliens in public institutions. According to his statistics, the foreign-born constituted one-eighth of the population but supplied "one-third of our criminals, one-third of our paupers, and one-third of our insane." Since states had no control over immigration, only federal action could resolve the problem. Pratt's resolutions received the unanimous endorsement of the Association. A few members directed abuse at immigrants. One called them "a mass of ignorance" humbled by the "shackles of caste" and poverty. Another referred to an inadequate mental capacity that made immigrants "incapable and unfitted" for the hardships and competition in a new environment, and susceptible to mental disease. This argument carried Darwinian overtones and typified the attitude of psychiatrists and other middle-and upper-class Americans toward immigrants.

The voices of an articulate few in the 1880s had become by the 1910s a well-orchestrated chorus of anti-immigrants, and for apparently good reason. Between the 1870s and 1910s an analysis of asylum statistics revealed a 50 percent drop in recovery rates, and the incidence of insanity in the United States showed a marked increase. Study after study of "the foreign-born insane" pointed to the relatively small percentage of foreigners in the total population and the large percentage of immigrant patients in mental hospitals. In 1903, 31.5 percent of inmates in mental institutions were aliens, yet they accounted for only 13.5 percent of the entire population. In urban areas the percentage was much higher: Philadelphia's foreign-born population of 24.7 percent supplied 44 percent of the city's indigent insane. To many psychiatrists a reading of these statistics pointed to one conclusion: immigration accounted for the high rate of insanity in America.

If immigration was indeed responsible for the soaring rate of mental illness, aliens must have had certain qualities that made them prone to insanity. A long-standing popular view in the psychiatric community held that immigrants represented "an inferior lot of beings," "illegitimate offspring," and "the off-scouring of all Europe." This general assumption soon evolved into a clear-cut ethnic or racial argument indistinguishable from the protestations of anti-immigrant organizations. It became noticeable after 1900, when psychiatrists contrasted the new immigration with the older Anglo-Saxon or "native American stock." The former represented "discordant elements," "other races," "a serious menace" to the nation's existence; the latter denoted settled, industrious, "law-abiding," "home-loving and stable" people.

Dr. Sidney D. Wilgus, chairman of the Board of Alienists of the Lunacy Commission of New York, curtly labeled the recent immigration "unnatural" because it included many types of defectives: epileptics, nervous and insane persons, criminals, paupers, and alcoholics. He went further and specifically identified its undesirable ethnic groups: Jews, Italians, and the Slavs of eastern Europe were "low-grade" persons without achievement at home and destined for failure, poverty and institutionalization in America. Wilgus and other psychiatrists attributed to these ethnic groups susceptibility to unique behavioral disturbances. The most serious mental illnesses affected Italians and Jews. Italians suffered from epileptic psychoses; Jews, more than any other "racial group," fell victim to manic-depressive disorders and dementia praecox. One psychiatrist argued that Jews had an "excessive incidence of mental disease" wherever they settled.

These designations were based on the findings of small, indiscriminate numbers of patients, yet they were used to identify the mental illness of an entire ethnic group. The studies failed to probe deeply to determine just why a particular ethnic group was or was not prone to a specific form of insanity.

Prevailing hereditarian and degenerative theories of insanity played key roles in the developing anti-immigrant ideology. Around 1900 interest was stimulated by the rediscovery of Gregor Mendel's laws of heredity, notably the idea of transmission of dominant and recessive characteristics. Numerous studies purportedly showed that between 30 and 40 percent of the institutionalized mentally ill had family histories of insanity, a statistic that pointed to a hereditary foundation of mental illness. Hereditary increasingly was linked to the theory of degeneracy, a concept imported from Europe in the 1880s. Some of its major theorists included the French psychiatrists Benedict Morel, J. J. Moreau, and Valentin Magnan; the British neurologist Henry Maudsley; and the Italian criminologist and psychiatrist Cesare Lombroso. Basically, degeneracy meant deterioration to an inferior level. An acquired pathological character was transmitted from one generation to another, and each succeeding generation produced more widespread and more severe defects, culminating in sterility and the dying out of the tainted family. In this country the concept received great publicity at the trial of Charles J. Guiteau, assassin of President James A. Garfield. Psychiatrists defending him argued that he had a family history of psychopathology and suffered from hereditary insanity.

The adherents of the degeneracy theory contended that it produced visible deformities. Labeled the "stigmata of degeneracy," these might include squints and tics, facial asymmetry, unusually large or small eyes, distorted ears, leathery skin, a "prematurely wrinkled" face. Moral stigmata complemented these physical features. The degenerate was dishonest, cunning, and revengeful; had no morals; and pursued a life pattern of self-gratification and debauchery. Degeneracy also carried psychic stigmata. Such types of mental illness as neurasthenia, paranoia, and "manic-depressive insanity," and certain psychological qualities including impulsiveness, excessive egotism, emotionalism, mental weakness, dejection, and mysticism were symptomatic of degeneration.

Psychiatrists voiced an increasing concern over the mentally defective, the prime example of degeneracy. A trace of mental retardation in someone's ancestry pointed to a virtually predetermined fate. A number of studies tracing family pedigrees drew considerable attention to the subject. Some of the popular ones were *The Nam Family* by Arthur H. Estabrook and Charles B. Davenport, *The Pineys* by Elizabeth S. Kite, *The Family of Sam Sixty* by Mary S. Kostir, and *The Kallikak Family* by Henry H. Goddard. Published between 1912 and 1916, these studies charted the courses of a various defects through several generations. The story invariably ended with widespread feeblemindedness.

Many psychiatrists identified the new immigrants as a main source of degeneration. To prevent these "degenerates" from forming "the nucleus for future crime and insanity," they called for laws that would curb the tide of immigration by screening out "undesirables" and deporting defective and insane aliens. The immigration statute of 1903 was a step toward the fulfillment of these objectives. It provided for the exclusion of insane persons, individuals with any incidence of insanity five years prior to arrival in America, those liable to become public wards, idiots, and epileptics. Anyone who became a public charge through causes stemming from a European background could be deported at any time within two years of arrival. Physicians of the United States Marine Hospital were given the task of determining the mental condition of all immigrants. Outside the psychiatric community the provision of the statute capturing the most attention dealt with the exclusion and the deportation of individuals subscribing to the doctrines of anarchism.

The physicians charged with judging the mental condition of arriving immigrants faced difficult problems. Within a few minutes they had to verify a person's mental ability and sanity. A psychiatrist from the Boston Society of Psychiatry and Neurology contended that the inspector's ability to "tell at a glance" an immigrant's nationality would facilitate the examination and insure an accurate prognosis. With such competency he would know that the stolidity expected of a Pole "might indicate dementia in an Italian."

Dr. Thomas Salmon, a physician at Ellis Island and later a prominent figure in the mental hygiene movement, presented more detailed guidelines. In his view the examination began with the ship's surgeon, who had the first responsibility for detecting insanity in an alien. During the voyage he had ample opportunity for observation. However, since he frequently shirked this duty out of ignorance or an awareness that the steamship company would be charged with the expense of transporting a rejected immigrant home, the task of the medical officer who watched the immigrants disembark became extremely important. Here, though only a cursory inspection was possible, a physician alert to the outward appearances of mental disturbance could pick out individuals who required a more detailed examination. For example, Salmon detained anyone who seemed "apathetic" or "supercilious" or "apprehensive"; his suspicions were aroused by "a hint of negativism or retardation, an oddity of dress, asymmetrical pupils, or an unusual decoration worn on the clothing." Old persons and individuals showing "stigmata of degeneration" were thoroughly questioned and reexamined.

A circular prepared by medical officers and approved by Salmon helped nonpsychiatric personnel to recognize any mentally ill aliens who slipped past the initial inspection. A few of the ascribed characteristics of the insane found in this document include evasiveness in answering questions, uncertainty, incoherence, misstatements of fact, and reticence. Salmon recommended that a psychopathic pavilion be established at Ellis Island to furnish facilities for observing suspected insane aliens, provide treatment for immigrants who were disoriented by their voyage, and supply accommodations for persons awaiting deportation.

The Immigration Act of 1903 and subsequent amendments failed to satisfy the restriction advocates within the psychiatric community, especially in New York. They argued that the Empire State was the destination of most immigrants. By receiving the largest number of aliens in its mental institutions, it suffered more than any other state from loopholes and lax enforcement of the law. This was not the cry of alarmists. The number of mental patients in New York state hospitals rose from over 16,000 in 1890 to over 33,000 in 1914, an increase of 108.4 percent. Approximately 9,000—over 27 percent—of the 33,000 patients were neither residents of the state of New York nor citizens of the United States. The cost of maintaining this large number of aliens approached $1 million per year. Statistical studies showed that the average hospital term of a mental patient in New York hospitals was ten years. Consequently, to care for this large number of aliens an estimated $19 million was needed.

For many New York hospital administrators and the Committee on Immigration of the American Medico-Psychological Association, the best possible relief from this "deplorable" situation rested with the enactment of tighter restrictive laws. Accordingly, they urged congressional action on a number of strict measures: chronic alcoholics and persons exhibiting mental instability should be barred from the country; American medical officers should be stationed on ships bringing immigrants to the United States; all immigrants should undergo a medical examination at the port of embarkation and a mental examination upon arrival; each immigrant should possess a certificate of health and character from his or her government; the alien's liability to deportation should be extended to five years. Psychiatrists also supported the demand of anti-immigrant groups for a literacy test. While not directly related to the problem of mental illness, they simply hoped that it would reduce the number of aliens entering the country, and therefore lessen the number of insane immigrants. The sense of urgency over this problem should have been allayed by Census Bureau statistics and other data that revealed only a superficial link between immigration and insanity. Unfortunately, in the 1910s this evidence went largely unnoticed.

The drive of the psychiatrists for rigid immigration laws received the support of a powerful eugenics movement. Capturing wide attention between 1905 and 1930 in both the scientific and the lay worlds, eugenicists had a dual purpose: to prevent the reproduction of "unfit" persons who suffered from such congenital defects as feeblemindedness and to promote racial improvement by encouraging the reproduction of "fit" persons. While the program's reformist and humanitarian connotations drew progressives, its emphasis on unalterable hereditary qualities attracted conservatives concerned with preserving America's "best stock." In either case eugenicists were imbued with a strong sense of self-righteousness and saw themselves as moral crusaders applying the principles of evolution and biology to achieve the noble goal of uplifting the human race. Throughout their campaign they clearly revealed class and racial biases. They scorned the lower classes and identified with the upper conservative classes, which alone possessed superior ability and accounted for all human progress. Many eugenicists regarded the Anglo-Saxon or Nordic as the "fittest race." In taking these stances they reflected the dominant values and social realities of this period when America's business, intellectual, and cultural elite arose from white, upper-class, Anglo-Saxon, Protestant stock.

The most prominent American eugenicist was Charles B. Davenport, a biologist who in 1910 established the Eugenics Records Office at Cold Spring Harbor, New York, to compile data and disseminate propaganda on eugenics. An excellent organizer and prolific writer, he tended to attribute all forms of social variance, including prostitution and crime, to genes rather than to social forces or environmental factors. He never tired of speaking before conservative organizations and genealogical societies on the need of America's best stock to marry well and produce "healthy effective children—and plenty of them." The *American Journal of Insanity* published one of Davenport's articles in which he traced the impact of Huntington's chorea on four family complexes. He identified immigrants as the carriers of the disease. Its effects were disastrous; in each generation the symptoms worsened, and some of its victims succumbed to "manic-depressive insanity."

In their efforts to prevent the propagation of "genetic inferiors," Davenport and other eugenicists promoted segregation in institutions, human sterilization, and strict marriage laws. Such proposals found support in the psychiatric community. Dr. John J. Kindred of River Crest Sanitarium on Long Island saw an intimate relationship between eugenics and mental illness. He defined eugenics as a "preventive against the continuation of race impairment" and outlined the kinds of marriages that would produce insane offspring. The children of two insane parents, for example, would be insane; one normal parent and one insane parent would produce normal children, all of whom would carry the "insane taint in their germ-plasm." Kindred favored sterilization of the "grossly unfit" and "eugenic marriages" as the best means of eliminating "preventable mental and other diseases."

In 1914, Dr. Carlos F. MacDonald, president of the American Medico-

Psychological Association, called for the sterilization of the chronically insane. A few psychiatrists had already experimented with the extirpation of the sexual organs of the mentally ill. The demand of some physicians for the "asexualization of the unfit," including the feebleminded, the criminal, and the insane, rang with urgency. Dr. Martin W. Barr, physician at the Training School for Feebleminded Children in Elwyn, Pennsylvania, said that "the time for cleansing has come"; he asserted that the removal of the testicles and the ovaries of "defectives" gave "absolute security" for maintaining the purity of the race. The perfection of the surgical techniques for vasectomy in men and salpingectomy in women added momentum to the sterilization campaign. The persistent pressures of interested physicians and eugenicists reached fruition in 1907, when Indiana passed the first state sterilization measure. Upon the recommendation of a board of medical experts, the law permitted the sterilization of convicted rapists and criminals, as well as any institutionalized insane, idiotic, imbecile, or feebleminded person. Other states followed suit, and by 1931, 30 had enacted sterilizations laws and approximately 20,000 sterilizations had been performed.

Psychiatric and eugenic interests coincided firmly on the issue of immigration restriction, one of the major political thrusts of the eugenics movement. Armed with their fervent attachment to Anglo-Saxon or Nordic superiority, eugenicists looked aghast at the new immigrants. For them immigration was a biological problem, and the country seemed bent on racial suicide in permitting "degenerate" aliens to "pollute" the nation's bloodstream. Psychiatrists reached strikingly similar conclusions: the exclusion of defective and insane aliens was of paramount importance to the nation. As progenitors of paupers, vagrants, criminals, and the mentally ill, their entrance would "terminate only with the extinction of the race."

Laymen and psychiatrists associated with the National Committee for Mental Hygiene, a reform group committed to improving the care and treatment of the mentally ill, expressed the same alarm and pressured Congress for action. For them success was achieved with the Immigration Act of 1917, which, in addition to a literacy test, contained a provision excluding chronic alcoholics and cases of "constitutional psychopathic inferiority." Commenting on the Act of 1917, Dr. Charles G. Wagner, the leader of America's institutional psychiatrists, referred to it as a "great benefit to the country." It kept out persons "unfit for the duties of citizenship and unfit to become parents of American children." Wagner had added the terms of the eugenicists to those of simple preventive medicine.

The Immigration Act of 1917 required suspected defective and insane individuals to undergo a thorough examination. In identifying a mental defective, the examining physician attempted to evaluate the subject's reasoning ability. The individual was first asked to answer simple questions—for example, when scrubbing a flight of stairs, would you begin at the top or bottom? The would-be immigrant was then asked to respond to absurd stories. A common one related an incident in which the police had found a young woman's body cut into 18 pieces; the police reported that she had committed suicide. Did the alien agree with the police report? A number of imaginary problems were posed. Imagine a man alone in a small boat hundreds of miles from land. Two fifty-pound boxes, one containing bread and the other gold, are in the boat. The sea is rough, and one of the boxes must be thrown overboard to prevent the boat from sinking. Which box should be discarded? In addition to such questioning, the immigrant was given memory tests, required to copy geometric forms, and complete wood-block puzzles.

One important criterion in determining sanity rested with the alien's ability to adjust to the new environment. It was assumed that a "properly balanced" person would not exhibit prolonged disorientation or nervousness. If such traits were displayed, an intense interrogation followed. Some of the questions asked included: "Is there anything wrong with your mind?" "Are you crazy?" "Does your mind work well?" "Have you ever been in a hospital for nervousness?" "Did anyone ever call you a fool?" "Why did you come to America?" "What happened to you during the voyage?" "Did people follow you or look at you suspiciously?" "When alone, do you hear strange noises or voices?" "Do you hear a voice from your stomach?" "Does God talk to you?" "Do you see visions?" "Do people make faces at you?" "Do you taste strange things in your food?" "Do you smell disagreeable odors?" "Does anyone arrange electrical wires or other devices to bother you?" "Does anyone control your mind?" "Do you feel something moving inside your head?" "Have you any enemies?" "Of what are you afraid?" "Are you a great person?" "Are you better than the other immigrants?" "Have you any special message to deliver?" These questions were taken from the *Manual of the Medical Examination of Aliens*, published in 1918.

The examination itself could be frustrated by its brevity; the language, social class, and ethnic barriers between the examiner and the alien; the absence of any family or historical data on the subject; and the attempt to isolate the immigrant's behavior from a broader social context. Still, the questions could at least help the examiner to identify the more obvious cases of mental disorder.

For the restriction advocates within the psychiatric community, the 1917 immigration law fulfilled the legal demands of either excluding or deporting the major types of mentally defective and insane aliens. Gradually their interest narrowed to matters related to enforcement of the act. On this issue they expressed bitter indignation over the apparent lack of congressional support for vigorous prosecution of the law. Dr. Spencer L. Dawes, a medical examiner for the State Hospital Commission of New York, accused Congress of criminal negligence. Its failure to appropriate sufficient funds negated the intent of the law. At all ports of entry, Dawes declared, immigration offices were understaffed and the employees were poorly paid. This situation turned the examination process into a travesty.

From his own observations at Ellis Island, Dawes claimed that immigrants passed through the inspection lines at a rate, in some instances, of one every seven seconds. They were simply counted and sent ashore. He attributed the laxity and indifference to the political pressures of Congressmen from districts heavily populated with the foreign-born. In lieu of the effective enforcement of the law, Dawes and other psychiatrists demanded that the federal government reimburse states for providing custody for alien public charges. The attorney general of New York requested that the federal government pay New York State over $17 million to cover the cost of maintaining its insane aliens.

The actual numbers of immigrants excluded and deported for reasons of mental deficiency or insanity substantiated the protests of the New York physicians. Considering the hundreds of thousands of aliens entering the country each year, the figures were almost negligible. Between 1919 and 1923, when more than 2 million people immigrated to the United States, fewer than 2,000 were denied admission for reasons of insanity, and approximately the same number were deported. These meager results, however, do not indicate the full impact of the restrictionists within psychiatry. Their activities, pronouncements, and apparently scientific assumptions and data significantly influenced lay opinion as well as the extreme anti-immigrant forces. In this oblique fashion, by giving professional validation to the prevailing prejudices against the new immigrants, they contributed to the reversal of America's traditional open-door immigration policy.

6
CHANGING PATTERNS

The opening decades of the twentieth century mark a watershed in the history of mental health care in America. Psychiatrists expanded their scope of activity beyond an asylum setting to embrace a concept of community care. Instead of remaining isolated behind hospital walls, they worked in schools, prisons, and courts, and supported the establishment of psychiatric hospitals, outpatient clinics, and psychiatric wards in general hospitals. They sought the aid and cooperation of general practitioners, neurologists, psychologists, social workers, and other professional and lay people interested in mental health issues. With this broad community base psychiatrists focused on preventive measures and developed an interest in the neurotic and acute cases of mental illness.

This reorientation of psychiatric goals occurred against a backdrop of social and intellectual ferment in the wider society. In American history the period between 1900 and 1917 is best known as the Progressive era, a time when a reform impulse agitated the major sectors of American life. The Progressives were middle-class reformers who believed that society could be made better. Representing an articulate, moralistic, and altruistic group eager to assert their leadership toward solving the problems of an urban, industrial nation, they struck at large concentrations of economic power, social inequities, and corruption in government (particularly on the municipal level), and offered innovations designed to make the political system more responsive to voter demands. Their basic premises were a fervent belief in progress, a conviction that human problems originated in a bad environment, and an assumption that a disturbed individual could be regenerated by controlling and reconstructing the social milieu. The environmentalism, hope, and enthusiasm of these reformers permeated the psychiatric community and stirred a spirit of optimism and innovation. Here the psychotherapy movement was Progressivism's dramatic manifestation.

Concrete achievements in science and technology added strength to the idealism of the Progressive era. The automobile, the radio, the electric light, and the airplane represent only a small sample of early twentieth-century inventions that demonstrated man's power over nature. While such technological marvels captured people's imaginations, medical science intoxicated Americans with miraculous breakthroughs that promised a healthier and longer life for present and future generations. Medicine made tangible progess toward conquering diptheria, cholera, tetanus, hookworm, and yellow fever; anesthesia and antisepsis made surgery more successful. These tangible achievements not only enhanced the prestige of medicine but also helped to confirm science as the new panacea for solving human problems. A widespread assumption held that the facts and methods of science could unravel any complex social issue.

If the optimism of the times and the faith in science furnished a general setting for change, a number of more specific factors within the psychiatric community spurred interest in preventive measures and community care. Some asylum physicians recognized the deficiencies and limitations of the mental hospital system. Neurologists made important contributions with the treatment of neurotic patients in their private practices. New theories and therapies of mental illness, along with popular "mind cure" movements, challenged traditional practices. The new trends in mental health care were represented by Dr. Adolf Meyer, who exerted a powerful influence over institutional psychiatry in the first third of the twentieth century. His work and the concurrent establishment of new types of facilities for mental patients added to the ferment and excitement of this reform period, which witnessed the proliferation of psychiatric interests and concerns, a new pattern in the history of mental health care.

An important stimulus for change developed from a growing awareness of institutional shortcomings. Here the most distressing fact remained the constant trend of increased admissions of patients and fewer recoveries. At most institutions only 20 percent of the total number of patients recovered, and of these the majority had resided in the hospital for less than one year. A sizable number of patients suffered from general paresis and other organically based illnesses that involved progressive deterioration. Long-term patients yielded to what psychiatrists later called "institutionalism," "hospitalism," or "institutional neurosis," a condition characterized by apathy, loss of individuality, deterioration of personal habits, lack of interest in the future, resigned acceptance of the status quo, absolute submission to institutional rules and orders, and an inability to anticipate an independent life outside the hospital.

In an effort to alter this condition and to prevent persons from sinking into chronicity, asylum physicians experimented with various methods of therapy, some reminiscent of moral treatment. These included special diets and physical therapies ranging from a massage to a Turkish bath. An ephemeral scheme called the "photochromatic treatment of insanity" required a patient to absorb sunlight filtered through stained glass windows. Musical therapy gained popularity. Patients at one institution formed an orchestra and played marches and light classics during meals. A method of care known as "tent treatment" received a short-lived but enthusiastic reception. Originally conceived to alleviate over-crowding and to isolate tubercular patients, it entailed the removal of a small number of inmates from wards to tents on asylum grounds. The close staff contacts, the availablility of reading materials and amusements, and the fresh air and sunshine contrasted with the idleness and monotony of stuffy wards. Tent treatment lost its original character and led to the construction of wooden pavilions with large sun rooms. Connected to the hospital, these structures became crowded, staffs were reduced, and doors and locks restricted patient movement.

This and other therapeutics demonstrated the efforts of some administrators to prevent the deterioration of their patients' health. Yet the fact remains that these attempts lacked a theoretical foundation and were too randomly applied to effect significant change in patient recovery rates. In 1907, Dr. Charles G. Hill, president of the America Medico-Psychological Association, gave expression to this state of therapeutic nihilism when he observed, "With all our boasted scientific advancement, our therapeutics is simply a pile of rubbish."

Another distressing element in the asylum milieu was the passion for clas-sifying patients into general categories of mental illness. In this process the work of Emil Kraepelin, a Munich psychiatrist, exerted a powerful influence. Krae-pelin's nosology, or grouping of mental disorders, represented a descriptive system based on the assumption that these afflictions could be identified and classified as easily as such physical diseases as malaria or the measles. In the early 1900s his research was hailed as a major scientific advance, and it generated intense discussion in American psychiatric circles. Its overall impact, however, increased pessimism regarding chronic insanity. Kraepelin believed that a physician had a "very narrow" capacity for curing mental illness. While he thought that recovery was possible in manic-depressive cases, he singled out dementia praecox, or schizophrenia, as a "hopeless disease."

In American mental institutions there was a tendency to place many patients in the category of dementia praecox. This situation resulted from the imprecise and overlapping nature of the symptoms of mental disorders. In examining a patient two physicians could offer different interpretations of his or her malady. One might argue that the inmate suffered from "melancholia," which was viewed as a treatable, curable affliction; the other physician might label the condition "dementia praecox." With that tag the level of hope decreased, a fatalistic outlook prevailed, and the patient became a chronic case impervious to therapy.

The classification process also diminished the patient's status through placement in a psychiatric slot rather than treatment as a person needing indivi-dual care. In short, the stagnation of asylum life, so vividly evident in the low curability rate, the therapeutic nihilism, and the emphasis on classification, encouraged some psychiatrists, particularly of the younger generation, to question the therapeutic value of the mental hospital and to look beyond this institutional milieu in search of alternative ways of treating and preventing mental illness. Dr. Walter Channing, an innovative psychiatrist of Brookline, Massachusetts, reached this conclusion when he commented in 1901 that "there is a big field for the psychiatrist outside the hospital."

Neurologists contributed to the reorientation of psychiatric goals. Throughout the later decades of the nineteenth century, this group of physicians vigorously attacked asylum psychiatrists for improper management of mental institutions, isolation from medicine, and lack of scientific research. This assault culminated in 1894, when Dr. S. Weir Mitchell, a noted Philadelphia neurologist, addressed a convention commemorating the fiftieth anniversary of the American Medico-Psychological Association and delivered a verbal spanking to institutional psychiatrists. The familiar themes and the fact that he had been invited to present a critical analysis took some of the sting out of his sharp remarks. Actually, by the mid-1890s the enmity between neurologists and psychiatrists had mellowed. Psychiatrists accepted criticism and admitted institutional faults; they engaged in more research, especially in neuropathology; and they actively recruited neurologists for asylum positions. By 1910 neurologists and psychiatrists were no longer antagonists. Both spoke of their common enemy, "the diseases of the nervous system."

The most significant contribution of neurologists to the future orientation of mental health care rested with treating neurotics and other acute cases of mental illness in private offices, an activity that brought psychiatric care to the community. Asylum psychiatrists dealt with psychotics; the clientele of neurologists consisted of the urban professional and business middle class, who suffered from what was termed "nervous disorders." These included hypochondria, insomnia, impotence, hysteria, and nervous exhaustion.

Intense debates over such fundamental problems as the relation of mind and body, the efficacy of somaticism, the importance of heredity and environment, the validity of therapies, and the physician's role in treating the mentally ill agitated the neurological profession. While neurologists clung to an organic view of insanity, they appreciated the importance of the social tensions of daily life in determining erratic or "nervous" behavior. S. Weir Mitchell suggested that the rapid social changes caused by modern industrial life produced uncertainties that confounded people and led them to seek medical help. He and other neurologists believed that those people could be cured through intensive private care.

Mitchell's method, the rest cure, drew international attention. It involved a proper diet, seclusion, and rest in bed. Assuming that any nervous disorder caused loss of weight, Mitchell prescribed fattening the patient with large quantities of good food. This would recoup physical strength, a basic requirement for restoring emotional control. The patient was removed from the surroundings in which the illness developed and was kept under the rigid discipline of the physician and attending nurse. Careful supervision of activities entailed the administration of daily massages and the avoidance of disturbing events. Shades were drawn and silence maintained; reading and other diversions, including visits, were prohibited. In this tranquil atmosphere the patient gained insight into the malady, attained self-control, and invariably recovered. The psychological thrust of the rest cure, particularly the manipulation of the patient's environment, presaged the acceptance of psychotherapeutic techniques in treating acute cases of mental illness.

New theories of mental illness altered the direction of early twentieth-century American mental health care. The most significant developments related to the investigation of insanity from a psychological standpoint. This interest stemmed from several sources. The new field of psychology, well-established by 1900, provided an important stimulus. Two outstanding psychologists—William James and G. Stanley Hall—exerted a profound impact.

James, the dean of American psychology, had direct experience with mental disorder. For several years he suffered from spells of depression and anxiety. During one severe attack he was tormented by the image of a patient he had earlier seen in an asylum, a young man who looked like a "Peruvian mummy," ". . . absolutely non-human." His identification with this wretched figure reduced him to "a mass of quivering fear," and for days James remained in a state of depression. He wrested himself from this condition through an act of will, an achievement that confirmed his belief in the power and freedom of the individual will. As a result of his emotional difficulties, James was sympathetic to mentally troubled persons and was drawn to the field of psychology.

In 1890 his seminal work, *The Principles of Psychology*, was published, and it became a popular college textbook. It synthesizes late nineteenth-century American and European psychology and contains many of James's most important ideas, especially his concept of the "stream of consciousness." We experience the world, James argued, as a continuum without breaks, as a flowing stream. Consciousness is a process of constant change and cumulative experience over which the individual exercises selective influence. This view of the mind as an active and adaptive instrument reflected the general thrust of James's psychology. He rejected the rigid, deterministic materialism of Social Darwinism and emphasized an individual's capacity to transform the environment.

This was an optimistic message rooted in concrete experience, the very essence of his system of pragmatism. Alert and receptive to new trends and ideas, James supported both the mental hygiene and the psychoanalytic movements. He encouraged and contributed financially to Clifford Beers, the prime mover of the mental hygiene campaigns. To Ernest Jones, a close disciple of Sigmund Freud, he commented, "The future of psychology belongs to your work." In short, James represented a refreshing and stimulating force characterized by optimism, unorthodoxy, and openness.

G. Stanley Hall played an important role in enlarging the scope and appeal of psychology. In 1878, Harvard University awarded him the first American doctorate in psychology. While a professor at Johns Hopkins University he established a psychology laboratory and lectured on such diverse topics as "disorders of speech," "illusions," and "the psychological aspects of insanity." Hall regularly took students of "psychiatric medicine" to observe patients at Bay View Asylum, Baltimore's institution for insane paupers. An active organizer, he was the founder of the *American Journal of Psychology* and the American Psychological Association.

In 1888, Hall left Johns Hopkins to become president of Clark University, a position he held for 31 years. Clark was a graduate school, and Hall made psychology its most important discipline. The main focus of his interests was education and child psychology. These subjects were vigorously promoted by summer seminars entitled "Higher Pedagogy and Psychology" and by Hall's own public and professional lecture tours and publications. *Adolescence*, published in 1904, was a major work that stressed the theme of the preteen years as the formative period of life, the most important and plastic age of growth and development. From his interest in child rearing and sex, Hall drifted toward psychoanalysis. He admitted that Freud had deepened his understanding of child development, and in 1909 he invited the noted Viennese physician and two of his disciples, Carl Jung and Sandor Ferenczi, to celebrate the twentieth anniversary of the opening of Clark University. The historic meeting enhanced the prestige of Hall and the university, and publicized psychoanalysis and the budding field of psychology.

Psychopathology remained important to Hall's psychology. He called for enlightened asylum care, supported psychotherapy, and worked to achieve a broader public and professional understanding of the psychological manifestations of mental illness. Speaking at the annual meeting of the American Psychological Association in 1905, he maintained that psychiatry was "coming our way." Its "subserviency to neurology" was abating, and there existed "unprecedented opportunity" for "psychology to influence psychiatry." This was a prophetic observation. Unaffected by the pessimism of institutional psychiatry, both James and Hall generated enthusiasm for their profession. They trained a generation of psychologists and educators to view the human being as a malleable creature who learned by habit, imitation, and association. This belief stimulated optimism and hope that psychological methods could help to treat and prevent mental disorders. Perhaps in expounding their theories through informal professional contacts with neurologists and psychiatrists, James and Hall had their greatest impact on psychiatry. They frequently took students, future psychologists, to observe psychiatric procedures at Worcester State Hospital. With other progressive psychologists they encouraged physicians to analyze mental disorders from a psychological viewpoint.

Disenchantment with somaticism stirred an interest in psychological causation and patterns of mental illness. The critics of the organic approach, however, did not demand the total abandonment of somaticism, but sought a change of emphasis. Continually to connect insanity to some anatomical lesion without concrete supporting evidence, they insisted, represented a fruitless exercise. Until a firm somatic foundation was built, they called for an exploration of the potentials of psychological observation and treatment. The eclectic, nondoctrinaire, and pragmatic nature of American psychiatry facilitated the shift away from somaticism, and a number of institutional psychiatrists actively promoted a psychological approach to the care and treatment of their patients. Dr. Edward Cowles, superintendent of the McLean Asylum in Massachusetts, viewed insanity as a "disorder of the mind" as well as a "disease of the brain." In his McLean laboratory he conducted clinical observations and studies to show that stress and fatigue created symptoms of mental illness. Cowles gave progress reports to his staff and encouraged their research through periodic seminars in which papers were presented and current psychiatric literature was reviewed.

Drs. C. B. Farrar and Steward Paton of the Sheppard and Enoch Pratt Hospital in Maryland, a progressive, private institution, avoided placing patients in "textbook categories." Attention to the individual's unique psychology and its development, they argued, would effect the most beneficial results. Dr. A. B. Richardson, superintendent of the asylum at Athens, Ohio, also favored a psychological approach to treatment. Influenced by William James, he believed that through intensive care a patient's bad habits could be modified and redirected into productive channels.

Several institutional psychiatrists probed the possible effects and functions of the unconscious. Dr. Charles W. Page, superintendent of the Danvers Insane Hospital in Massachusetts, analyzed the "adverse consequences of repression," noting that repressed desires can surface to the conscious level in a sudden surge of "mental energy" and cause bizarre behavior. Dr. Charles P. Bancroft, superintendent of the New Hampshire Asylum, reached similar conclusions in a study on "subconscious homicide and suicide."

All of these excursions into varied psychological treatments and ramifications of mental illness represented innovations and indicated that some psychiatrists not only recognized the limitations of somaticism but also searched for alternatives. This new thrust had another implication. It broadened the interests and domain of psychiatry beyond the asylum and into the community, where the observations of family dynamics and social settings might reveal a fruitful prognosis for the treatment, cure, and prevention of mental disorders.

This environmentalism found expression in a vigorous psychotherapy movement that gained wide popularity in the decade before American entrance into World War I. The general ferment within psychiatry and neurology, the partial eclipse of somaticism, and the reforming ethos of Progressivism facilitated the acceptance of the idea that mental disorders could spring from social processes. When a physician engaged in psychotherapy, he became an important environmental force actively involved in altering a patient's behavior. He could manipulate a patient's milieu through therapies ranging from hypnosis to persuasion. Most patients proved unreceptive to hypnosis; persuasion, suggestion, and reeducation were more typical and acceptable methods. Here the physician engaged in discourse with the patient, giving advice on how to overcome problems and encouraging the patient to adopt new habits and a new outlook that would aid recovery. Much of the literature of psychotherapy consisted of morale-boosting suggestions that physicians could pass along to their patients. In some instances the recommendations included reading works of such authors as Marcus Aurelius or Ralph Waldo Emerson.

Conservative critics within the medical profession argued that the psychotherapist assumed the role of a priest, a faith healer, a charlatan, or a quack. While this was an unfair accusation, many physicians were alarmed over the practice of psychotherapy by laymen, especially in the churches. The efforts of laymen to comfort neurotics threatened the physicians with the loss of patients. For psychotherapy did indeed strike an unusually wide response outside the medical world. The Emmanuel Movement, for example, was characterized as an experiment in religious psychotherapy. Its founder, Rev. Elwood Worcester of Boston, believed that America faced a major crisis of "nerves and national character." To prove his point, he itemized a list of growing problems, including the increase in the rates of mental illness, suicide, alcoholism, drug abuse, venereal disease, prostitution, and divorce. This situation could be checked and reversed, he preached, by inaugurating a crusade that combined liberal Christianity and the techniques of psychotherapy. Worcester's movement spread to many Protestant denominations and received publicity in newspapers and magazines. Even *Good Housekeeping* covered the story in its "Health and Happiness" feature. Journalists were muckraking all areas of American life, and eagerly exploited new developments in psychiatry. In the opening years of the twentieth century there appeared a flood of articles and books explaining and offering cures for mental illness.

A growing professional acceptance of psychotherapy accompanied its spreading popularity in the lay community. By 1910 the subject received much attention from state medical societies as well as specialists in nervous and mental disorders. Psychiatric and medical journals carried an increasing number of articles on the new therapy. Some of the leading and most outspoken physicians in American psychiatry and neurology actively promoted it. Notable were James Jackson Putnam, professor of neurology at Harvard University; Morton Prince of Tufts College Medical School; Lewellys F. Barker, professor of medicine at Johns Hopkins University Medical School; Smith Ely Jelliffe, owner of the *Journal of Nervous and Mental Disease*; and William Alanson White, superintendent of St. Elizabeth's Hospital for the Insane in Washington, D.C. Strategically located within the profession, these men firmly established and gave respectability to the psychotherapeutic method of treatment, a strong factor in the preparation of a receptive climate for psychoanalysis.

In theory and practice the work of Adolf Meyer exemplified the new directions of early twentieth century American psychiatry. Throughout his long career Meyer displayed a unique commitment to improving mental hospital life and developing programs for community care and prevention of mental illness. He became one of the country's leading institutional psychiatrists, a catalytic agent for charting a new course in mental health. Born near Zurich, Switzerland, in 1866, Meyer chose a medical career rather than follow the religious calling of his father, a Zwinglian minister. Medicine, unlike the ministry, he wrote in his diary, would provide an opportunity for studying "the whole of man." He studied medicine at the University of Zurich, spent a year taking advanced training at Paris, Edinburgh, and London, and then returned to Zurich to complete a doctoral thesis on the structure of the forebrain of reptiles.

In 1892, at the age of 26, Meyer received his medical degree and, lured by dreams of opportunity and independence migrated to America. He went to the University of Chicago, searching for an academic position that would offer him time for research. He found, however, an honorary fellowship without stipend, and met the practical demands of life by working in a neurological dispensary. On the university staff were outstanding and stimulating faculty members including John Dewey, George Herbert Mead, and Charles Horton Cooley. Basically environmentalists and pragmatists, they placed the individual in both a historic and a cultural context, and argued that the individual represented a dynamic entity capable of changing the social environment as well as of being influenced by it. Meyer made lasting friendships with them and absorbed many of their ideas.

In 1893, Meyer accepted the position of pathologist at the Eastern Illinois Hospital for the Insane at Kankakee. Here he observed some of the basic problems of American institutional psychiatry: overcrowded facilities, political jobbery, and a small, complacent staff committed to somaticism. The dull pattern of hospital life was especially irksome, and he complained about the medical staff's being "hopelessly sunk into routine and perfectly satisfied with it." Meyer's activities enlivened this torpid atmosphere. As pathologist he took more interest in "the living patient" than in autopsy findings. His reports to the governor of Illinois, describing the reforms needed for improving state hospitals, reached partial fruition in 1895, when the state initiated the practice of holding competitive examinations for medical internships at public asylums. This drive to upgrade mental hospitals and institutional staffs remained one of Meyer's paramount concerns. Positions in asylums, he noted, had gained a reputation for being "breeding places" for "inaccuracy" and "laziness."

Meyer left Kankakee in 1895 to become pathologist, and eventually clinical director, of Worcester State Hospital in Massachusetts. There he undertook a search for energetic, ambitious, and dedicated physicians alert to recent developments in their fields and precise in their clinical observations and research. The successful recruitment brought to Worcester such outstanding individuals as Dr. Isador Coriat, a founder of the Boston Psychoanalytic Institute, and Dr. Albert M. Barrett, later head of the Psychopathic Hospital at the University of Michigan. In addition to a high-quality staff, Meyer maintained a system of complete, exact, and uniform patient records, hoping to gain a better understanding of mental illnesses through the accumulation of empirical data. Above all, this activity related to the central goal of integrating research with the everyday care and treatment of patients.

Meyer scorned traditional pathologists who engaged solely in postmortems and devoted all their time to examining dead tissue. He commented that any connection between autospy findings and mental disorders was spurious without clinical or psychological observations of patients. While at Worcester he established ties with leading physicians and psychologists in Boston and Cambridge, including Morton Prince, James Jackson Putnam, William James, and August Hoch. Always concerned with teaching psychiatry, he conducted classes at nearby Clark University and held "clinics" at the hospital for the students of G. Stanley Hall and William James. Some of these students later helped to develop the field of clinical psychology.

Meyer left an imprint on Worcester, a practical legacy divorced from the arena of innovative therapeutics or ideas. He gave the hospital a new ideal, a set of goals, that helped to change its image. The emphasis on research, a staff with high medical standards, and the interaction with the broader medical and academic world militated against the inertia, custodialism, and pessimism associated with the hospital. In short, he jolted Worcester out of its lethargy and set a high standard for institutional psychiatry.

Meyer continued this mission in New York when, in 1902, he became the director of the Pathological Institute of the New York state hospital system. From this commanding position he coordinated the pathological work of the state's 13 mental institutions. A seven-year tenure allowed him time to complete constructive administrative changes, notably in establishing cooperation and collaboration among hospitals, in maintaining uniform case records, and in initiating programs for training staffs. He frequently visited the upstate hospitals, where he held conferences and consultations, went on ward rounds, and encouraged the staffs to engage in case discussions. Preoccupation with these administrative matters did not thwart Meyer's dedication to teaching. He lectured at Cornell University Medical School and to the physicians from the state hospitals. They came to the Pathological Institute to take short courses in both the theory and the practice of psychiatry. In 1907, for example, Meyer offered a course for assistant hospital physicians that reviewed recent literature and developments in psychopathology. Other courses dealt with research techniques in the histopathology of the central nervous system and the methods of keeping patient histories.

For all of this vigorous activity, Meyer was credited with making New York's asylums progressive institutions. In 1913 he became the director of the new Henry Phipps Psychiatric Clinic in Baltimore, part of Johns Hopkins University Medical School. It was here that Meyer spread his message to some of the nation's best medical students, physicians, and psychiatrists, an activity that marked the culmination of his professional career.

Meyer rejected a rigid somatic interpretation of behavioral disorders, and postulated a holistic concept integrating psychology with biology. This "psychobiology" centered on the individual's reacting and adjusting to concrete environmental settings. It represented a pluralistic approach that refuted mind-body dualism and viewed the individual as a physical and social being, the product on a unique environment and life experience. "Man is fundamentally a social being," Meyer wrote, and could best be understood by studying the total personality and entire life with all of its social ties and conflicts. This view, with its implication that social factors produced mental illness, helped to take psychiatry out of the pathological laboratory and to put it in the community, where, Meyer believed, "things have their beginnings." Psychiatrists must study "the atmosphere of the community" from which patients come and to which they return, a practice that Meyer developed early in his career. As a young practitioner he had felt a need for more information about his patients; and he sent his wife, a hospital volunteer, to visit their families at their homes. Her work soon became "indispensable," and demonstrated the importance of reaching beyond the hospital in order to acquire a greater sensitivity to the problems of the mentally ill.

In expanding psychiatric interests and practices, Meyer advocated a comprehensive plan of prevention and treatment that began with a mental hospital dedicated to curative rather than administrative matters, and intergrated fully with the community. It would maintain close contacts with the public by cooperating with the press, promoting a lecture and visitation program, and distributing literature about the etiology of mental illness. These steps, Meyer insisted, and a policy of encouraging voluntary admissions would facilitate prevention and help to dispel some of the stigmas associated with mental hospitals. Schools, courts, social agencies, and charity and church organizations also occupied important places in his drive. Meyer envisioned a total community commitment and participation that even included an attack on such sources of social pathology as alcoholism and prostitution. This widespread movement would militate against the traditionally myopic policies of state hospitals and would relate psychiatry to the problems of everyday life.

Central to Meyer's community program was the psychiatric clinic, a new institution flexible enough to function as an agency for preventive and educational work as well as for conducting research and teaching. Most important, its location in the community permitted wide utilization of its facilities. All cases would be served, from the mild to the most severe. Some would be admitted for a few days, for examination and observation; most would be treated on an outpatient basis while living at home. This status favored the development of an intimate relationship with the physician, who, unburdened of administrative duties and large numbers of cases, had time to offer individualized care and to study each patient's social background. The social workers on the clinic's staff took the responsibility for observing a patient's home, place of work, and outside interests.

An important change in early twentieth-century mental health care was the establishment of new types of facilities for the care and treatment of patients. The Henry Phipps Clinic under Meyer represented one example of this trend. It was private, well-endowed, and associated with the Johns Hopkins University Medical School. A more popular and widespread institutional development originated in Albany, New York, where the first psychiatric ward in a general hospital opened in 1902. Designated "Pavilion F," it was a separate two-story building, the first floor for women and the second for men. Each floor was divided to segregate the "quiet" from the "turbulent" patients. Dr. J. Montgomery Mosher, its director, received the title "attending specialist in mental diseases." He referred to the pavilion as a place for the treatment of persons afflicted with "incipient or transitory mental disturbance." These patients were admitted on a voluntary basis, and Mosher claimed that most of them had "normal minds" that responded to "proper treatment." Their condition resulted from the stresses, worries, and discouragements of life; if neglected, they would deteriorate and fall into a state of hopeless incurability.

A general hospital had the obligation of caring for acute cases of mental disorder, just as it had for any type of physical disease. Mosher cited statistics to prove the effectiveness of his pavilion. In a six-year period over 1,300 patients were admitted; the majority returned home either recovered or improved, and only 126 were committed to asylums. This new pavilion at Albany marked the beginning of a trend of extending the services of the large metropolitan hospitals to psychiatric patients.

In 1906 the University of Michigan opened the first university psychopathic hospital at Ann Arbor. It was a small building capable of providing accommodations for only 40 patients, 20 of each sex. Dr. Albert M. Barrett, the director and a former student of Adolf Meyer, characterized it as "a receiving, non-custodial institution" that stood midway between a general hospital and a state asylum. It had two functions: to conduct research on "the phenomena and pathology of mental disease" and to treat persons "bordering on insanity." The subsequent research consisted largely of laboratory work sent from the Michigan asylums, and it had the strict somatic aim of establishing a correlation between anatomical findings and clinical symptoms.

For Barrett the hospital's most important duty was the care and treatment of patients suffering from acute mental disorders. He specified that the types of persons best suited for treatment included voluntary cases, juvenile delinquents, and individuals sent for observation. Unfortunately, the public nature of the hospital made it impossible to limit admissions to curable cases, and Barrett frequently complained about the large number of chronic patients entering the institution. He did not want the hospital transformed into a custodial facility. Especially frustrating to him was the lack of sufficient space for the hospital to segregate patients according to mental condition. Depressed and apprehensive patients required a peaceful atmosphere and continual supervision; the violent and noisy needed an isolated area to avoid disturbing others; the convalescent wanted a cheerful setting and relaxed staff control. The cramped quarters also forced the hospital to discharge patients rapidly. An unfortunate situation developed: those patients who responded slowly to treatment were finally transferred to an asylum. Barrett repeatedly pleaded with the state legislature to appropriate the necessary funds for the construction of a larger facility.

Doubtful about finding cures for the majority of chronic patients in mental institutions, Barrett voiced the point of view, increasingly common to twentieth-century psychiatrists, that prevention was "the most promising and rational point of attack upon the problem of insanity." He contended that an effective assault could be launched when better and additional psychiatric education and training were established. In this regard the hospital initiated a weekly lecture on insanity to seniors in the University of Michigan Medical School, and small groups of students received instruction in the laboratory and at the bedside. By 1918 this institutional program had expanded, and every senior took 45 hours of clinical lectures on psychiatric medicine and 16 hours of practical experience in the wards. Barrett followed a pattern set by Meyer in New York by conducting courses for physicians from the state asylum. He and his staff covered such subjects as "the development of the central nervous system" and "psychological experiments in relation to the insane," In short, a major thrust of the hospital's prevention program was the training of medical students and physicians in the latest developments in psychiatric theory and practice.

Outpatient service was also one of the hospital's important activities. Aware of environmental influences upon mental health and the importance of detecting mental illness in its incipient stages, Barrett extended his work to Detroit, where a clinic was attached to the Wayne County Juvenile Court. There a psychologist and a social worker assisted a psychiatrist and court officers in the disposition of cases. This team, especially the social worker, studied the family and social settings of patients before and after treatment. In 1918 it provided services to almost 1,000 patients.

Barrett took pride in his work and met with much success in treating acute cases. In the hospital's *Fifth Biennial Report*, he recorded that only 25 percent of his patients went to asylums; the rest presumably returned to a normal life. More important, his hospital established a pattern of interaction for the professions concerned with the issues and problems of mental illness. The Ann Arbor facility and the other new psychopathic institutions brought together psychiatrists, neurologists, psychologists, and social workers in a stimulating, innovative environment.

In 1912 the first psychopathic hospital associated with a mental institution opened as a department of Boston State Asylum. Its prime mover, Dr. L. Vernon Briggs, a young physician-reformer, wanted an institution free from the custodial atmosphere of an asylum. This "observation hospital" would permit the study and the treatment of acute cases of mental disorder, including voluntary and emergency patients. It would especially help two types of distressed persons: those needing treatment who were frequently arrested for disorderly conduct and detained in a jail or police station, and those who suffered from mild forms of mental disturbance and could not receive treatment unless they were declared insane and committed to an asylum. In either case the psychopathic hospital offered a refuge.

Research was a major hospital goal. The first director, Dr. Elmer E. Southard, professor of neuropathology at the Harvard Medical School, fulfilled that aim, giving Boston Psychopathic a high reputation for psychiatric investigation and training. In most respects his research had a somatic orientation. For example, he conducted an exhaustive comparative analysis of the brains of normal and mentally ill subjects in search of a link between brain disease or structure and mental disorder. He and his staff contributed to such areas of neuropsychiatric research as encephalitis, meningitis, epilepsy, and anaphylaxis. This work received an added impetus from the laboratory studies of Drs. Joseph W. Moore and Hideyo Noguchi of the Rockefeller Institute that showed a casual link between syphilis and general paresis. Published in 1913, their findings marked a major breakthrough for neuropathology. With paretics forming a significant proportion of patients in mental hospitals, somaticists drew encouragement. Here was a model that might have application for other types of psychiatric disorders. Stimulated by the work of Moore and Noguchi, Southard and other physicians in mental hospitals devoted more attention to investigating brain syphilis. The Massachusetts State Board of Insanity directed the state's mental institutions to expand research in that specific area.

While dedicated to somatic research, Southard admitted the importance of studying social factors and environment in the etiology of mental illness. He referred to social psychiatry as "the outstanding development" in the last 25 years. In a number of ways he advanced this new field of professional activity. At professional meetings and in journals, he continually called for cooperation and coordination between physicians and social workers. In addition to establishing a training program for social workers at Smith College, he employed them at Boston Psychopathic and appointed Mary C. Jarrett as director of social work. She was an outstanding member of her profession and originated the term "psychiatric social worker." The activities of this type of mental health person strengthened a tie between the hospital and the community. To facilitate a physician's diagnosis, the social worker compiled the patient's history from investigations of the home environment and later made aftercare studies of readjustment to a job and normal life.

The example of Mary Jarrett and others promoted the expansion of outpatient services and stimulated the growth of her specialty. Many clinics and hospitals included psychiatric social workers on their staffs. While largely devoted to acute cases of mental disorder, they also became absorbed in the problems of juvenile crime and delinquency. In this field the work of Dr. William Healy had a lasting impact. Progressive social workers knew of his activities at the Juvenile Psychopathic Institute in Chicago and of his writings, particularly *The Individual Delinquent*. Healy tested the validity of prevailing theories of criminology, notably degeneracy and hereditary assumptions. He found no evidence to support either principle, and concluded that delinquency had many causes. An observer could be misled by a facile theory that oversimplified the problem with superficial, unscientific, and largely irrelevant data. In short, Healy educated both physicians and social workers to the complexity of social deviancy; he advised them to ignore general theories of behavior and to analyze each case objectively, on its own terms. He represents an excellent example of the social psychiatrist as progressive reformer, a physician who saw a close relationship between psychiatry and criminology, and devoted his professional life to finding humane and scientific, rather than punitive, answers to delinquency.

Dr. Thomas Salmon, a prominent figure in the mental hygiene movement and a president of the American Psychiatric Association, placed Healy's activities in a broad framework. Speaking before the New York Neurological Society in April 1917, Salmon praised Healy for setting an inspiring example. His work encouraged the founding of such pioneering psychiatric facilities as a clinic at Sing Sing Prison and a "psychopathic laboratory" at police headquarters in New York City. For Salmon, Healy had established "the usefulness of psychiatry" to criminology. This demonstrated that psychiatry was capable of solving a social problem. Indeed, it was a tool for social betterment, a means for ameliorating some of society's most difficult problems.

By 1917 many psychiatrists shared Salmon's perspective. The rhetoric and institutional boundaries of psychiatry had moved beyond the narrow and restrictive range of asylum practitioners of the 1890s. Now the progressive psychiatric outlook embraced a research orientation, an environmental etiology, and an involvement in community affairs, particularly in the schools and courts. The outline of a team approach was evolving with psychologists, physicians, and social workers employed together in clinics and psychiatric and outpatient wards of asylums and general hospitals. Focusing on prevention and care of acute cases of mental illness, these mental health workers generated enthusiasm and optimism for the present and future status of psychiatric care.

7
PSYCHOANALYSIS AND MENTAL HYGIENE

The changing patterns of early twentieth-century psychiatry facilitated the acceptance and growth of psychoanalysis and mental hygiene, two movements that dramatically altered the course of mental health care. Psychoanalysis was formally introduced into America in 1909 when Sigmund Freud lectured at Clark University in Worcester, Massachusetts. In the same year the mental hygiene movement was launched in New York City with the formation of the National Committe for Mental Hygiene. These two movements struck a response in the medical and lay communities. Each captured a devoted following, infused a new ideology into psychiatric care, and sustained the optimism and hope of progressive reform. While psychoanalysis was widely popularized, often in diluted or distorted forms, its concrete application was largely restricted to a select group of physicians with an affluent clientele. Mental hygiene, on the other hand, found broader support and became a large, diffuse movement that expanded the concept of mental illness and enhanced the prestige of psychiatry. Its effort to promote mental health involved psychiatry in community affairs, diverting attention from the problems of asylum life.

A brash, pioneering spirit pervaded the early practitioners of psychoanalysis. For them Freud's ideas, notably the concept that the unconscious was the major factor in determining human behavior, represented something new and different. Deriving his notions from listening to patients, Freud concluded that mental disorder was caused by unconscious conflicts over the desires, wishes, and ambitions rooted in early-childhood psychosexual experiences. A healthy maturation process channeled conflict into constructive outlets; an unsuccessful sublimation produced mental illness. This was a refreshing contrast to the dull classification systems and existing unproductive therapeutics. In a short period of time, psychoanalysis spread rapidly, attracting some of the best and brightest physicians in America.

After Freud's lecture-visit to Clark University, psychoanalytic ideas penetrated the medical and psychiatric communities along several avenues. Many of the leaders of the profession attended the Clark Conference and carried away positive impressions. Professional journals contributed to the growing awareness. G. Stanley Hall's *American Journal of Psychology* published the lectures Freud had delivered at Clark. The *Journal of Nervous and Mental Disease*, the *Journal of Abnormal Psychology*, the *American Journal of Insanity*, the *New York Medical Journal*, and the *Boston Medical and Surgical Journal* carried information and articles that alerted their subscribers to Freud's ideas. At professional society meetings, notably at the sessions of the New York Neurological Society and the Eastern Medical Society, psychoanalytic concepts were transmitted through discussions and scholarly papers.

In 1911 two new professional societies were founded for the specific purpose of organizing and propagating the new discipline: the New York Psychoanalytic Society and the American Psychoanalytic Association. Freud received attention in medical education: his ideas appeared in textbooks on nervous and mental disease and in courses at medical schools. Among the prominent physicians promoting psychoanalysis were Morton Prince, the Boston doctor who founded the *Journal of Abnormal Psychology*; Ernest Jones, Freud's biographer; James J. Putnam, professor of neurology at Harvard; A. A. Brill, who translated Freud's work into English; Smith Ely Jelliffe, owner of the *Journal of Nervous and Mental Disease*; and William A. White, superintendent of St. Elizabeth's Hospital in Washington, D.C. In 1913, Jelliffe and White established the *Psychoanalytic Review*, the first psychoanalytic journal in English.

As psychoanalysis gained support and influence, it became embroiled in professional controversy, notably the debate over the significance of organic and psychological factors in the etiology and treatment of mental illness. By stressing early life experiences and sex as major determinants of personality traits, it buttressed the environmental or psychological viewpoint, thus lending support to the psychotherapy movement. In fact, psychoanalysis was seen as a type of psychotherapy, and it found a place in the eclectic milieu of American psychiatric practice. Physicians frequently diluted or misinterpreted its doctrines in their search for innovative techniques that promised effective therapeutic results. Nevertheless, psychoanalysis strengthened a basic premise of psychotherapy: if mental illness was caused by environmental factors, the cure was obvious. Treatment entailed psychologically readjusting the patient to those conditions or removing the patient from the pathological milieu.

Intense opposition to this view came from conservative somaticists, who presented the most vitriolic arguments against psychoanalysis, denigrating it for disregarding biological knowledge and research. At the 1914 annual meeting of the American Medico-Psychological Association, Charles W. Burr, a conservative

Philadelphia physician, called psychoanalysis "the unscientific moonshine of madmen." According to Burr and others the mentally ill were best treated by "full feeding and simple physiologic measures"; the promise of better future care and treatment rested with biochemical studies of "auto-intoxications, metabolism, . . . and internal secretions." Psychoanalysts curtly countered such remarks by labeling these critics "neurotic" or "ignorant"; but many physicians, particularly in mental hospitals, accepted the conservative argument. To these practitioners the Freudian approach neglected the physical needs of patients, engaged in frivolous techniques, and wasted time.

Debate went beyond the divergences of opinion between somaticists and psychotherapists, and revealed the distinct levels of psychiatric practice, each with a unique clientele. Psychoanalysis appealed chiefly to physicians in private practice, notably neurologists outside the mental hospital milieu who wanted to innovate with Freud's teachings. It became identified as a therapy best suited for middle-and upper-income persons, a class bias implicit in Freudian practice of that day. Presumably inarticulate persons with low moral standards and intelligence could not be psychoanalyzed. Only intelligent, educated individuals, whose strong sense of morality produced conflict and neurosis, responded to therapy. This type of person was a member of the professional or business class, and was assumed to be prone to mild nervous disorders. Such an individual also had the financial means and leisure required for psychoanalytic care, and received that treatment in private clinics or offices located in exclusive urban districts.

The basic technique of psychoanalysis placed the patient in a demanding situation. The analyst adopted a generally nonauthoritarian, nondirective role and listened to the patient, who rested on a couch, the emerging symbol of psychoanalysis. The psychoanalytic method was individualistic and humanistic, allowing the patient total freedom of expression. It utilized new techniques, particularly free association and such concepts as wish fulfillment and repression. It demonstrated the impact of the unconscious on the patient's everyday life. By delving deeply and comprehensively into a patient's life history, it not only showed the importance of childhood and sex habits but also helped to pinpoint motives and life patterns. In the discourse with the physician, the patient gained insight into his or her difficulties and worked out his or her own solution. This could be a painfully slow process requiring sessions several times a week over a period of months, perhaps years. The expense was considerable. In the 1910s, for example, the clients of a leading psychoanalyst in New York City, Dr. A. A. Brill, paid between $200 and $500 a month for his services. Brill justified the high cost with the argument that the treatment kept his patients out of a mental hospital.

Only a few institutional psychiatrists practiced psychoanalysis. Under the inspiration of Adolf Meyer, the New York State hospital system, especially its Pathological Institute at Ward's Island, was influenced by Freudian ideas. Meyer was an eclectic who favored several approaches to psychiatric care, and he wanted his younger staff members to be familiar with psychoanalytic practices. Whenever afforded the opportunity, he recommended these techniques to physicians in state hospitals. Freud's ideas were evident at the more progressive facilities for the mentally ill. Albert M. Barrett at the University of Michigan Psychopathic Hospital and E. E. Southard at Boston Psychopathic Hospital advocated psychoanalysis, and insisted that a Freudian perspective be represented on their staffs. In short, psychoanalysis had a minimal, sporadic influence on institutional psychiatry. It affected the therapeutic programs only at the most professionally advanced hospitals. The majority of mental hospital patients were not considered proper subjects for Freudian analysis. They were diagnosed and treated by physicians steeped in Kraepelin's nosology and somatic therapeutics.

In contrast with the elitist appeal and practice of psychoanalysis, the mental hygiene movement captured a large following and exerted a profound impact on the delivery of mental health care. It emerged at an opportune time for voluntary public health organizations. Medical and lay efforts to improve health conditions and to control and eradicate disease were achieving great succcess, notably in the crusades against tuberculosis, hookworm, and syphilis. The campaign against tuberculosis brought physicians and social workers together in an enthusiastic and massive effort at prevention. Here much of the educational effort stressed the relationship between disease and environment. Notable professional and lay people supported the National Tuberculosis Association, and by 1909 over 300 anti-tuberculosis societies existed in the United States.

While the work of Charles Wardell Stiles of the U.S. Public Health Service virtually eliminated hookworm as a major health problem, the drive against venereal disease encountered the Victorian avoidance of discussing sex openly, a fact that thwarted its initial efforts. This reluctance was overcome, however, by a growing awareness of the serious and often horrible effects of the disease. Led by Dr. Prince Morrow, a highly respected New York dermatologist, a social hygiene movement flourished. Campaigning among physicians, social workers, and women's groups, he demanded that the public be informed about how easily the innocent, especially women and children, could be ravaged by syphilis and gonorrhea. Morrow's movement called for sex education in the schools, disseminated educational material on venereal disease, and struck at prostitution. These efforts at and achievements in controlling and preventing communicable diseases formed a model for the mental hygiene movement, and stirred hope that mental illness might be conquered.

From its very beginning the mental hygiene movement was dominated by one individual, Clifford Whittingham Beers of New Haven, Connecticut. His autobiography, *A Mind That Found Itself*, published in 1908, described his battle with mental disorder, the institutional care and treatment he received, and his plans for organizing a society to promote mental hygiene. His book was widely received and went through six editions and fourteen reprints by 1937. With sensitivity and perception Beers analyzed his malady. Its first manifestations occurred in childhood, when his "healthy boyish side" competed with "a nature" that displayed "morbid tendencies." The condition often compelled him either to feign happiness or to mask inner troubles "under a camouflage of sarcasm." Aside from this behavioral problem he had a normal childhood and attended the public schools, where he developed interests in business and tennis. In June 1894, the month of his graduation from high school, an older brother was stricken suddenly with epilepsy. The event marked the beginning of the mental breakdown of Clifford Beers, and he became obsessed with a fear that he too would someday contract epilepsy. Throughout his years at Yale University, this "overwrought imagination" was concealed; he broke down only once, during a recitation in German, when he "sat as if paralyzed until the class was dismissed."

Upon graduation from Yale, Beers took a position with an insurance company in New York City. While he was striving for success and financial gain in business, his mental health remained erratic and he suffered from "nervous" days, weeks, and even months. A severe attack of the "grippe" left him in a state of depression, unable to work. At times "terrifying sensations" seized him: his hands shook, and he could not speak or read. This condition intensified when he returned to New Haven. Thinking he had become an epileptic, and unwilling to accept that apparent fate, Beers made plans to commit suicide. After considering death by drowning, poisoning, and severing his jugular vein, he jumped out a window 30 feet above the ground. A last-minute decision to drop from the windowsill by his hands saved him from serious injury. His broken bones and strained spine healed, but his mental condition deteriorated, and he remained under a haze of delusions for three years. All his senses seemed "perverted," and he suffered from "hallucinations of hearing" as well as "phantasmagoric visions." Fears of persecution contributed to his frenzied state of mind. On the train trip to the asylum, for example, he saw conspiracies everywhere: the passengers knew about his mental condition, the newspapers carried stories of his "crimes," the police had him under constant surveillance.

In *A Mind That Found Itself* Beers related his experiences in three Connecticut mental institutions: a private profit-oriented asylum, a private nonprofit hospital, and a state hospital. The first, he claimed, was a "fire trap" in which the administration engaged in crass penny-pinching and sacrificed the comfort and health of the patients in order to make a profit. Here Beers was restrained in a "muff" at night, spat on by one attendant, and physically abused by others. He was treated by an incompetent and cruel physician. In June 1901, after a short and difficult furlough at home, the family transferred Beers to a private nonprofit hospital, where he stayed for 15 months. Initially he remained mute and meek, and thought that the friends and relatives who visited him were imposters; on occasion he showed suicidal tendencies. A change in his condition occurred when he no longer saw his brother as a detective in disguise. Now, instead of being depressed and suspicious, he became elated and developed delusions of grandeur. In that state he displayed stubborn independence and often defied the instructions of asylum personnel. Contentious attendants and physicians, easily provoked by such a boisterous patient, made the situation more difficult. Their refusal to acknowledge some of Beers's requests or to tolerate his new, excitable nature produced violent episodes. He was choked, kicked, kept in a straitjacket for a long period of time, placed in a padded cell, and force-fed.

In November 1902, Beers's relatives committed him to a state hospital. His condition seemed static, and they hoped that a new environment would improve his mental health. Beers later wrote that a major factor in his recovery was the concern and devotion of friends and relatives who never allowed him to waste away in a custodial institution. At the state hospital Beers enjoyed the change, and found pleasure in constant and rapid conversation with personnel and patients. While this verbosity irritated many attendants, he stirred alarm with blunt statements about a wish for banishment to the violent ward. This urge sprang from several sources: a craving for excitement, an escape fantasy, and a "reckless desire to investigate violent wards."

Actually, Beers had a sincere interest in exposing the malpractices of asylum life and in reforming mental instuitions. He wondered if the abuses he had experienced while a patient in private asylums would also occur in a state hospital. He was not disappointed. After an abortive effort at barricading himself in his room, he was taken to the violent ward, stripped to his underwear by "brute-force type" attendants, and placed in a cell ten feet long and six feet wide. He remained in this cold and poorly ventilated compartment for three weeks and experienced a series of nightmarish events. In the early and dark hours of the morning, the "unearthly noise" of inmates in other cells kept him awake. Attendants goaded him. He was choked, struck, kneed, and kicked; he usually saved himself from serious injury by feigning unconsciousness.

Other patients in the violent ward took abuse. They received blows from broom handles and "a heavy bunch of keys." Every day Beers heard the beatings and the "incoherent cries for mercy." He observed several factors that contributed to the problem of violence in mental institutions: the lack of sufficient exercise for inmates, the administrative repression of the reasonable desires and requests of patients, and attendants who viewed any act of kindness as an expression of cowardice. Two types of patients were subjected to violence: The noisy and troublesome and the weak and helpless. Those persons who required little care or treatment were left alone.

Beers was among the latter; he avoided confrontations with the staff and spent time reading, drawing, and writing. While occasional delusions of grandeur disturbed this tranquillity, his general condition improved. A transfer out of the violent ward gave him more liberty, including freedom to walk, accompanied by an attendant, into the nearby town. He renewed old relationships and eagerly wrote letters to relatives and friends. The new correspondence included a letter to the state governor that described abuses ranging from the violence inflicted on inmates to the difficulties patients encountered in receiving mail. Beers knew that the hospital administration had deliberately destroyed some of his mail. Throughout the spring and summer of 1903, he enjoyed additional leisure and freedom, and in September was discharged in fully restored health.

Beers adjusted to normal life with ease. Reinstated in his former position in New York, he avoided humiliating interviews with employers biased against former mental patients, and devoted all efforts to fulfilling business duties, eager to prove to others and himself that he had the capacity to earn a living. Still, he could not forget the recent past, the experiences in the asylums. These memories were made more acute through a chance reading of Victor Hugo's *Les miserables*. The French author's plea for the suffering underdog aroused in Beers a zeal to work for reforming the management of the mentally ill, the "miserable ones" he had left behind. Emulating Hugo's example, he resolved to write a book exposing the system of care and treatment under which he had suffered. It would draw public attention to the plight of the insane just as *Uncle Tom's Cabin* had crystallized opinion about slavery. What Beers really envisioned was the establishment of a reform organization dedicated to the amelioration of the conditions of the mentally deranged. The book would mark the first concrete effort toward creating that agency. Working within a favorable social and professional climate, he sought and received criticism and advice from outstanding psychiatrists and psychologists. William James, for example, recognized the importance of the manuscript to both scientists and laymen, and urged Beers to publish it. The end result, *A Mind That Found Itself*, created an immediate sensation.

The reviews of the book illustrate the contemporary attitudes of educated laymen toward mental illness. In shockingly simplistic terms most reviewers made an absolute distinction between sanity and insanity. Mental illness was defined as the loss of all human attributes, and its obvious feature was a violent disposition. Here is the old stereotype of the insane person as a violent beast. Another striking and lamentable element in the commentaries was the overwhelming pessimism expressed regarding the prognosis of mental illness. The reviewer in *The Nation*, for example, commented that insanity was "an unpreventable and incurable disease." This is the type of sentiment Beers would try to overcome.

Beers wanted an organization that, like the National Society for the Prevention of Tuberculosis, could crystallize opinion, rally support, and achieve concrete results in resolving a major public health problem. A pioneering step in this direction occurred in May 1908, when the Connecticut Society for Mental Hygiene was launched in New Haven. Its prospectus identified the society as a "friend" of the insane, an organization committed to improving the conditions of persons confined in mental hospitals and dedicated to fostering the mental health of the public. In February 1909, Beers capped the enthusiasm and success of this pilot state project by founding the National Committee for

Mental Hygiene (NCMH) in New York City. It received the support of progressive psychiatry, and a succession of outstanding leaders of the profession served as its president. Beers became executive secretary and functioned largely as a coordinator, seeking and accepting professional advice and formulating programs.

The new organization was backed by leaders in psychiatry, finance, social work, religion, education, and philanthropy. Prominent among these were William James, the Harvard philosopher and psychologist; Lewellys F. Barker and Frederick Peterson, two outstanding neurologists; August Hoch, an innovative New York psychiatrist; William H. Welch, a Johns Hopkins University physician frequently called the "Dean of American Medicine"; Jacob Riis, the social activist and author of *How the Other Half Lives*; Julia C. Lathrop of Hull House in Chicago; Henry Phipps, financier and philanthropist; Cardinal Gibbons of the Archdiocese of Maryland; Russell H. Chittenden, director of the Sheffield Scientific School at Yale University; Jacob Gould Schurman, president of Cornell University; and Dr. Livingston Farrand, executive secretary of the National Tuberculosis Association and later a president of Cornell.

This widespread endorsement showed that NCMH had strong community support, a factor that contributed to its early successes. It received generous financial aid from such socially prominent persons as Henry Phipps, Mrs. Willard Straight, Mrs. Elizabeth Milbank Anderson, and members of the Harriman, McCormick, and Vanderbilt families. There were also contributions from the Rockefeller Foundation, Commonwealth Fund, Milbank Memorial Fund, Julius Rosenwald Fund, and the Carnegie Corporation of New York. This aggressive community and financial backing contributed to NCMH's rapid organizational growth: by 1917 many state societies were affiliated with it, a Canadian society had been established, and it had its own quarterly journal, *Mental Hygiene*.

NCMH initially focused attention of state hospitals, exposing abuses, demanding higher standards of care, conducting surveys of institutions, and calling for liberal commitment laws. It identified with the wider roles and functions of the progressive state institutions, notably in the employment of social workers, the development of outpatient clinics, and the use of aftercare and follow-up studies for determining the effectiveness of treatment. These activities, the mental hygienists argued, extended the scope of the hospital, closely relating it to the community and to the environmental conditions that caused mental disorders. The traditional institution of restricted and limited aims was scorned. In a letter commending *A Mind That Found Itself*, William H. Welch of Johns Hopkins University advised Beers to emphasize in his program the need for psychopathic hospitals and wards. These facilities, he contended, especially when affiliated with a university, provided the best care and treatment, and were always preferable to the state mental hospital.

The downgrading of the public mental institution represented a dominant theme in mental hygiene literature. It obviously reflected a general belief that many asylums were human warehouses offering inferior care. Mental hygienists wanted an identification with something more positive and hopeful than the typical state institution. The asylum, along with the prison and the poorhouse, quartered the "results of failure"; and the primary work of mental hygiene rested with preventing "such failures." However understandable this view might be, it contributed to maintaining the status quo in mental hospital care. Ideologically it relegated the chronic mentally ill to further oblivion and reinforced the custodial role of the asylum.

NCMH engaged in vigorous educational campaigns. This was a common practice of the prevailing progressive reform movements, including those for child labor, housing, and public health. Its drives were based on carefully researched investigation of existing conditions. This was extremely useful work, representing the first time such vital facts were widely distributed. For example, NCMH prepared a summary of laws relating to the care and commitment of the mentally ill and a directory of institutions housing dependent persons such as the alcoholic, the epileptic, the feebleminded, and the insane. It collected information on psychiatric instruction and clinics. With the financial support of the Rockefeller Foundation, it conducted a number of studies aimed at discovering mental variancy of specific populations. NCMH's analysis of 608 admissions to Sing Sing Prison in Ossining, New York, revealed that 30 percent were mentally deficient. It studied the frequency of mental disorders in Nassau County, New York, and the causes of delinquency at the Children's Court in New York City.

The information gathered from these and other studies and surveys was disseminated through public lectures, magazine articles, pamphlets, and exhibits, and had the desired effect. NCMH's nationwide campaigns stimulated a rapid proliferation of popular mental hygiene literature, and its bibliographic and public information center became a consultant service for all areas of mental health.

Preventing sickness was a noble, altruistic, and optimistic ideal of the mental hygiene movement. Much of the effort dealt with problems associated with milder forms of mental illness, with persons suffering from neuroses who could not "live happy and efficient lives." A president of the Connecticut Society for Mental Hygiene maintained that the emotional difficulties that frustrated normal daily living and upset inner harmony constituted "the supreme problem of mental hygiene." Mental health was equated with "more individual happiness" and "better social adjustments." Lewllys F. Barker, a professor of medicine at Johns Hopkins University and the second president of NCMH, expressed a typical mental hygiene dream: "We want all people . . . to feel better, to think better, and act better than they do now."

Barker's vision was shared by others in the movement who rejected the past as a dismal era symbolized by the custodial asylum. For them the founding of NCMH in 1909 signified the "first great step" taken in "the field of human behavior." Convinced of the organization's goodness and righteousness, they projected a bright and hopeful future for mental health care. This confidence permeated the movement and found many outlets. Psychiatrists wary of extravagant claims in NCMH literature were chided. Editorials in *Mental Hygiene* outlined glowing progress reports and insisted that the accumulation of scientific facts about behavior was providing a foundation for initiating wiser programs for the mentally troubled.

The self-assurance of the mental hygienists stemmed from their conviction that mental disorders and related social problems originated in childhood. They obviously knew, then, where to initiate the preventive effort. The criminal, the juvenile delinquent, the alcoholic, the drug addict, and the insane person were not made in one day. In most instances it took years of faulty habit formation to produce the maladjusted individual. These ideas, derived largely from Freud and the growing interest in early behavioral problems, militated against the pessimistic hereditary notions of human development and, coupled with the goal of prevention, encouraged intervention in the education of the child both in the family and in the school.

A properly brought-up child would not suffer from any behavioral disorder. Dr. William A. White of Washington, D.C., a leading psychiatrist and a strong advocate of Beers's movement, referred to childhood as "the golden age of mental hygiene," a time when a program of prophylaxis would have a striking effect. His program involved the application of an objective psychology that viewed the child in terms of his or her own psyche rather than as a small adult; it included an awareness of the child's personal environment, especially the relationships to family members. Essential also was the concrete application of the observer's insights to the child's education. Above all, White and the mental hygienists saw the public school as an important institution for channeling any preventive effort. They demanded more medical inspections and psychological testing of children in the schools.

Teachers received sharp criticism. In a paper delivered before the 1925 annual meeting of the National Conference of Social Work, Dr. Ralph P. Truitt, an official of NCMH, identified the teacher as a "barrier to mental hygiene." While admitting that "she" worked long hours, caught in a web of monotonous routine, heavy clerical work, and large classes, Truitt saw her as a policewoman, a rigid, narrow person blind to child psychology. Reducing the teacher's work load and allowing her more flexibility, he contended, would mark a major step toward achieving a good mental hygiene program in the public schools. The teacher also needed training that would help her create a healthy classroom atmosphere, notably instruction in how to recognize and correct unproductive and destructive student behavior.

Another suggested method for assuring mental hygiene in children involved applying the propaganda techniques used by the American government during World War I for arousing the people's patriotism. Mental hygiene themes could be propagated by means of posters, slogans, motion pictures, and other types of publicity. Used widely in the schools, this effort presumably would improve both the morale and the mental health of the next generation of American citizens. A more typical and practical endeavor occurred on the state and local levels of the movement. Papers on such topics as "Mental Hygiene and the Public Schools," "Nervous Children and Their Training," and "Fate of Mental Hygiene for Teachers" were presented at symposiums on education held by state societies of mental hygiene. Invariably these sessions produced broad, bold, repetitive declarations: many mental cases could be prevented by the recognition and correction of behavioral anomalies in childhood; schools should have more power to influence the mental health of children; the school represented a challenge, a social laboratory, a place where new theories of mental illness could be tested for the purpose of charting a better future for mental health care.

Implied in these mental hygiene generalizations was an assumption common to early twentieth-century American reform drives: take certain steps, and any social problem will be resolved. Temperance people, for example, believed that the elimination of the saloon would curb alcoholism and reduce corruption in politics. This was a simple solution for a difficult issue. The mental hygienists followed the pattern by providing a facile answer to a complex problem: a concerted preventive attack on mental disorders in childhood, largely through the schools, would dramatically diminish the numbers of mentally ill persons and improve the health of the nation.

The years after World War I witnessed a remarkable growth of professional and popular interest in child development. Operating in that favorable milieu, NCMH's concern for child rearing gave impetus to the child guidance movement and to the developing field of child psychiatry. Its program was built largely on William Healy's successful work with juvenile delinquents, and received the financial support of the Commonwealth Fund, a philanthropic agency. In 1922, NCMH launched a five-year pilot project that subsequently led to the establishment of numerous child-guidance clinics. This type of institution encouraged the team approach: psychiatrists, psychologists, and social workers functioned as a unit. Each assumed a special responsibility; each contributed to the assessment of individual cases and to the determination of proper treatment procedures. The team aimed at helping the child before he or she violated the law. The clinic also became an important training place for workers in guidance and child psychiatry. Child-guidance clinics proliferated rapidly, and many large cities established full-time permanent facilities; in small and medium-size communities hundreds of part-time services were set up.

A vague, multifarious quality characterized the mental hygiene movement. Many of the aims and programs of NCMH remained obscure and impossible to attain. Perhaps the mental hygienists lacked a sense of the limits of the possible and could not establish clearly defined goals or specific areas of competency or jurisdiction. The concept of mental hygiene lacked precision. Much was said about what mental hygiene could do, but little about what it actually was.

Mental hygiene meant "progress" and was deemed good for everyone, rich and poor, young and old, sane and insane. It dealt with "personal and social adjustments of all sorts," and went beyond the area of mental illness to the fostering of those conditions that contributed to "happier and more efficient living." Mental hygiene helped normal persons who operated at only 50 percent efficiency became "70% efficient." Papers delivered before mental hygiene conventions often dwelt on topics related to self-understanding and "positive living." Mental hygiene was called "a force for the common welfare" that promoted "life enrichment." It was capable of "releasing and directing the best energies of human beings." It represented "the laws of mental health"; indeed, mental hygiene embraced "all the manifestations of human activity."

This ebullience was carried to the resolution of national and international problems. The issues involved in factory sanitation, the employment of women and children, and the designation of dangerous occupations fell within the field of mental hygiene. In labor-management disputes, mental hygiene formed the basis for a new and better understanding; "bad" mental hygiene produced industrial unrest, but almost any dispute would be solved if the opposing participants were "free from inferiority complexes and defense reactions." E. E. Southard of Boston Psychopathic Hospital attributed industrial discord to agitators "of abnormal mental make-up" who found support among emotionally sick and feebleminded workers. The cure for labor unrest, he believed, rested as much with mental hygiene as it did with economics. The same principle applied to international relations. The League of Nations, an international organization established in 1920 to promote peace and settle disputes by arbitration or conciliation, was called "a great experiment in mental hygiene" because it provided a forum for the open, frank discussion of international problems and relationships.

Clearly, for some proponents mental hygiene was a cure-all, a panacea for any issue. The ambiguity and diffuseness implicit in this broad concept contributed to the proliferation of the movement's aims and activities, dissipating its energies and thwarting its effectiveness. On the other hand, by promoting broad goals and programs, the mental hygiene movement received wide support from professional and lay people. Psychiatrists, medical administrators, psychologists, and social workers formed the bulk of its constituency, and it absorbed the basic approach of each specialty. Each became part of the mental hygiene team. Through promotional and educational campaigns, the movement linked itself with parents, teachers, clergymen, employers, and judicial and legal personnel, including officials of penal and reformatory institutions. In short, mental hygiene became an extraordinary eclectic movement capable of incorporating new trends and techniques as well as uniting diverse types of people in a cooperative effort. It could bring different things to each of its constituents: to the social worker, the guidance counselor, the teacher, the lawyer, the psychotherapist in a private clinic, as well as the judge presiding over a juvenile court. This eclecticism and diversity muted criticism and maintained a substantial lay and medical following.

The mental hygiene movement was a prime molder of public opinion on all issues related to psychiatric care. Its literature popularized a concept of the mentally healthy person. Such terms as "wholesome," "sound," "balanced," "adjusted," "integrated," "successful," and "happy functioning" helped convey an image of the normal individual. The ideal person was given a number of attributes. One sign of mental health was ambition, a desire to get ahead in life; a lack of a competitive spirit represented a symptom of maladjustment. But striving for goals should never exceed an individual's capacity to achieve them. Another good quality was "personal independence," and "healthful recreation" promoted mental health. Likewise, participation in church social events, summer camping, scouting, and YMCA signified mentally healthy recreation. Happiness was a sign of mental health; it could be achieved through self-control, prudence, and applying one's insight and reason to the solution of personal problems. The normal person was one who could react to the physical and social environment "in an effective, consistent, and integrated manner," and who displayed "mental poise," "calm judgment," "an understanding of leadership and fellowship." Some of the more obvious signs of a mentally disturbed individual were "day-dreaming," "odd attachments," "unwise enthusiasms," "moods," "seclusiveness," and "unusual interest in religion and abstract questions."

This normal-abnormal motif in mental hygiene literature not only revealed a middle-class bias; it also established a standard of mental health, a definition of mental illness. Professionals who applied it were placed in the difficult role of being arbiters of normality. A basic outlook of the mental hygiene movement was also revealed in the creation of this ideal personality, the concept of human nature that held that behavioral patterns originate within the individual, largely divorced from social reality. This view, derived from traditional psychological and medical thought, was well represented in the NCMH literature. Physicians and psychiatrists accepting that concept wrote much of the publicity material and stressed the biogenetic, rather than the sociological, determinants of behavior.

This tendency dampened any potentially radical thrust of the movement. To be sure, there was discussion of the environmental factors in the etiology and prevention of mental illness, but this approach was neglected; it was dissipated in rhetoric rather than substantive action. Instead of thoroughly analyzing the social conditions of psychopathology, conformity to a model—an ideal child or the normal person—was emphasized. Attention went to an individual's reflexes, instincts, guilt feelings, inferiority complexes, anxiety states, and emotional conflicts, with only superficial reference to the social setting. In sum, by turning inward, by calling for the reconstruction of the individual rather than of society, mental hygiene played down the elements of sociological causation in mental illness, a factor that circumscribed the effectiveness of its preventive work.

The most significant outcome of the mental hygiene movement was the power and prestige it gave to psychiatry. This developed out of the experiences of NCMH during the American involvement in World War I. It helped to screen the mentally ill or deficient for the armed services and established facilities for treating mentally disordered soldiers. It assisted in the creation of the Division of Psychiatry, Neurology, and Psychology within the Army Medical Corps. Dr. Thomas W. Salmon, the first president of NCMH, went to Europe as a psychiatric consultant to the American Expeditionary Forces. He studied "war neuroses" and "shell shock," and participated in organizing psychiatric wards in military hospitals. The phenomenon of shell shock drew wide attention. Identified as a neurosis without a somatic cause, it was a good advertisement for the advocates of an environmental etiology. The extensive publicity it received quickly educated people to its frequency and painful effects. Here was a condition that alerted the public to the anguish mental illness could bring. The effort involved in treating and coping with shell shock helped to change the public image of the psychiatrist, who acquired status and recognition in combatting the new "war wound." This appreciation extended into the postwar years and encouraged psychiatrists and the public to anticipate a continued and effective drive against mental illness.

After the war NCMH developed a program of rehabilitation and hospitalization for mentally ill veterans, an activity that stimulated the new field of psychiatric social work. In the 1920s social work and mental hygiene converged. The leading professional social work organizations, such as the National Conference of Charities and Correction, had mental hygiene departments; psychological elements of casework were emphasized; and mental hygiene courses formed part of the curriculum in schools of social work. In this area of professional education, NCMH made a striking impact. It promoted the teaching of psychiatry and mental hygiene in medical and nursing schools on both the graduate and undergraduate levels, and mental hygiene education was developed for associations of teachers, parents, lawyers, and public health personnel. More important, NCMH joined with leading psychiatrists to create a national examining board to certify specialists in psychiatry and to fix standards of psychiatric training.

There were other areas of activity. NCMH organized the first international congress on mental hygiene, which met at Washington, D.C., in May 1930. It encouraged the growth of facilities for the mentally deficient and the adoption of state programs for identifying, registering, and educating the feebleminded. It worked to replace the label "insanity" with the term "mental illness." Its influence also was felt in the renaming of the agency controlling the administration of the mentally ill. The State Board of Insanity became the Department of Mental Hygiene, a change that signified concern for promoting mental health as well as setting policy for mental hospitals. The NCMH publicists proclaimed that it alone had established "mental disease . . . as a leading public problem and a major concern of medicine."

This arrogant statement reflected reality. By 1934, its twenty-fifth anniversary year, NCMH exerted a strong impact on every aspect of mental health and related problem areas. Affiliated with 52 state and local mental hygiene societies, its programs and activities revealed the new directions of American mental health care. The mental hospital, once the central concern of reformers and psychiatrists, was looked upon as a low-priority item, something "old-fashioned" and lusterless. The past and present were of peripheral interest; the mental hygienists bet on the future. All of their hope and optimism went into preventive work, in anticipation of opening new vistas for the mentally troubled and dependent, an outlook promising too much, and presaging failure and disappointment. Like proponents of curability in the nineteenth century, the mental hygienists raised false hopes and unrealistic expectations, and their diffuse aims and activities meant that little time would be left for resolving one of the most difficult of problems: the condition and care of the chronically insane. This large mass of patients was written off. In effect, the mental hygiene philosophy of prevention rationalized custodial care for the chronically ill, who were easily shunted aside and forgotten in the drive to prepare for a greater and healthier future.

Preventing mental illness has remained an elusive goal. While a child can be inoculated against polio, there is no easy way of rearing one to be free of mental illness. Child-guidance work has not changed the upward trend of numbers of psychotic and neurotic children. And behavioral disorders strike anywhere—in the best as well as in the worst of homes. All of this cold evidence has deflated the mental hygienists' exaggerated promises of success. In addition, mental hygiene set the stage for future difficulties by promoting an ideal concept of normality. The person who deviates from the norm may indeed be healthier, happier, and more creative than the individual who conforms to an ideal standard. In short, the utopian vision of mental health encouraged a search for abnormalities and established a pattern of discovering illness where it had never been found.

PHOTO SECTION

PHOTO CAPTIONS

1. A transorbital lobotomy. To show the depth of the instrument, the leucotome, in the frontal lobe, the second leucotome is held outside the skull to indicate the position of the tip of the first. *American Journal of Psychiatry* 107 (1950): 120-21.
2. A phantom drawing of a transorbital lobotomy, showing the instrument penetrating between the eyeball and the upper eyelid, through the orbital plate and into the white matter of the frontal lobe. *American Journal of Psychiatry* 105 (1949): 736-37.
3. An overcrowded ward, about 1940, in an Ohio mental hospital filled to twice or three times its normal capacity. Ohio Historical Society.
4. The Utica crib, a nineteenth-century invention for restraining recalcitrant patients. Ohio Historical Society.
5. The spray shower, a form of hydrotherapy, was widely used in mental hospitals, notably in the 1920s and 1930s to relax and "sedate" noisy patients. National Archives.
6. Adolf Meyer (1866-1950), a leading twentieth-century American psychiatrist and a director of Henry Phipps Psychiatric Clinic, Baltimore. National Library of Medicine.
7. Benjamin Rush (1745-1813), a practitioner of venesection and an advocate of humane facilities for mental patients. He wrote the first significant American text on mental disorders and later became known as the "Father of American Psychiatry." National Library of Medicine.
8. Dorothea L. Dix (1802-1887), the leading nineteenth-century lay reformer and crusader for the humane care of the mentally ill. National Library of Medicine.
9. The "Original Thirteen." Archives of the American Psychiatric Association.
10. The tranquilizer chair (about 1800). Designed as an alternative to the "mad shirt," it subdued the "maniacal" patient. National Library of Medicine.
11. Physical exercise in a violent ward (about 1900). Ohio Historical Society.
12. A wet pack was designed for calming an excited patient. Ohio Historical society.
13. A print of the State Lunatic Hospital, Worcester, Massachusetts, about 1839. Under the direction of its first superintendent, Dr. Samuel Woodward, a

practitioner of moral treatment, this state institution gained a national reputation for curing patients.   Edmund V. Gillon, Jr., *Early Illustrations and Views of American Architecture* New York: Dover, 1971, p. 229.

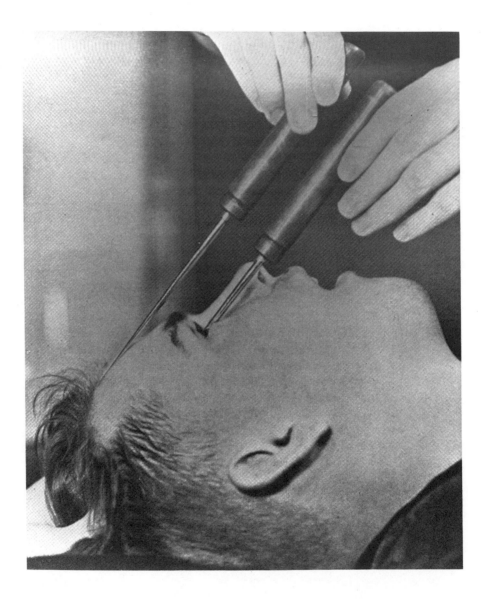

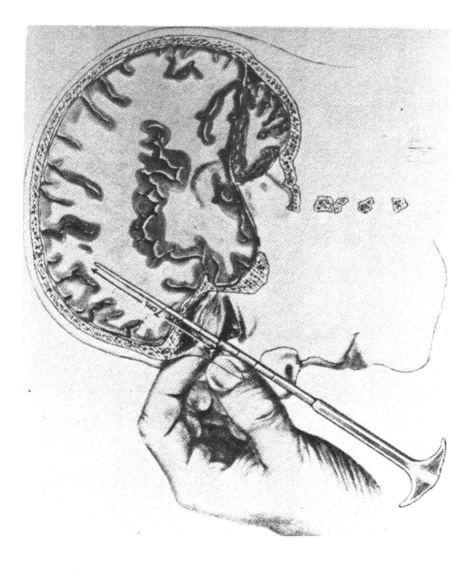

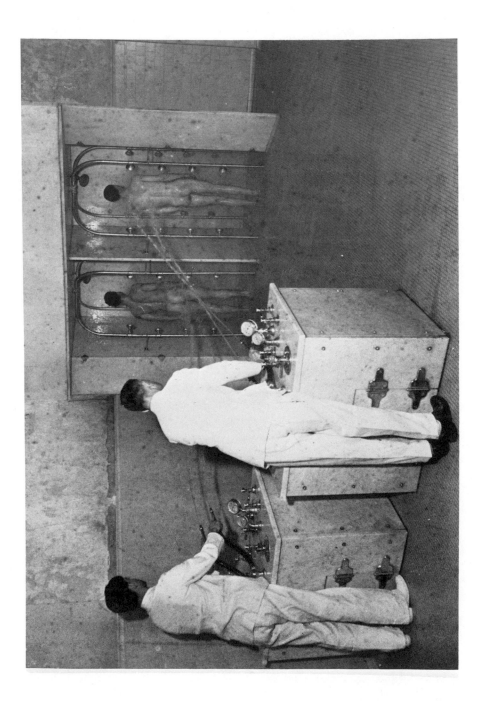

ADOLF MEYER

BENJAMIN RUSH

DOROTHEA L. DIX

The Thirteen Founders

The Association of Medical Superintendents of American Institutions for the Insane 1844-1891
American Medico-Psychological Association 1892-1919.

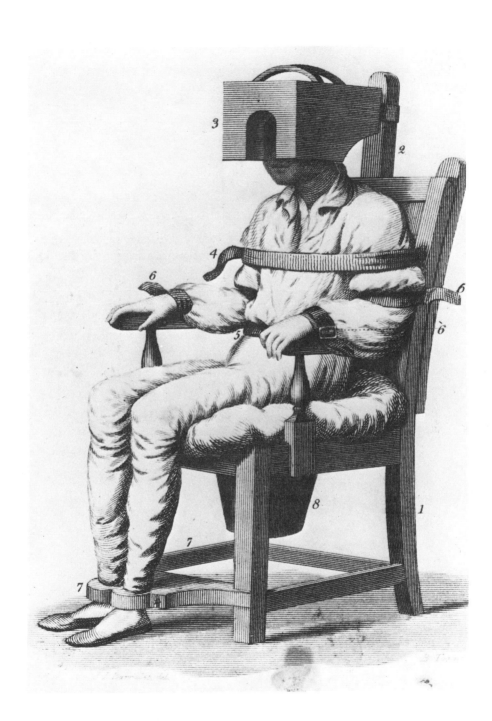

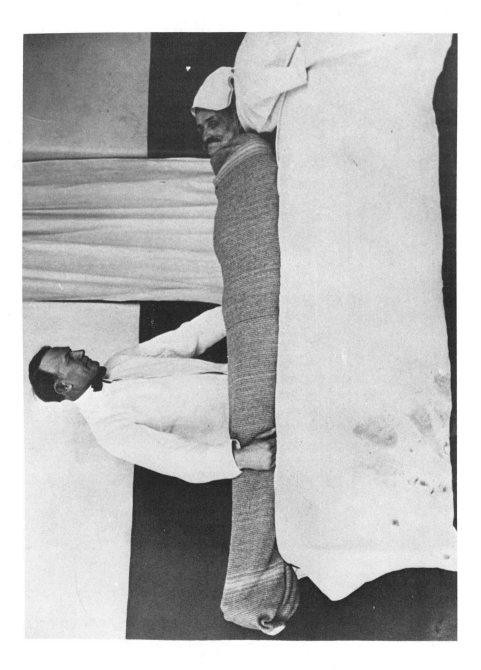

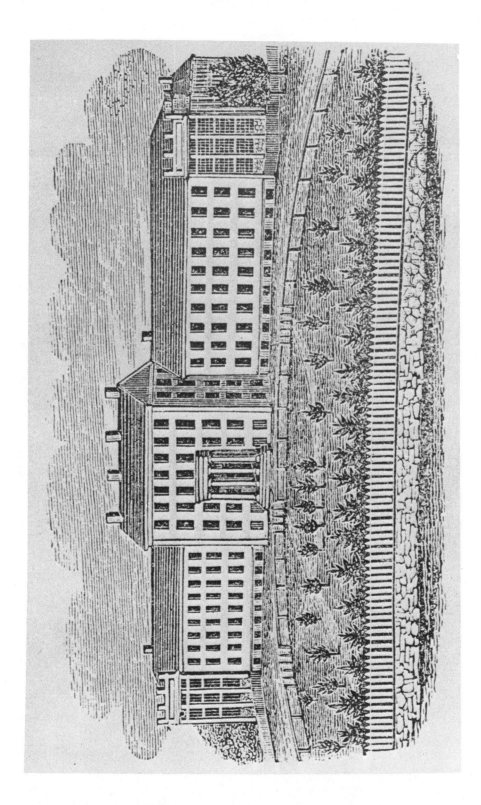

8
INSTITUTIONAL DILEMMAS

The 1920s and 1930s were difficult years for institutional psychiatry, a period when mental hospitals struggled with such perennial problems as overcrowded facilities, inadequate personnel, and public apathy. There were constant expressions of disappointment over this state of affairs. In 1921, Dr. Owen Copp, president of the American Psychiatric Association, deplored the deficiencies in the institutional delivery of psychiatric care. Succeeding presidents echoed his cry. In 1939, Dr. Richard H. Hutchings remarked that the impaired standards of state hospitals threatened to bring them down to the level of poorhouses. While efforts at upgrading mental hospitals had little discernible effect, there was interest in expanding psychiatric education in medical schools, alerting general practitioners to mental health issues, and treating more mental patients in general hospitals. A marked feature of this concern was the participation of physicians from other fields of medicine. In the early 1930s the Great Depression became the nemesis of the state hospital system, as reduced funding caused most institutions to plunge further into custodialism.

The mental hospital of the 1920s was an essential, self-contained unit of society. No critic called for its dissolution. Treatments were offered that purportedly brought relief to patients in distress. The most persistent feature of the institutional care of the mental patient was occupational therapy, a type of treatment that mushroomed in the 1920s. In 1922, 4.8 percent of the patients in New York's 13 state hospitals received occupational therapy, and by 1927 the percentage rose to 31.9. Systems in other states showed a similar trend. Diversions of any sort had long been recognized as having a beneficial effect on mental patients. Work was part of the routine at Tuke's York Retreat in England and at the Frankford Asylum in Pennsylvania. It became an essential ingredient of moral treatment in the United States. Occupational therapy expanded out of a need for meeting the disabilities and handicaps of the veterans of World War I. The profession had a scholarly journal, *Archives of Occupational Therapy*, and a national organization, the American Occupational Therapy Association.

In the view of occupational therapists, two factors determined the success of a program introduced in a mental institution. First, treatment represented a branch of medicine and required the supervision of physicians as well as of specialists in handling mental patients and trained in the fundamentals of teaching arts and crafts. Second, the program had to be initiated with the hospital's most receptive and intelligent patients. Upon completing simple jobs, patients advanced to more complicated tasks, and their places were then filled with less promising beginners. In effect, an occupational therapy school was established with a definite line of promotion. A physician placed each patient in the appropriate grade. Progress brought a promotion, and failure meant assignment to a less demanding task. One administrator commented that the patient's mind was led as a child's from kindergarten to a higher grade until recovery was complete.

Mental health authorities acclaimed the efficacy of occupational therapy. The *American Journal of Psychiatry* documented its beneficial results, asserting that it had "unquestionable" value. Dr. C. S. Miller of Jackson State Hospital in Louisiana referred to it as "one of the greatest helps we have in handling mental cases." Dr. Henry Frost of Boston State Hospital in Massachusetts, claimed that it helped some of his more difficult patients return to normal life. Horatio Pollock of the New York State Department of Mental Hygiene stated that occupational therapy was the "best available method of treating the vast majority of chronic mental patients" and, if introduced on a large scale, it would transform any hospital into an active therapeutic center.

Pollock and other advocates of occupational therapy believed that it struck at the root of all evil in mental institutions, the problem of enforced idleness. Patients condemned to a monotonous existence devoid of activities or diversions exhibited bad temper and developed untidy and destructive habits. Occupational therapy countered this torporous condition by giving the patients' energy outlets ranging from such simple endeavors as sorting colors or sandpapering parts of wooden toys to projects of stimulating technical exactitude. Calisthenics and games complemented work therapy. Varied physical education and recreation included tug-of-war, horseshoe pitching, shuffleboard, handball, tennis, basketball, soccer, and baseball. Some persons, especially severe cases of paranoia or schizophrenia, could not be reached through an activities program. Nevertheless, those chronic inmates who engaged in work and recreation seemed to deteriorate less rapidly, and the acutely disordered had a faster convalescence. Occupational therapy simply enabled many patients to forget their troubles, lose their delusions and hallucinations, and concentrate on a concrete task.

Hospital administrators recognized the economic value of occupational therapy, a potent factor accounting for their enthusiastic and wide acceptance of it. Employed patients had little time for mischief, and in economic terms this translated into fewer broken chairs, tables, lamps, and windows. A ward of patients on a regimen of definite duties also reduced the cost of supervision. The smaller staff maintained discipline and worked in an atmosphere free from the need for constant vigilance over restless patients lost in aimless activities. Occupational therapy contributed to the economical administration of a hospital by justifying the employment of patients in every area of institutional life. This source of cheap labor was eagerly exploited by economy-minded administrators who directed patients to the tasks necessary for maintaining the hospital.

At many institutions patients, under the guise of occupational therapy classes, did the general plumbing, carpentry, and electrical repair work. They replaced downspouts, plastered walls, painted rooms, reupholstered chairs and couches, and fixed damaged tables and broken lamps. They performed other basic services. A typical example occurred at Colorado Psychopathic Hospital, where patients did laundry, baking, and sewing. Kalamazoo State Hospital in Michigan operated on a policy of reclamation, allowing nothing to be thrown out that could be used again; patients cut old clothes into rags that were woven into rugs. This was a general practice at other institutions, where inmates made the hospital's furniture, clothing, and linens. At Watertown State Hospital in Illinois, patients made window shades, screens, bedsprings, baskets, chairs, tables, brooms, brushes, coat hangers, pillows, pillowcases, sheets, quilts, bath towels, table napkins, curtains, dresses, overalls, trousers, suits, scarves, and mittens.

An important feature of a hospital work program was the use of patient help on the institution's farm and garden. In their annual reports superintendents recorded how much activity saved money and kept patients employed. Lists of the farm goods raised and consumed by patients showed the number of bushels of vegetables, dozens of eggs, gallons of milk, and pounds of meat. Alton State Hospital in Illinois raised enough ducks and geese to provide Thanksgiving and Christmas dinners for every patient and employee. More often hogs, chickens, and cows were raised. Hogs had the dual advantage of providing an excellent source of meat while being easily fattened on the hospital's garbage. In addition to furnishing food for the institution's kitchen, the farm offered employment that could be easily adjusted to the patient's skills and mental condition. The patient could hoe a garden, clean a barn, milk a cow, and can vegetables. Once the inmate found an enjoyable job, he or she was encouraged to develop a proficiency in it. The farm, in short, performed two functions: it was a business enterprise that furnished the basic supplies for sustaining the institution, and it was a therapeutic work outlet, contributing to the restoration of the patient's mental health.

Hydrotherapy ranked second to occupational therapy as the most extensively used type of treatment in mental hospitals. Its equipment included the needle-spray shower, the steam bath, and the whirlpool bath. Its chief form was the continuous bath, in which the patient was suspended in a hammock in a bathtub filled with constantly changing water. An air pillow supported the head. The patient's mental condition, the "period of excitement," determined the duration of the bath. He or she usually remained in the water for one or two hours and was then placed in bed until the excitement returned. This alternation between bath and bed could extend for days and weeks. The cold pack, used in conjunction with the continuous bath, involved wrapping the patient between two rubber sheets wrung with cold water. Two blankets were drawn around the patient and a cold, wet towel was applied to the head. After 45 or 60 minutes, the pack was removed and the patient given a needle-spray shower at a temperature of 100 to 110 degrees F. for one minute, followed by a ten-second shower at 70 degrees F. Finally the patient was dried and dressed.

The continuous bath and the cold pack calmed patients, especially those suffering from the "excitements of dementia praecox." Institutional staffs always preferred quiet patients who accepted discipline and were not destructive. They justified hydrotherapeutic measures on that point: it kept patients passive during the day and helped them sleep at night. A state hospital psychiatrist commented: "Nothing is more important than quietness." To maintain a peaceful atmosphere, he argued, a continuous bath or a cold pack administered to a noisy patient several times a day was always the better alternative to allowing that patient to disturb an entire ward.

The somatic view of mental illness dominated state hospitals. The patient was seen as having a medical problem. The fact that patients frequently suffered from bodily ailments and disorders offered enough evidence to suggest that something physical indeed produced mental distress. At most institutions a new patient had a physical examination that often revealed a common pathology, such as infected tonsils or abscessed teeth. Staff physicians coped with appendicitis, perforated ulcers, diabetes, influenza, every kind of heart disease, tuberculosis, syphilis, and pellagra, as well as dislocations, fractures, and wounds.

A common prescription for the quick relief of patient stress was a thorough cleansing of the intestinal tract. A "colonic irrigation" secured "proper intestinal elimination" and produced "beneficial results." Rectal examination was routine procedure because some patients placed foreign objects in that region, causing infection. Physicians listened to and investigated physical complaints; patient laments were not to be dismissed as the ravings of a distorted imagination or the utterances of an unbalanced mind.

State hospital practice witnessed some medical experimentation. The reputed connection of schizophrenia to endocrine disorders or thyroid dysfunction or changes in the vasomotor system produced therapies of dubious results. There were other treatments including prolonged narcosis or sleep therapy, fever therapy, the removal of various organs for focal infection, and vasectomy. Catatonic patients were given injections of the salts of maganese, cadmium, and cesium. In these cases the results were "indefinite." This sample of experiments characterized the basic thrust of institutional research: the continued groping for a somatic solution to mental illness. Speculation was not dampened by the unproductive fruits of research. On the contrary, after surveying the recent literature on treating schizophrenic and manic-depressive patients, one psychiatrist boasted: "We will continue unabashed, always hopeful that tomorrow may bring the happy answer." In fact all psychiatric therapies were strictly empirical.

Psychotherapy did not flourish in public mental institutions. Too many obstacles thwarted its development as a major therapeutic measure in the armamentarium of state hospital practice. The small number of psychotherapists preferred private practice to a career in a state hospital, where salaries were low and the majority of patients suffered from chronic disorders. Some mental hospital patients were suitable for psychotherapeutic work, notably first admissions and the neurotic. Yet superintendents showed little interest in psychotherapy. A survey of attitudes of hospital administrators toward this type of therapy, conducted by the American Psychiatric Association in 1933, revealed indifferent and negative responses to it. Superintendents indicated no present or future need for it, and the study concluded that psychotherapy would gain importance in state hospitals only when it received more recognition from universities and medical schools.

A few mental institutions inaugurated unique types of therapy. At Danville State Hospital in Pennsylvania, the directress of nurses supervised a therapeutic regimen called "normal living." It involved relating the hospital routine as nearly as possible to the patient's former life patterns, with the stipulation that he or she receive a well-balanced program of rest, sleep, nutrition, recreation, and work. Worcester State Hospital in Massachusetts established a program of grading and promoting patients. Designed to encourage a patient's initiative, to help break the routine and conformity of institutional life, the grading was based upon behavior. A series of posters displayed throughout the wards explained the plan, and each poster carried the line: "Patients are sent home only from Grade B." The most disagreeable behavior was designated Grade F, and its poster read: "Mute and Resistive, Silent or Too Talkative, Excitable and Disturbed, Not Cooperating, Not Working or Playing." Grade E behavior was characterized as "Working and Playing Poorly, Lazy and Shiftless, Too Proud of Own Ideas, Not Very Cooperative, Careless of Clothing." With Grade C the patient was on parole, "Working and Playing Well, Getting New Ideas and Interests, Making the Best of Everything, Cooperating Well and Obeying Rules." Grade B meant "Going Home" and Grade A signified recovery, with the patient "Able to Act Like a Normal Person, Able and Willing to Work, Able to Get Along with Family and Friends." According to the Worcester staff, this treatment produced significant results: it aroused patient interest, stirred a sense of group consciousness, and encouraged hope. The movement from one grade to the next gave the patient a sense of accomplishment and enhanced self-esteem.

The innovative methods employed at Danville and at Worcester, along with the diversity of other accepted and experimental treatments in state hospital practice, reflected a strong trend toward developing special therapies. These activities received extensive publicity in the professional psychiatric journals and generated lively discussion at local medical society meetings. The publications and the debates, however, could not obscure the many factors that undermined effective treatment efforts.

One destructive influence was the lack of knowledge of the nature and causes of psychoses. The uncertain, fragmentary, underdeveloped state of etiology made it difficult to determine and delineate the proper methods and principles of treatment and research. With psychotics constituting the vast majority of an institution's resident population, staff members, especially younger ones, succumbed to pessimism upon finding themselves unable to attack the root causes of patient disorders. The inability to engage in significant research added another dimension to the plight of young physicians. While no official scorned research, interest in basic administrative problems dominated state hospital life. Superintendents were kept busy finding room for more patients, attending to the needs of the physical plant, and maintaining harmonious personnel relations. Medical staffs conscientiously discharged routine responsibilities and accepted the poor prognosis for most of their cases. Treatment was largely physical: a judicious use of some type of occupational therapy in conjunction with hydrotherapy.

This institutional pattern militated against research and encouraged a "brain drain," keeping away psychiatrists devoted to scientific work. Their talents were better utilized in the expanding number of psychiatric research centers, notably psychopathic hospitals, well-endowed private clinics, and university clinics. Others searching for a congenial and lucrative setting found opportunity in private practice, at every level of the educational system, and in the developing specialties of child guidance, industrial psychiatry, and forensic psychiatry. An ironic condition ensued: the lowest salaries and the most pessimistic attitudes in psychiatry were found among state hospital physicians.

The inadequate number and the low quality of nursing and attendant staffs continued, as in the nineteenth century, to work against effective treatment programs. With only a skeleton nursing staff at many mental hospitals, the nurse played a small, unimportant role in caring for patients. Attendants carried the daily burdens and responsibilities of the ward routines. Superintendents frankly confessed disdain for these "poorly trained," "uncultured" employees and made repeated efforts to upgrade personnel through institutional training schools. Some administrators inaugurated a recruitment campaign designed to attract quality persons. Booklets that outlined the aims and accomplishments of the state hospital system were distributed at high schools, YMCAs, and general hospitals. Advertisements in newspapers and medical journals outlined the desirable features of service in mental health care. Other means suggested for improving staffs included a physical and mental examination process to screen out the unfit and the psychopathic; an adequate salary scale; good living conditions and recreation facilities within the institutional environment; and incentives and promotions that would reward good work and stimulate an interest in the career potentials of state hospital service.

Unfortunately these suggestions remained unattainable goals. Financially pressed mental hospitals could find neither enough professional nurses nor sufficient candidates for their own schools. Competent, motivated nurses and attendants were appalled by the salaries and unwilling to live in small, unattractive, poorly furnished quarters just off patient wards. Consequently they looked for career advancement outside of mental hospitals.

Following the pattern of the other institutional personnel, social workers, too, showed a decreasing interest in state hospital employment. They were introduced into the asylums before World War I to perform aftercare services. Their utilization of the casework technique helped to determine the impact of societal factors on a patient's mental condition, thereby facilitating a proper diagnosis. The war, the rapid growth of the mental hygiene and child-guidance movements, and the development of community clinics opened new vistas for psychiatric social workers. Many of them became attached to school systems, welfare agencies, courts, penal institutions, and general hospitals. All of these positions were considered more desirable and more interesting than work in state hospitals where the large number of long-term chronic patients discouraged even the most resolute workers. For the mental hospital the practical result was a rapid turnover of social work personnel. Vacancies simply went unfilled; a reduced staff remained overworked, sunk in routine, and largely isolated from the profession.

Overcrowded facilities also handicapped the treatment process. An excess of most difficult types of patients filled the wards. Their numbers continually increased and created a condition that produced irritation and conflict, and retarded improvement and recovery. To cope with the large number of patients, hospital procedures continued to be standardized and mechanical. Stereotyped routines that enforced order over the mass of inmates eclipsed the basic institutional objective, the treatment of the individual patient. The inmate's life pattern became artificial, almost abnormal, and was adjusted to the institutional interest of harmonious employee relations. When the patient ate an afternoon supper and went to bed early in the evening, this was for the convenience of the employees.

A treatment procedure could contribute to a smoothly running hospital even though it caused confusion and pain to the patient. To encourage sleep, for example, a patient might be given a hypnotic. The maximum and beneficial effect of the drug, however, was not allowed to run its course because hospital routine required that the patient be awakened at a specific time. In another instance, hydrotherapy was usually applied in the daytime, often in the morning, when patients were most active and restless. It actually had the greatest value in the evening, just before bedtime, when it soothed the patient, permitting sleep without the aid of a hypnotic. Again institutional needs took priority over patient comfort, a direct and detrimental effect of understaffed and overcrowded wards.

A perennial fact of institutional psychiatry has been the tremendous diversity in the quality of mental hospitals. Throughout the 1920s and 1930s the ebullient rhetoric frequently delivered before professional meetings disguised the variety and the reality of state hospital life. The caliber of an institution profoundly affected the delivery of psychiatric care. At many mental hospitals a lack of personnel, of facilities, and even of imagination prevented the adoption of innovative, progressive therapies. Southern institutions lagged noticeably behind the rest of the nation. The mentally disturbed still languished in jails and poorhouses. State expenditures for mental health care were at best minimal, and in several instances the allotted figures were less than half of the national average. The quality of personnel ranked low, with no specialists, not even occupational therapists, to examine and treat patients.

Institutions in the South were custodial operations lacking extramural services or contacts with the community. Independent state surveys testified to this grim portrait of asylum life. Texas state hospitals were tagged "merely brickwalls for custodial care"; Louisiana institutions were "grossly inadequate from the standpoint of personnel . . . physical plant, equipment, and method"; Kentucky placed patients in "antiquated firetraps" where they were "packed like sardines in a box." In other southern states, and in many northern and western ones, similar conditions prevailed.

On the brighter side, New York and Massachusetts had the best state hospitals. In both states excellent medical schools, established professional societies and journals, strong reform traditions, and public and political support combined to work for the maintenance and improvement of mental health facilities. The more typical mental hospitals operated in Illinois and Pennsylvania. Elgin State Hospital in Illinois and Danville State Hospital in Pennsylvania ranked highest in their states.

In the private sector the Menninger Sanitarium of Topeka, Kansas, gained a national reputation for quality care and treatment, notably in cases of alcoholism and drug addiction. Karl Menninger and his father Charles founded the clinic in 1920, and brother William joined in 1926. During and after World War II the Menningers transformed this small, regional facility into a major international center for psychiatric training and research.

St. Elizabeth's Hospital in Washington, D.C., was one of the nation's best mental institutions. Operated by the federal government, it was a large hospital handling over 4,000 patients. Dr. William A. White, its superintendent, was a bold, innovative psychiatrist and administrator who worked for humane care of patients, promoted research, and maintained a large, high-quality medical and nursing staff. St. Elizabeth's typified a new trend toward better-quality care at federal rather than state mental hospitals. Federal facilities for treating psychiatric patients, notably veterans, had grown steadily since World War I. In 1939 there were over 30,000 beds in the hospitals of the Veterans Administration assigned to neuropsychiatric cases. This development gained more significance during and after the American involvement in World War II, when the federal government moved aggressively into mental health care.

The major problems confronting mental institutions prompted concern, debate, and action from diverse groups within the psychiatric and medical communities. Seeking solutions to the dilemmas of hospital care were the American Psychiatric Association, the American Medical Association, state medical societies, university medical schools, general hospital administrators, general practitioners, mental hygiene groups, and state hospital superintendents. While there was little coordinated activity among these groups, and a comprehensive reform program never appeared, their common interests included improving the standards of public mental hospitals, opening general hospitals to more mental patients, providing additional psychiatric training at medical schools, and educating general practitioners to psychiatric problems. A marked feature of this drive was the interest and participation of state medical societies, particularly in regard to ameliorating the inadequate conditions in the state hospital system.

The American Psychiatric Association had long been concerned with upgrading state hospitals, and in 1925 it promulgated its list of standard operating procedures for mental institutions. Some of the recommendations included adequate, well-qualified medical and nursing personnel, complemented with a staff of consulting specialists; the maintenance of an efficient system of clinical records; the periodic staff review of each patient's progress; the establishment of an outpatient clinic; the removal of all political influence from state hospital appointments. These proposals were actually long-standing principles of hospital care, and were designed to educate and prod administrators into accepting higher standards of achievement.

Just as in the nineteenth century, a major thrust of the Association's 1925 demands focused on providing adequate physical facilities for patients and staff. This recommendation struck a notable response from administrators, who were always preoccupied with hospital buildings. From their discussions and writings the basic outlines of a new psychiatric architecture emerged. The Kirkbride model, which created the large, imposing building with extended wings, received a general rejection. It had produced too many "massive monastery and prison-like structures." Progressive superintendents and hospital architects wanted buildings that could relate directly to the institution's fundamental purpose: the treatment of the patient. Individualized care could not be attained in buildings with large wards and day rooms. A structure composed of a large number of single rooms with small doors would facilitate individual attention and avoid treatment en masse.

The creation of a home atmosphere was also fundamental to a good mental institution. Hospital life should be pleasant and devoid of the usual institutional appearance and trappings associated with feelings of gloom and isolation. Patient surroundings must be bright, cheerful, comfortable, safe, and sanitary, without any dark passages or corners, gloomy rooms, and hiding places. Windows should permit ample sunshine and air to enter, and be guarded with an ornamental grill rather than prisonlike steel bars.   Nothing in the interior should excite the patient. Adequate soundproofing according to the reports, could muffle disturbing noises; pleasant, restful visual experiences could be achieved by harmonious color schemes, by concealing ugly plumbing fixtures, and by placing radiators in wall recesses.

The application of these two principles—the provision of single rooms for patients and the creation of a domestic atmosphere within the institution—was only partially achieved in a few places, notably Fairfield State Hospital in Connecticut, Payne-Whitney Psychiatric Clinic associated with Cornell University Medical College, and Veterans Memorial Hospital and Kings Park State Hospital in New York. The main trend in state hospital construction did not follow this lead. Largely for economic reasons, few new public hospitals appeared in the interwar period, and the basic building pattern consisted of adding wings to existing structures.

Although annexes did not relate well to the existing buildings, which had been fashioned after the ideas and architectural designs of an earlier period, the new additions helped to relieve the crowded wards. Finding enough physical facilities to segregate the different types of patients was a major administrative concern. The physical space allotted to patients remained quite constant throughout the 1920s and 1930s. An important part of the typical mental hospital was the administration building, which provided facilities for receiving and diagnosing patients, typically housing about 5 percent of the resident patient population. These persons represented acute cases whose term at the institution would be only a few weeks or months.

Another building or wing was necessary for handling surgical cases. It accommodated perhaps 2 percent of the patient community. Those inmates suffering from contagious diseases, notably tuberculosis, numbered 5 percent and were isolated in a small building or "cottage." Others, the "quiet and moderately disturbed," made up about 45 percent of the patients; some could work, while most needed prolonged treatment. The "depressed, disturbed, and violent" constituted about 20 percent of the cases and required careful supervision in a controlled physical setting. The aged, infirm, and feeble accounted for 18 percent of the inmates. They were more or less in a helpless, dependent condition, needing special provisions in a separate building. A small wing housed the remaining 5 percent, who were convalescents or epileptics. The administrative goal of providing separate facilities for different groups was not always attained. When space was not available, institutions simply separated the quiet from the noisy. The quiet lived together in large wards; the violent and actively disturbed were isolated in small wards and rooms.

These unfortunate conditions reinforced the public view of the state hospital as an institution of last resort, an undesirable place without therapeutic value but of great social untility. Administrators defended their institutions with a public relations effort that stressed two themes: the necessity of a positive, warm reception for the patient, and the identification of the mental institution as a hospital rather than an asylum. The patient's first impression of an institution was deemed a vital factor in establishing rapport with the staff. To elicit a favorable response, the initial reception was arranged without delay or the annoyance of any disagreeable sight and sound. The receiving area conveyed a cheerful sitting room atmosphere, furnished with carpeting, tables, lamps, a couch, a rocker, chairs, and pictures. In meeting the patient the staff displayed poise and tact, and showed concern for his or her comfort. The purpose of the institution and the patient's role in it were carefully explained. All of this helped to put the patient at ease and to reassure the family and friends, giving them a positive experience with a mental institution.

Public relations were further advanced by emphasizing the institution's hospital role. Progress in mental health care, from the asylum to the hospital ideal, was stressed. The asylum concept stood in the past and evoked images of custody and isolation; the mental hospital represented the present and the future, and it brought hope, treatment, and service to society. Its standards, services, and equipment compared favorably with those of a good general hospital. For many mental institutions, of course, this was rhetoric, a public relations effort designed to screen institutional realities and to neutralize unfavorable public opinion.

An important development in the interwar era was the growing acceptance of mental patients in general hospitals. The practice was unorthodox in the early 1920s but standard policy by the late 1930s in over 100 general hospitals. The administrators who accepted this new responsibility saw it as a rescue mission: a few weeks, even months, of sympathetic attention in a general hospital would restore an individual's mental health and save that person from death or, worse, indefinite commitment to a state mental institution. The general hospital offered treatment supervised by physicians and nurses, not attendants. One general hospital administrator succinctly stated the dissimilarity of the two types of institutions: "Cure rather than care epitomizes the difference between the custodial asylum and the psychiatric section of a general hospital."

A patient's removal to a general hospital also avoided the stigma associated with the mental institution. A family sending one of its members to a general hospital could avoid public awareness of the malady. Also, hospital care permitted a neurotic person to get immediate treatment, avoiding the sometimes lengthy commitment procedures.

Some hospital administrators opposed the new admissions policy. They argued that the bustle of a city hospital, with visitors constantly coming and going, had a disturbing effect on mental patients. Might not patients also be disoriented by the lack of outdoor facilities or the attitudes of an uninformed staff, who might see them as nuisances, as constantly complaining persons impossible to please or comfort?

But criticism was muted by the successful demonstrations of psychiatric departments in such general hospitals as St. Agnes Hospital in Philadelphia, Miller Hospital in St. Paul, St. Mary's Hospital in St. Louis; and Christ Hospital in Topeka. In these institutions a number of factors combined to create a high quality of care: trained and experienced staffs, good accommodations in an attractive setting, ample hydrotherapy equipment, and provisions for occupational therapy, the socialization of patients, and the necessary dietary regimes. It was a standard policy of hospital physicians that they dealt with the "nervous," not the insane. They took curable cases and left the chronic for the state mental hospital.

This limitation was not necessarily essential. At Henry Ford Hospital in Detroit, Dr. Thomas J. Heldt, director of the Psychiatric Department, admitted all types of mental cases. He believed that the general hospital could relieve the overcrowded and understaffed mental institutions, and gained a national reputation for putting that idea into practice. At Henry Ford psychotic cases were handled with the proper facilities, notably in hydrotherapy rooms, and with an understanding administration. Most patients came on a voluntary basis and received the early treatment that prevented more serious disorders. This service, in Heldt's view, had tremendous educational value. It militated against the popular bias that a mentally disturbed person required isolation. The public could see the general hospital as a place for treating mental patients as well as those suffering from physical illness. Having mental patients at Henry Ford was an invaluable educational experience for the staff. They learned the principles of caring for the mentally disturbed, an essential requirement of their training; and medical students and nurses could study mental patients and learn how psychiatry related to general hospital practice.

Heldt's interest in making the general hospital a learning center for professionals and the public was an expression of a wider interest in upgrading psychiatric training. The inadequate conditions at state hospitals drew attention to the quality of psychiatric education in medical schools. Some associated inferior care with insufficient educational preparation. Although this was too facile an argument, it reflected the state of psychiatric education. At many schools psychiatry received little attention: a few courses offered in the senior year, followed by a visit to a state hospital. Deans of medical schools and professors of medicine criticized psychiatry for its inexactness, therapeutic inefficiency, and isolation from medicine.

But they recognized a need to attract more persons into the field, and in the early 1930s they inagurated some important changes in the medical school curriculum. Psychiatry would be taught throughout the student's college career, not simply in the senior year, and the curriculum included courses in psychobiology, medical psychology, and psychopathology. A student had a variety of options for clinical experience: work in a psychopathic or Veterans Administration hospital, an outpatient department of a general hospital, or the traditional state hospital. The classroom stressed an eclectic point of view, a genetic-dynamic approach, such as that advocated by Adolf Meyer, who held that a long accumulation of unhealthy reactions produced mental disorder. Proper diagnosis of a patient involved an examination of the total biography, a summation of reactions to physical, organic, and environmental forces. This approach stood in contrast with the traditional Kraeplin type of psychiatry, which had dominated medical schools and was oriented toward diagnosis and classification. A major objective of the changes in the curriculum was better preparation of the student for psychiatric problems and conditions in general practice.

The general practitioner was recognized as a key figure in preventive psychiatry. Ideally he stood in a position to abort an illness before it reached an advanced stage. As a friend and adviser to the family, he knew its history and morale as well as the desires, conflicts, and frustrations of its members. Such intimacy enabled the general practitioner to notice signs of disorder. He could intervene promptly, explain the problem to the family, and save an individual from a life of frustration and neurosis. The general practitioner was seen as a warrior-physician who stood on the first line of defense, carrying out measures that allowed the maladjusted person to recover without hospitalization. This portrait was divorced from reality. Many a general practitioner was negative and hostile toward the mental patient, whom he saw as a weakling with unreal, intangible problems that could not be stated in concrete medical terms. This kind of patient might be an annoyance, a malingerer who wasted the doctor's time; such a person should be sent home with a placebo and advised to forget about the symptoms.

Mental hygiene groups and many state medical societies worked to change such attitudes. They wanted the general practitioner to become an effective agent of prevention, and argued that his reeducation and cooperation might diminish the numbers of mentally ill sent to state hospitals. State medical journals offered guidelines on coping with mental patients, and the advice given was remarkably consistent. Above all, the general practitioner must be able to recognize neurotic symptoms. The neurotic patient might tire easily, be irritable and supersensitive, have headaches, generalized pains, and sleepless nights. Other symptoms might include chronic diarrhea or constipation, along with attacks of vertigo, nausea, and vomiting. A neurotic might be anxiety-ridden, filled with worry and fear. It was important to accept these symptoms as indications of a real illness, as real as pneumonia or appendicitis. The etiology of the disorder might remain obscure. While searching for a physical pathology, the doctor must remain open to possible psychopathological influences, including family disturbances, financial reverses, and frustrations resulting from the burdens and responsibilities of business and professional life.

General practitioners were advised about the role of age in mental disorder. Each decade of life was assigned a type of mental disturbance that physicians could detect and diagnose, and for which they could offer a reasonable prognosis. Feeblemindedness emerged in the first ten years; the second decade brought dementia praecox, notably in the form of antisocial, introverted behavior. In the third decade manic-depressive symptoms were evident, with such signs as inferiority feelings coupled with inefficient, irresponsible actions. Paranoia surfaced in the thirties and forties, followed by general paralysis in the fifties. The last two decades of life witnessed melancholia and arteriosclerosis.

In treating the mental patient the general practitioner was advised to handle only neurotic, borderline cases. Psychotics required immediate commitment to a state hospital. While the neurotic looked for sympathy and understanding, the doctor's reassurance played only a minor role in the recovery process. A specific regimen should be administered, with careful supervision of daily activities to assure a proper balance of work, rest, exercise, and recreation. The elimination and digestive processes needed special attention. Most important, the patient must talk, relating his or her story freely and fully to the doctor, who offered advice and administered appropriate therapy. If more mental cases received treatment from general practitioners, it was argued, many nervous breakdowns would be prevented and the patient population at state hospitals would be noticeably reduced.

Whether better-informed general practitioners would indeed limit admissions to mental institutions remained academic. The Great Depression of the 1930s upset plans and programs, and struck a devastating blow at the state hospital system. Budgets were drastically reduced; preventive work was retarded; community services were curtailed; plans for institutional expansion were abandoned. The most severe strain on the already overcrowded wards was a general increase in the numbers of patients admitted and retained. The Depression did not produce a sudden surge of psychotics requiring institutionalization. The unsettling economic conditions caused a rise in patient populations by forcing the mental institution into the role of a relief agency. It had to accept some of the unemployed and elderly, the outcasts of an economically depressed society. With millions out of work, thousands of families with unemployed breadwinners suffered humiliation and misery, and did not want a former patient back in the household. Without a job such a person became a liability, a burden the family passed back to the state hospital. Superintendents constantly reported difficulty in paroling patients.

The elderly posed a more difficult problem. Older, economically unproductive family members suffering from mental disorders were shunted to the state hospitals, where they formed a growing segment of senile and arteriosclerotic patients. Superintendents were alarmed and distressed by this trend, recognizing that patients stricken with the psychoses of advanced age required only minimal custodial care. Their prognosis pointed to slow, steady deterioration, with no hope of improvement. Commenting on this condition, Dr. Richard H. Hutchings, in his 1939 presidential address before the American Psychiatric Association, noted that state hospitals were becoming "vast infirmaries for dotards." The change to an older patient population gave the mental hospital an additional stigma; housing fewer young and curable cases, it became a home for the aged, a place for the unwanted and worn-out who were alienated and disengaged from the youth-oriented culture of America.

During the Depression the federal government granted some aid to state hospitals. The Public Works Administration, and later the Works Progress Administration (WPA), two New Deal agencies designed to provide employment through public building, initiated several projects. Buildings were repaired or painted or remodeled; new utility systems were installed; storage buildings were erected; grounds were landscaped. The WPA spent over $11 million improving facilities at three New York mental institutions: Creedmore State Hospital, Brooklyn State Hospital, and the New York State Psychiatric Institute. While these projects put men back to work, the WPA also intervened in the lives of patients with educational, recreational, and occupational therapy programs. It sponsored classes in art, handicrafts, beauty culture, cooking, and sewing. Under the guidance of WPA workers, patients participated in group games, including baseball, and held dances, carnivals, and picnics. A WPA theater group at the psychiatric clinic at Bellevue Hospital in New York City stimulated patient interest in composing dramas related to their own troubles. Weekly concerts by WPA musicians helped brighten the atmosphere of St. Elizabeth's Hospital in Washington D.C. The projects of the federal government aided some institutions and a few patients, but did not signify a major assault on the problems of institutional psychiatry. Their key objective was employing people rather than providing better care and treatment for mental patients.

In 1936 the dilemmas of institutional psychiatry were elaborately documented in a study conducted by an imposing group of professional organizations and agencies: the American Psychiatric Association, the American Medical Association, the U.S. Public Health Service, the American Board of Psychiatry and Neurology, the American Neurological Association, the National Committee for Mental Hygiene, the Canadian National Committee for Mental Hygiene, the Canadian Medical Association, and the Rockefeller Foundation. Based on an analysis of 226 hospitals from Maine to California and from Florida to British Columbia, the findings revealed the distressing conditions of the state hospital system in the midst of the Great Depression. Most institutions functioned as custodial pesthouses and only a few as treatment centers. The basic institutional dilemmas remained: overcrowded facilities, inadequate personnel (notably the lack of proper nursing staffs), and minimal research and pathological work. A very small number of hospitals met the standards set by the American Psychiatric Association.

Conditions at mental hospitals represented only one barometer that measured the effects of the Depression on mental health. A major concern of the psychiatric community, including mental hygiene groups and general practitioners, was the frequency with which mild cases of mental disorder were treated outside of institutions. Nearly universal opinion proclaimed that the economic malaise had caused a massive, almost epidemic increase of neurotic disturbances. The most serious maladjustments occurred in households of the unemployed, where the loss of a stable income produced an explosive emotional environment damaging to every member of the family, especially the children. Harried parents became irritable, impatient, critical, quick-tempered, suspicious, self-centered, and selfish, creating an atmosphere of fear and insecurity. Children grew sullen and disobedient, and vented their hostility in actions ranging from school truancy to stealing. Without employment and guidance, they developed habits of idleness that could only augur badly for later life. Mental hygienists, consistent in their emphasis on the young, predicted that the toll of mentally ill children would be heavy, the natural result of growing up in deprived circumstances. Several psychiatrists forecast a foreboding future of an ever-increasing ratio of mental disorders, noting that it took time for major psychoses to develop. In short, widespread personality disturbances and maladjustments represented the danger signals of serious mental illness that would mature in the future.

The sense of alarm about the increasing incidence of mental disorders persisted throughout the 1930s. Editorials and statements of eminent physicians in professional journals proclaimed that mental illness represented a major health problem. In 1939 the president of the American Medical Association, Dr. Rock Sleyster, stated that "mental disease is imposing in scope," and that on any day in America over 1 million people were incapacitated in mental hospitals and several million were handicapped by neurotic disturbances. U.S. Public Health Service reports presented alarming statistical predictions of the number of persons born in a particular year who would be destined for a mental institution 25 years later. State medical society journals published disturbing projections of the rates of mentally ill persons. The *Virginia Medical Monthly*, for example, claimed that of the thousands of American babies born each day who reached adulthood, one out of 125 would go insane and only 12 out of 125 would become "fairly normal." These pessimistic forecasts and the professional awareness of the meager results of institutional care created a milieu receptive to shock treatment. Introduced into the state hospital systems in the late 1930s, the dramatic shock methods offered a possible way out of the major institutional dilemmas.

9
SHOCK TREATMENTS AND LOBOTOMY

Shock treatments brought relief from the tedium of mental hospital life. Imported from Europe in the late 1930s, the new therapy was enthusiastically embraced by American institutional psychiatrists who assumed that here, at last, was something that could have a demonstrable, positive effect on the most hapless of mental patients. The term "shock" suggests that the treatments produce upheaval in the central nervous system, although the exact nature of the upheaval remains unknown. There were three basic types, occurring in chronological sequence: first came the insulin method, followed by the use of Metrazol, which was replaced by electroconvulsive therapy or electroshock therapy. Almost simultaneously with these treatments a surgical procedure, prefrontal lobotomy, was adopted throughout the country. The term "psychosurgery" soon evolved and embraced all refinements and modifications of the original lobotomy technique. It has been defined as "the neurosurgical treatment of behavioral disorders." Shock treatments and lobotomy were used extensively between 1936 and the mid-1950s, when the rapid acceptance of pharmacotherapy diminished their popularity.

In 1933, Dr. Manfred Sakel reported on his work at the University Clinic in Vienna with the hypoglycemic or insulin shock treatment of schizophrenia. After using large doses of insulin to alleviate the withdrawal symptoms of morphine addicts, he employed the same technique on schizophrenic patients with striking effect. Confused and excited patients who had been restricted in a cage bed for weeks, Sakel contended, returned to normal life without psychotic symptoms. His subsequent reports confirmed the initial results: an unusually high percentage of patients made complete recoveries, and many others regained sufficient health to return to the community. Sakel's astonishing claims electrified the world of American institutional psychiatry, and in 1936 he was invited by the New York State Department of Mental Hygiene to demonstrate his treatment process at Harlem Valley State Hospital in Wingdale. In a six-week course he would teach 40 American physicians his approach to treating the mentally ill.

The basic aim of Sakel's treatment was to induce a state of hypoglycemia, a condition of abnormally low blood sugar, through doses of insulin. Increasingly large amounts were administered until the patient lapsed into a coma. Before the patient lost consciousness, the symptoms of hypoglycemia intensified; they included increased perspiration and salivation, accompanied by complaints of hunger and thirst. Some patients became drowsy, while others grew restless, tossed and turned, and shouted. Alterations in perception were common; sucking movements, forced gasping, tremors, twitchings, and epileptic seizures were observed. The shock phase of the treatment occurred when the patient went into a coma, remaining totally unresponsive to outside stimuli. Hypoglycemia was terminated by administering a carbohydrate solution orally or intravenously. Sugar was used, dissolved in water, tea, or fruit juice.

This whole procedure, from the initial injection to recovery from coma, took five or six hours. While the frequency and duration of the treatment varied with the patient's condition and the physician's opinion, it was usually given five times a week, with two rest days, until 50 or 60 comas had been applied. Every healthy patient was deemed suitable for treatment. Those suffering from tuberculosis, diabetes, kidney or liver disease, diseases of the pancreas, thyroid, or adrenal glands, and, most important, cardiovascular diseases were excluded. From a psychiatric viewpoint the selection process was simple: Sakel indicated that his treatment helped to cure schizophrenia; insulin had little effect on the manic-depressive and involuntional psychoses.

At Harlem Valley, Sakel admitted that the theory behind his work remained vague and was perhaps even wrong. However, he testified that the effects of the treatment were impressive, noting that remarkable changes occurred in psychotic cases. The violent, confused patient suddenly became lucid, lost all hallucinations and delusions, and grew calm. As the treatment progressed, the psychosis receded, eventually disappeared, and a normal consciousness dominated the personality. There was no doubt about the connection between treatment and patient improvement. Sakel proclaimed that psychiatrists now possessed "an instrument with which they can break through the barrier and attack the psychosis." His enthusiasm spread to mental hospitals and clinics, where psychiatrists eagerly practiced the new theory. Their initial reports identified the insulin method as the "best available therapy" that produced "striking," "beneficial" results. Such pronouncements were reminiscent of the curability claims of the asylum superintendents of the pre-Civil War period. The press echoed the new professional optimism and gave additional publicity to the remarkable rates of recovery among patients hitherto inaccessible.

In fact, no practitioner ever matched Sakel's results, and for good reason. The terms used to designate a cured person were vague, and varied from hospital to hospital and from one examiner to another. The "recovered" and "much improved" cases were frequently lumped together in a category called "remissions." An important time factor, the length of the patient's illness, clearly affected the remission rate, a fact Sakel admitted. Short-term patients, troubled for six months or less, responded to the treatment more favorably than those suffering for over one year.

Some serious complications dampened the initial enthusiasm. These occurred during the treatment procedure and included a certain percentage of fatalities, cardiovascular and respiratory disturbances, vertebral fractures, and the occurrence of prolonged coma. Follow-up studies over a period of years revealed less favorable results, demonstrating that the treatment had little long-range sustaining effect. This led many observers to the skeptical conclusion that the insulin method offered no major answer to the schizophrenic condition. From a practical administrative viewpoint there was an additional problem: the insulin treatment process was inefficient. It tied needed physicians and nurses to a handful of patients over a lengthy time period, a fact that contained its spread.

The hypoglycemic treatment of schizophrenia peaked in the late 1930s and early 1940s. For a short time another shock method, Metrazol convulsive treatment, attracted attention and captured some support. It was developed by Dr. Joseph L. von Meduna of the Leopold Field Hospital in Budapest, Hungary, who migrated to the United States in 1939 to become an associate professor of psychiatry and neurology at Loyola University in Chicago. The object of his method was to utilize the apparently beneficial effect that convulsive seizures had on the schizophrenic process. The treatment was quick and simple, and Meduna claimed a 90 percent remission rate with patients who had been ill for less than a year, a figure that subsequent workers never reported.

The drug Metrazol was injected intravenously, and within 30 or 60 seconds convulsions began. Before the patient lost consciousness, a terrifying sensation occurred which frequently terminated with a sharp, piercing outcry. After convulsing, the patient went into a brief comatose sleep and awoke in a confused state, experiencing memory failure and sore muscles. The whole procedure lasted only a few minutes, and Meduna asserted that patients were up and around within an hour after treatment.

Metrazol required less care, preparation, and supervision of the patient than the insulin method. Its practitioners documented "gratifying," "promising," and "spectacular" results. The drastic nature of the treatment and its many complications, however, sharply curtailed its acceptance and wide application. One difficulty was the unpredictability of the convulsion. The intensity varied from individual to individual, and at times nothing happened, leaving the patient anxious, restless and nauseated for several hours. The convulsion itself could not be easily terminated—the effect of a fixed dosage simply had to run its course. The injuries suffered by the patient in the treatment process constituted a more serious drawback. The damage wrought by the epileptic-like seizures could be severe, and included dislocation of the shoulders or the jaw, the loosening and breaking of teeth, and fractures of the humerus, the femur, the spine, and the vertebrae.

The most unpleasant feature of the Metrazol treatment was the patient's fear of it. The attitude stemmed from experiences during the brief period between injection and convulsion, when sensations of impending death, of sudden annihilation, of being overpowered and killed were felt. This anguish was observed in the patient's facial expressions of terror and horror. After such an experience the patient wanted neither to discuss the treatment nor to pass through it again, a fact that obviously limited its therapeutic value.

Electroconvulsive therapy (ECT) avoided this painful reaction by immediately rendering the patient unconscious. Dr. Ugo Cerletti, a professor of neuropathology and psychiatry at the University of Rome, developed the method, presenting his findings in 1938. His work had a curious history. Although Cerletti had for years induced epilepsy in dogs by means of electrical current, he was reluctant to conduct the same experiment on humans, believing that the procedure was dangerous and evoked images of the electric chair. Chance intervened to alter the direction of his research. He investigated a rumor that hogs were electrocuted at a slaughterhouse, and discovered that electricity simply had knocked out the animals, making it easier for the butcher to stab and bleed them. Elated by this discovery, he continued experimenting, resolved now to use a human being. Chance again interceded. The police commissioner of Rome sent to Cerletti's clinic a man in a disordered mental condition who had been arrested at a railroad station for boarding a train without a ticket. This man became the first human recipient of induced electric convulsion. After 11 applications of ECT, he appeared well, although his wife reported that at night he often answered voices no one else heard.

The simple and direct procedure of ECT facilitated its rapid acceptance and wide application in American mental institutions. The patient was given the treatment early in the morning. He or she was placed comfortably on a bed or examining table without straps or other types of restraining devices. Attendants and nurses stood along both sides, ready to prevent the patient from falling or being hurt during the convulsions. An electrode was attached to each temple, and current from a normal electric light circuit was passed between the electrodes for a fraction of a second. The patient immediately lost consciousness, had a generalized convulsion corresponding to an epileptic seizure, and then passed into a brief sleep lasting four or five minutes. About 15 or 20 minutes after treatment, he or she was able to walk. Usually the patient was given the treatment three times a week. For hospital administrators ECT had the decided advantage of being inexpensive. One physician could administer it to 30 or more patients in two hours.

Initially there were many complications. Although less severe than Metrazol, ECT produced fractures, dislocations, cardiovascular disorders, complications in the respiratory system, and a few fatalities. The development of a satisfactory muscle relaxant minimized these difficulties, the rate of fractures was noticeably reduced, and attention focused on the patient's state of mind. Here there was a universal problem: a condition of amnesia accompanied the emergence from the post-convulsion sleep. This memory impairment had an unnerving effect on the patient. He or she awoke with a headache, feelings of dizziness and nausea, blurred vision, and had no idea who he or she was, where he or she was, or what had happened. Everything seemed new, strange, unfamiliar, and unreal. Slowly the disorientation left, the shattered self acquired some of its former identity, and from the attending physicians and nurses the patient grasped his or her whereabouts and the nature of his or her condition. At that point partial amnesia remained, its length varying with the invidual. Some experienced impairment for hours, others for several months, and a few had irretrievable losses.

The ease and simplicity of delivering ECT to the patient expedited its adoption at outpatient clinics and at the offices of private physicians. Some of the most ardent enthusiasts of ECT worked on that level, and testified that the "borderline," neurotic patient showed the most positive and striking response to the treatment. An enormous professional literature buttressed this position with claims that ECT kept a mentally disturbed person out of a hospital, enabling him or her to remain at home and continue working. In papers delivered at professional meetings throughout the 1940s and early 1950s, psychiatrists exuberantly testified about the efficacy of ECT. The results of the treatment "were unparalleled in the history of psychiatry"; improvement of a patient's mental health was "often unbelievable."

One psychiatrist asserted that the increased use of ECT had caused a decrease in the rate of suicides. Others claimed that all types of mentally disturbed individuals displayed immediate and dramatic behavioral change: the depressed patient became euphoric, the extremely agitated individual became calm, hallucinating paranoids lost their false perceptions and beliefs. Even if relapses occurred, ECT proponents argued, the defeatism of the past was being dissipated. Optimism in treating the mentally ill now had a "valid basis," with ECT proving itself far superior to any other form of therapy.

This arrogant enthusiasm permeated mental institutions and had a bandwagon effect on hospital administrators. Other forms of treatment were deemphasized or discarded, and a remarkable optimism developed as mental health workers rushed to give ECT an extensive trial. At one state hospital, for example, over a five-year period 2,050 patients received ECT, with a total of over 28,000 electrically induced convulsions administered. Very few hospitals considered that the treatment had no value.

While ECT became the most popular and widely used shock method, insulin and Metrazol were not completely abandoned. Combined shock treatments, usually ECT and insulin, were assumed to be beneficial. A patient might be given 20 insulin comas followed by a series of electric shock convulsions. If the response was judged inadequate, a different combination of treatments might be tried. At several institutions a special building was designated an insulin-Metrazol-electroshock unit. Pilgrim State Hospital on Long Island, a large institution that received about 150 patients a month, used an eight-ward building where there were proper facilities for each type of shock therapy. Insulin-treated patients were kept in large wards where all cases could be easily observed. Metrazol was administered in a special room early in the morning, when other wards required little nursing attention. ECT was handled in several small rooms on an assembly-line arrangement so that 12 to 20 patients could be shocked each hour. This central treatment unit, administrators boasted, brought efficiency and economy to the shock therapy process, and it effected good public relations, with relatives of patients expressing gratitude that Pilgrim had such a facility.

The establishment of shock units encouraged the development of a policy known as "maintenance treatment," which became standard procedure at many mental hospitals. It simply consisted of inducing shock in those patients who showed no lasting remissions. The treatment was given weekly, biweekly, or even daily, depending on the patient's mental and physical condition. Administrators claimed that this policy simplified the management of difficult cases and produced high staff morale. While the effects were most noticeable on chronic wards, where the mere movement of patients to treatment rooms aroused staff interest, an unfortunate pattern of care evolved: there was an almost reckless commitment, indeed capitulation, to an indiscriminate application of shock therapy to every patient on the chronic wards. Practitioners of maintenance treatment believed that all schizophrenics needed some form of shock, contending that it avoided reliance on such disagreeable measures as force-feeding and the use of restraining devices. One authority asserted that it could be continued for years without damaging patients, citing a case of a man who received 248 convulsions over a long time span without apparent ill effect. Presumably this person and the other human beings on the chronic wards had a hopeless prognosis, and without shock treatment they remained in a vegetative state of existence. Shock brought them to a level where they could establish contact with the hospital environment and perhaps engage in occupational therapy.

A reaction set in against shock treatment. This fact illustrates and repeats a dominant pattern in mental health history. The difficult, obscure nature of mental illness, coupled with the many, frequently fruitless methods of treating it, led psychiatrists to grasp any new therapy that promised good, perhaps even spectacular, results. This enthusiasm diminished when the therapy produced conflicting, less promising results, and within a brief period of time it became another accepted or rejected method in a psychiatrist's armamentarium. While shock treatment followed this trend, it sparked an acrimonious debate between proponents who extravagantly praised it and opponents who condemned it. This polarization surrounding the topic acquired an emotional aura, making it difficult to evaluate the therapy objectively and to place it within a proper perspective.

Certainly the theoretical underpinning of shock treatment remained elusive. While the obscurity shrouding the action of this method was admitted, even by its strongest advocates, all sorts of hypotheses were offered to explain why it apparently benefited some patients. The somatic-oriented psychiatrist presumed that convulsive shock altered brain and nerve tissue; the psychologically inclined therapist suggested that it purged the patient of guilt feelings or enabled him or her to experience death and rebirth emotionally. Many argued that shock literally knocked a pathological state out of the brain, and that memory impairment was actually a positive development. The patient "forgot" the pathological state. As speculations and experience accumulated, the inadequacies of these theories became obvious, and a consensus was reached on one point: shock therapy operated on a symptomatic rather than an etiological level. For example, ECT gave apparent relief to cases of involutional melancholia. A 1960 report viewed it as a "boon" to these sufferers, yet "why it is effective and how it works, no one knows for sure."

An amazing number of studies on shock treatment lacked scientific objectivity and consistency, a fact that frustrated efforts to synthesize and compare the results of individual reports. The types of patients examined, the actual treatment procedure, and the method of evaluating the response to treatment, varied from study to study. The classifications denoting positive results to treatment, notably "greatly improved" and "much improved," were so broad and vague as to be virtually meaningless. No time limit was set to determine whether the patient benefited from shock or from some other therapeutic measure. Misleading figures cited the immediate remission rate, implying that shock had unusual efficacy. In fact, a wide discrepancy existed between immediate effects and long-term results. In many instances shock shortened the time period spent in institutions after the first admissions, yet caused a very high readmission rate. It made the patient dependent on continued treatment that involved lengthy institutional readmissions, thereby negating the impact of the initially brief hospital stay.

Another characteristic of shock therapy literature was to water down unfavorable or controversial results. While fractures and dislocations received some attention, many studies overlooked the more subtle complications of treatment. Certain hazards were minimized, notably the danger of too many shocks. There was a direct relationship between the number of treatments a patient received and brain damage, including cerebral hemorrhages.

The more shocks administered, the greater the risk of permanent injury to the patient. Psychological changes appeared most ominous. A general emotional flattening occurred. The individual's sense of humor, social finesse, intuition, and capacity for inventiveness and ingenuity were altered, marking the beginning of a process of personality deterioration. The pattern of dullness persisted, and the patient gave little attention to personal needs, adopted sterile, rigid attitudes, showed no concern for the future, and could not concentrate on anything but the most trivial of matters.

A very serious after effect was the loss of skills to perform tasks previously handled with routine ease. This inability to perform once-familiar tasks or to recall information meant that the patient could not return to former employment. Here was a severe, humiliating blow, damaging to a person's self-esteem and sense of security. Still another painful situation was the frequent and dramatic chance of diagnosis occurring during the course of treatment. Before the therapy was administered, for example, the patient might be diagnosed a schizophrenic; after receiving shock therapy he or she became a manic-depressive case. Assuming that these were accurate assessments, shock obviously changed behavioral patterns and perhaps only scrambled psychotic symptoms. This effect again suggested the formulation of a deteriorating pattern of behavior and offered an explanation for the increased frequency of readmission.

In 1947 a sharp and objective critique of shock treatment, notably ECT, was made by the Group for the Advancement of Psychiatry (GAP), a progressive psychiatric organization established the year before. Approximately 150 American and Canadian psychiatrists, all members of the American Psychiatric Association, formed the core of the group, which aimed at stimulating research and utilizing psychiatry to solve social problems. In the GAP report a number of abuses in the practice of ECT were condemned: the administration of ECT by physicians and personnel untrained in its techniques, the indiscriminate application of ECT to patients of all diagnostic categories, and the total reliance on it to the neglect of other types of therapeutic measures. The report called for the establishment of uniform criteria for evaluating the results of clinical research, long-term follow-up studies, the integration of physiological and psychodynamic research, and special research projects correlating brain damage with the number and intensity of shocks administered. In short, GAP believed that the abuses of shock treatment warranted widespread professional attention: the treatment obviously had limitations, and future research would determine its proper role in mental health care.

The criticism of progressive psychiatrists failed to dampen the enthusiasm of ECT practitioners, who claimed that it was benign, beneficial, and had absolutely no contraindications. While admitting that shock was not the panacea for all psychoses, they stressed a point sensitive to hospital administrators: the alternative was custodial care. Here was the fundamental reality of mental hospital life. The injection of shock methods into the therapeutic practice of institutional psychiatry created a new hospital milieu, an atmosphere that seemingly militated against the custodialism of the past. Shock therapy brought action and movement; it stirred interest in treating patients who appeared to be forever lost in some psychotic oblivion; physicians were required to oversee its administration, a fact that encouraged young psychiatrists to remain in an institutional setting; and the treatment and its effects aroused curiosity, stimulating research at the mental hospital. In this kind of setting, the more disagreeable side of shock therapy, the view from the patient's end, could be easily overlooked.

Lobotomy developed coincidentally with the shock methods of treating mental disorders, and it generated conflicting opinions equal to the controversy surrounding the use of insulin, Metrazol, and ECT. In the ancient past the Incas may have had a practice of trephining, a technique of cutting circular sections in the skull. They assumed that these openings in the bony calvarium allowed evil spirits to escape, curing the afflicted of insane delusions. While this practice has historic and anthropological interest, psychosurgery represents a modern development evolving out of a specific milieu of clinical experience, observation, and research.

In 1888 the first brain operation on a psychotic patient was performed by Dr. Gottlieb Burckhardt, superintendent of the insane asylum at Prefargier Switzerland, who aimed at changing a violent, assaultive individual into a docile, harmless person. The removal of parts of the cerebral cortex had the desired effect: the patient lost his aggressiveness. While Burckhardt made ablations on other agitated psychotics and recommended the continuation of the operations, the resistance and opposition of the medical community, especially after one of his patients died, stopped his work. A similar response occurred in Russia in 1910, when Dr. Ludwig Puusepp, a St. Petersburg neurosurgeon, achieved little success after operating on three manic-depressive patients. In each case he cut the fibers between the parietal and frontal cortexes on one side of the brain.

After World War I laboratory research on the cerebral functions of animals, notably monkeys and chimpanzees, had a direct influence on human neurosurgical procedures. The reports indicated that the animals became extraordinarily placid after damage to the frontal area of the brain: all kinds of frustrated behavior, including temper tantrums, virtually disappeared. The dramatic behavior change was best illustrated by Drs. Carlyle Jacobsen and John Fulton at Yale University in their experiences on Becky, a chimp. Involved in a test using a delayed-response procedure, she was exceedingly frustrated and upset whenever she made a mistake. She often flew into a rage, defecating and urinating on the floor. After receiving a "frontal operation," Becky became exceedingly gentle and showed no concern when she made an error. The results of these animal experiments were complemented by studies on humans who received brain injuries and required surgery. After the operation they displayed a definite loss of anxiety.

Within this general milieu of clinical experimentation, Dr. Egas Moniz, a professor of neurology at Lisbon University, performed the first frontal lobotomy on a human. At the Second International Neurology Congress, meeting at

London in the summer of 1935, he learned of the work of Jacobsen and Fulton, and asked if their procedure had application to humans. With his lobotomy, performed in December 1935, Moniz made that application; and he viewed the operation as "a decisive moment," hoping to prove that by cutting "certain cell-counting structures" in the brain, "certain symptomatic complexes of a psychic nature" would disappear. In other words, he anticipated the surgical destruction of the psychosis in the patient's brain. His patient was a 63-year-old woman, a former prostitute with a diagnosis of involutional melancholia, who exhibited depression, anxiety, and paranoia. Two months after the operation Moniz declared her cured. In 1936 he performed 20 lobotomies and claimed that one-third of the patients were cured, one-third improved, and one-third showed no improvement. He buoyantly asserted that the operations left no adverse physical or psychic effects on the patients. Until an assault by a patient cut short his professional life, making him a hemiplegic, Moniz supervised some 100 lobotomies. In 1949 he received the Nobel Prize in Physiology or Medicine for utilizing prefrontal lobotomy on psychotic cases.

Moniz's frontal lobe surgery precipitated adoption of psychosurgerical techniques in America. In September 1936, Drs. Walter Freeman and James Watts of George Washington University in Washington D.C., who knew Moniz and were aware of the neurological research on animals at Yale University, performed the first lobotomy in the United States. They became the staunchest American advocates of psychosurgery; Freeman had performed over 3,500 lobotomies by the mid-1950s. An aggressive lobotomy campaign quickly developed and produced an extensive literature. Proponents of lobotomy candidly admitted that it represented "an operation of last resort," a therapeutic measure to be utilized only with the awareness that it invariably changed behavior and could produce such unfavorable results as convulsive seizures, incontinence, and persistent inertia. The surgery should be done after all methods of therapy had failed and there was no hope of spontaneous recovery. Indeed, the decision to operate was often based on the hopelessness of a patient's condition.

While schizophrenics represented the largest group subjected to psychosurgery, a patient's symptoms rather than the psychiatric category became the prime criterion for determining suitability for lobotomy. Dr. Walter Freeman characterized the ideal candidate: an anxious, introverted totally self-absorbed individual who suffered from severe hypochrondriasis, fearing heart disease or cancer or syphilis; this person brooded over an uncertain future, could not relate to others, had attacks of uncontrollable violence, and often displayed suicidal tendencies, seeing death as the best and only solution to his or her troubles. Clearly the agitated, the compulsive, the anxiety-ridden were favored. On the other hand, it was believed that surgery could not help the depressed or the elderly.

The actual operation involved the severing of the fibers connecting the frontal lobes and the thalamus. No brain tissue was removed. The theory justifying this surgery was vague and simplistic, a fact that reflected the lack of understanding of the physiology underlying thought processes and emotions. The explanation included the Pavlovian assumption that conditioned reflexes were established in the cerebral cortex; it involved the idea that learning produced fixed connections between nerve cells. Abnormal stabilization of these conditioned patterns caused psychiatric symptoms. Relief came by destroying these fixed connections in the brain, notably those tied to the frontal lobes. Many psychosurgeons further believed that shock treatment disorganized the patterns and that lobotomy, the cutting of the nerve fibers, prevented them from reforming. Freeman and Watts maintained that the frontal lobes represented the centers for insight and foresight, and the thalamus supplied the emotional element associated with those functions. The severing of the thalamic connection blunted the intense emotional involvement of the patient in the psychosis. Some psychosurgeons advanced the claim that the operation obliterated one's past, freeing the patient from unpleasant and awful memories and, at the same time, making him or her indifferent to the future and to other people's opinions.

While the theoretical justification for lobotomy remained elusive and later was rejected, the results of the operation were dramatic and concrete: a definite postoperative condition and personality emerged. In the days and weeks following surgery, the patient was confused and apathetic; blood pressure dropped, and body weight increased at a striking rate. The lobotomized patient ate ravenously and remained overweight; gave monosyllabic responses to questions in a flat tone; had a blank expression; lost control over bowel and bladder; had to be fed like an infant. During the daily routine of convalescence such a patient played aimlessly with a doll or a ball, or wrote a letter that simply repeated a phrase over and over.

Many of these manifestations of lobotomy were transitory, disappearing or modifying sharply within a few months after surgery. However, the psychological changes were most obvious, more permanent, and often disheartening. The lobotomized patient lost something: soul, or spirit, or driving force, or sparkle; clearly some flavor of the personality was gone. That patient's interests narrowed; he or she procrastinated, lived without goals on a day-to-day basis in an euphoric state without rancor or emotional involvement, and was strikingly uninhibited. No longer self-conscious, his or her tactless, outspoken, childlike behavior irritated and embarassed others. On the other hand, the lobotomized patient forgot insults, and angry flare-ups and other displays of aggression quickly dissipated. Psychosurgeons argued that the patient's generally contented, but intellectually and emotionally flat, demeanor compensated for the immaturity and brief unpleasant outbursts, thus reconciling family and friends to the new condition.

The response of the family was important to the physician facing the decision of whether to keep the patient hospitalized. Most administrative psychiatrists opposed an early discharge, arguing that an institution provided shelter, supervision, and the proper therapy necessary to facilitate the patient's rehabilitation. Experience soon demonstrated that lobotomized patients, who quickly forgot advice and lacked effective emotional attitudes, responded poorly to psychotherapy. ECT and occupational therapy were the basic treatment methods employed. A difficult therapeutic challenge was preparing the patient for employment. After surgery some patients returned to work, but most found holding a job to be awkward and difficult. They lacked persistence and energy, and could not conform to a work routine. They arrived late, were frequently absent, and were poor workers. Any position requiring responsibility, planning for the future, and constant contact with people was impossible for most lobotomized cases. Here again administrative psychiatrists pointed to an important institutional role: the hospital maintained these patients, sheltering them from the strains of a competitive society and from the discouraging and distressing attitudes of the family.

Lobotomized patients who could not return to society became the focus of strong criticism leveled at psychosurgery. Hospital administrators and neurosurgeons countered this attack along several avenues. For example, there was a tendency among psychosurgeons to ignore or gloss over such negative effects of lobotomy as operative hemorrhages, infections, blunted emotions, convulsive seizures, and, in a few instances, deaths. On occasion physicians issued blanket denials of any undesirable side effects. Apparently good results from state mental hospitals muted criticism. A report from Willman State Hospital in Minnesota, which analyzed the effects of lobotomy operations on 46 patients, recorded "striking" results; after surgery the "tense and pinched expressions" on the faces of patients disappeared. From Delaware State Hospital a similar study concluded that lobotomy was an effective measure for reclaiming difficult cases. Other state institutions reported that it gave relief to patients under intense and perpetual tension.

Consistently, while concluding that the operation relieved the patient's apprehension, these studies emphasized its administrative utility. Many hospital officials saw lobotomy as a means of controlling their most destructive and dangerous patients. Indeed, the altered behavior and consciousness of the lobotomized person, the emergence from the operation different from the former self, became an administrative as well as a therapeutic goal of psychosurgery. Superintendents admittedly selected candidates for the operation on the basis of their troublesome behavior. Surgery remained the procedure of last resort, to be performed after other therapeutic means had proved fruitless, but a combative patient who tore off clothing and engaged in repeated confrontations with hospital personnel was identified as a potential lobotomy case.

This position was easily justified. Proponents of lobotomy held the view that the uncommunicative, destructively active, and intractable patient required radical intervention. It was deplorable to remain indifferent to the sufferings of such individuals. A desperate problem necessitated an equally desperate means of solution. Confronted daily with the most extreme forms of mental illness, administrators found lobotomy a reasonable and ethical alternative for the patient trapped by unbearable obsessions and doomed to a grim lifetime in the back ward of a mental hospital. A basic value judgment was made: the physician opted for the operation that could transform the patient into a superficial and placid person who could live on a clean ward and associate harmoniously with others.

Until the mid-1950s lobotomy captured a large following among psychiatric practitioners, with over 50,000 operations completed by 1955. Leading professional journals cautiously approved of it, editorializing that surgery offered "a better future" for many types of chronic patients. The federal government contributed to the upsurge of psychosurgery, especially after August 1943, when the Veterans Administration urged the neurosurgeons at its psychiatric facilities to obtain training in prefrontal lobotomy operations. After World War II overcrowded mental institutions, the shortage of trained psychiatric personnel, and the large number of psychiatrically disabled veterans returning from the war encouraged an easy acceptance of any positive report on lobotomy and promoted its use.

For a few years lobotomy reached boom proportions, notably after 1948, when Freeman introduced the transorbital leucotomy operation, a relatively simple procedure that could be performed in a physician's office. With a mallet the doctor tapped the transorbital leucotome, a surgical ice pick, through the bony cavity above the eye and into the brain. The handle of the leucotome was swung in the appropriate way to sever the fibers at the base of the frontal lobes. James Watts, Freeman's collaborator, disapproved of this procedure, warning that its simplicity misled people into believing that it was only a minor operation. In fact, he observed, any technique involving the cutting of brain tissue represented major surgery.

Watts critique, along with other criticisms of "ice pick" surgery, did not diminish the use of lobotomy. The legal profession and the general public ignored the issue, placing it under the discretionary control of the surgeon. Lobotomy operations declined with the introduction of pharmaceutical therapy. Tranquilizers and antidepressant drugs controlled psychotic behavior in a less drastic and more effective way than the surgical method.

Psychosurgery did not die, however. In the 1960s it entered a new era, the electronic age. This generation of psychosurgeons conceded that the "classical" frontal lobotomy was an "inadvisable treatment" that produced too many disturbing effects, notably an impaired intellect and blunted emotions. The new psychosurgeons attributed the failures of the past to a lack of technical sophistication, a limitation they had overcome with the development of subtle instruments and procedures for entering the brain with geometric precision. Stereotaxic coordinates, for example, could locate any point within the brain. Once the target was determined, an electrode was attached to a fine wire and directed toward it through a tiny hole drilled in the skull. Left within the brain, the electrode could be used for several purposes: a weak electric current passing through it stimulated tissue; a strong current produced lesions. Signals sent from an outside electronic device to the implanted electrode could change brain activity, thereby manipulating behavior. This technique was called ESB, electrical stimulation of the brain. Dr. José Delagado, a Yale physiologist, dramatically demonstrated its power when he halted the charge of a bull by pushing a button. While scientists debate whether the impulse sent to the electrode in the bull's brain dissipated his aggression or simply confused him, the fact remains that ESB clearly changed the bull's behavior.

With the stereotaxic method psychosurgeons gained access to the deepest regions of the brain, and much of the focus of their experimentation shfted from the frontal lobes to the limbic system, specifically a limbic structure known as the amygdala, the supposed center of "aggression." In this area surgical intervention, an amygdalotomy, was first performed on animals and later on epileptics, the mentally retarded, and hyperkinetic children. Some surgeons placed emphasis on the part of the brain known as the cingulum, a small, fibrous tissue that connects the front brain with the midbrain. A cingulotomy on a monkey relieved anxiety and tension, making it easy to handle. Other physicians specialized in ultrasonic irradiation, in which ultrasonic beams destroyed white matter, and multiple-target surgery, in which lesions were made in various brain areas. An operation known as orbital undercutting avoided disrupting fibers and blood vessels, and permitted the lifting of lobes to allow selective cutting beneath the orbital area.

Psychosurgeons maintained that the increasingly sophisticated techniques and procedures effectively controlled and limited any brain operation, making only localized lesions necessary. They also insisted that surgery benefited patients who could not be helped with other forms of therapy, notably those suffering from intractable pain or obsessive-compulsive fixations. Medical critics countercharged that the new psychosurgery represented only a milder version of the lobotomies of the 1930s and 1940s. The effects were still irreversible, and the operations represented experiments, not sound therapy. One brain researcher asserted that psychosurgery was simply operating "with your eyes closed." Other critics, largely from the legal and other nonmedical professions, worried about the social and political implications of psychosurgery. A maelstrom of opinion focused on its potential misuse as a method of deviance control, claiming that it could be directed to change the "abnormal" behavior of prisoners, sexual deviants, minorities, the poor, and the underprivileged. Critics forecast an Orwellian future in which psychosurgeons utilized their skills in the service of a totalitarian elite seeking to stifle dissent and eliminate individual liberty.

The reservations of the medical profession and the bold criticism of civil liberties have restrained psychosurgeons, keeping them alert to professional and public censure. Still, an estimated 500 to 600 operations have been performed annually. There is a dilemma here. While criticism of psychosurgery should neither threaten brain research nor diminish respect for a clinical judgment, is a permanent surgical treatment the best way to control behavior that in time could run itself out? Ultimately the dilemma of psychosurgery transcends medical ethics; it is a societal problem, a political responsibility to conserve an individual's integrity and identity.

10
WORLD WAR II, EVOLVING THERAPEUTIC ENVIRONMENTS, AND THE PROMISE OF PSYCHOPHARMACOLOGY

World War II was a catalyst for change in American psychiatric practice. It exposed the shortage of all types of mental health workers. Public consciousness of psychiatric issues was raised, notably about the wide prevalence of mental illness. The federal government was brought more directly into the arena of mental health care. The war also accentuated the long-standing policy of indifference and neglect toward public mental institutions. With the priorities and the interests of American society focused on questions of survival and security, state hospitals operated on austerity budgets and remained absorbed in the routines of custodial care. Invariably ugly and oppressive conditions developed.

At the end of the war, a number of dramatic exposés received national attention and revealed a chilling and shocking portrait of the state mental hospital system. The grim, deteriorating conditions of institutional life, however, did not elicit indignant denials, or countercharges of misrepresentation of fact, or self-pitying statements of despair and despondency. On the contrary, the obvious failure of the mental institution galvanized some administrators to develop programs for returning more patients to the community. Their interests centered on experimenting with the social environment of the hospital and the creation of a therapeutic milieu within the institution. This work was eclipsed in the mid-1950s with the introduction of drug treatments that had a sensational impact on hospital life, promising a millennium in mental health care.

World War II dramatized critical psychiatric issues. Public interest and concern were especially aroused over the problem of men rejected for military service. Of the 15 million men examined at induction centers, over 1 million were found inadequate because of mental disorders; in the course of the war, over 600,000 men received medical discharges for some psychiatric reason. Military authorities pressed psychiatrists to explain this excessive loss of manpower and to adopt measures to reduce it. The high number of psychiatric rejects represented a major and foreboding indicator of national health, a fact that public health administrators viewed with alarm.

An unexpected development of the American wartime psychiatric experience was the high incidence of neurotic disorders among soldiers. Many believed that the war would produce an epidemic of psychotic reactions and that military hospitals, like civilian institutions, would quickly become overcrowded with patients disabled by the most severe psychiatric illnesses. About 10 percent of all cases hospitalized in military establishments represented psychotic disorders. The large number of men suffering from all kinds of neuroses demanded a sharpening of diagnostic categories. Actually, mental health workers had long recognized the need to clarify professional nomenclature. Diagnostic labels and interpretations lacked precision and varied with the psychiatrist. Although a patient's condition remained constant, the diagnosis might change each time he or she moved to a different hospital. The vague terminology also meant that statistical complications lacked significant value, especially when related to the incidence of different types of mental disorders at different military installations.

New labels added more confusion: the World War I misnomer "shellshock" was updated with the term "combat fatigue" or "battle fatigue," a concept that avoided a mental illness label and connoted rapid recovery. Could not any person overcome fatigue with adequate rest and relaxation? This facile impression, along with the loose, vague, all-encompassing nature of "battle fatigue," further aggravated the problem of clarifying psychiatric terms and concepts.

The continuing surge of neurotics determined the course of treatment. Of necessity, group psychotherapy became the major method, an approach facilitated by the military ethos of collective living. Numerous wartime studies of men under combat stress showed that a soldier's identification with his squad or company sustained good mental health. An individual with weak or no loyalty to a group was vulnerable to neurosis. Army psychiatrists emphasized that group psychotherapy gave a distressed soldier security; it permitted an open discussion of his problems and encouraged him to develop new and positive relationships. Along with group psychotherapy, military psychiatric practice included recreational, educational, and occupational therapy; and whenever possible, ancillary personnel administered these programs, a practice that reaffirmed the team approach to treating the mentally ill.

Phenomenal recovery rates were reported and were attributed to early and vigorous intervention. At some army treatment centers, 60 percent of first admissions returned to duty within a few days; another 30 percent went back to their units within a few weeks. Here was gratifying evidence for army psychiatrists who believed that intensive, short-term care would dramatically increase the rates of recovery from mental illness. Military psychiatrists also claimed success with a treatment procedure known as narcosynthesis, often administered in areas close to combat zones. Sodium pentothol or sodium amytal, intravenous sedatives placed the patient in a state of narcosis, a semiconscious condition in which he was encouraged to relive his traumatic battle experience. The drug allowed him to cope with the emotions and memory of the terrifying combat incidents in a rational manner and, with the aid of a psychotherapist, gain insight into his problem.

Still another wartime change was the closer identification of psychiatry with medicine. Propinquity in military installations permitted easy and harmonious contact with all types of specialties, including surgery and internal medicine. A stimulating cross-fertilization of ideas ensued, and psychiatrists welcomed the opportunity to stress the importance of emotional factors in human conduct and illness. Their view won support. As the war progressed, medical administrators gave increased recognition to psychiatry, recognizing its contribution in handling neurotic soldiers. Medical acceptance was complemented by other authorities who demanded that psychiatrists be attached to military prisons, courts, and training centers. Indeed, requests for psychiatric services went beyond the necessities of proper selection, classification, and assignment of soldiers; there was demand for research on such subjects as leadership, motivation, morale, and group relations. These interests showed a new and major trend of military psychiatry: a concern for the prevention of mental disorders.

One of the most striking World War II developments for American psychiatry was the increased expansion of the federal government into mental health areas. The government created an extensive system of hospitals, and established training and research facilities that greatly enlarged the power and scope of psychiatry. Until World War II, federal programs in mental health remained largely within the Public Health Service, and included such activities as the medical inspection of aliens, a few projects and surveys on delinquency and crime, the study of the nature of drug addiction, and the treatment and rehabilitation of addicts. While there was only one significant federal mental institution—St. Elizabeth's Hospital in Washington, D.C.—psychiatric patients were treated in many Veterans Administration (VA) hospitals.

During World War II aggressive federal intervention in the mental health arena was demanded by swelling number of military psychiatric casualties and the severe shortage of trained personnel. Beginning in April 1945, with the appointment of General Omar Bradley and Major General Paul Hawley to head the VA, a strong psychiatric program was launched. The VA began the largest hospital building program in American history, providing for the construction of 69 general hospitals, each with its own psychiatric unit, and 16 mental hospitals. Construction of the mental institutions would follow specific guidelines: each would provide facilities for 1,000 to 1,500 patients and be located near an urban or suburban medical center. Drab, stereotyped asylum architecture would be avoided. Surrounded by gardens, a typical residential building would contain small dormitories, large day rooms and visiting rooms, and special treatment units and conference rooms designed for instruction and observation. There would be a gymnasium, a swimming pool, and a theater, as well as occupational training shops and educational rooms. While research and the training of psychiatric personnel were vital to the new VA hospital, the treatment of patients would remain its basic function.

Along with the extensive VA building program, the Mental Health Act of 1946 expanded the federal government's role in the care and treatment of the mentally ill. This legislation identified mental illness as a major public health program and marked the beginning of a national mental health program operating along three avenues: research into etiology, prevention, and treatment; training of personnel, including psychiatrists, psychologists, social workers, and nurses; and the improvement of local and state mental health services, especially outpatient clinics. It also established the National Institute of Mental Health, a new agency opening in 1949. A comment on the Mental Health Act in the *American Journal of Psychiatry* observed that federal intervention in psychiatric care was the only viable course for resolving "a disgrace to our civilization," the dismal condition of the nation's mental hospitals.

Shocking revelations about mental institutions represented another legacy of World War II. The exposures resulted from an unusual government policy. Beginning in 1942, Selective Service officials assigned conscientious objectors to work in state mental hospitals, and by the end of the war about 2,500 had served as attendants. These were idealistic men, devoted to their principles and work, who became deeply disturbed over what they saw. They observed the frequent beatings of patients with rubber hoses or wet towels, the vermin-covered walls of patients' cells, the tasteless, starch-laden food served on greasy platters, the general inactivity and apathy of patient life. Resolved to alter these conditions, they exchanged ideas through a bulletin, *The Attendant*, and developed plans for reform. In 1946 the former conscientious objectors met in Philadelphia and established the National Mental Health Foundation. It would awaken and enlighten the public about the desperate need to raise standards of care and treatment in mental hospitals.

The National Mental Health Foundation was only one expression of public and professional indignation and concern. In May 1946, *Life* published a bold photographic essay called "Bedlam USA"; it was later reprinted in the *Reader's Digest* under the title "The Shame of Our Mental Hospitals." A story in *Woman's Home Companion*, "What Is Wrong with Our Mental Hospitals?" became the subject of radio debates. Twentieth Century-Fox made a movie out of *The Snake Pit*, a best seller by Mary Jane Ward, a former mental patient. Throughout the country many newspapers reported on mental institutions. *The Kansas City Times*, for example, ran a series of articles by Charles W. Graham, who recorded the deleterious effects of apathy on patients in Missouri and Kansas state hospitals. Patients, he noted, simply sat in rocking chairs, "hopelessly rocking away their hours, days, and months and years."

Mike Gorman's stories in the *Daily Oklahoman* later became a book, *Oklahoma Attacks Its Snake Pits*. Albert Deutsch, a journalist-historian, completed the most comprehensive of these newspaper surveys, *The Shame of the States*, a compilation of his articles in the New York newspaper *PM*. He made a nationwide tour and observed that "shameful conditions" existed everywhere. At Milledgeville State Hospital in Georgia, Deutsch commented, a patient lost in a nearby swamp would get well as easily as one left in the institution. The crowded facilities at Napa State Hospital in California, he stated, destined patients to idleness and slow deterioration. At Philadelphia State Hospital in Pennsylvania, he walked through the wards and was reminded of pictures of Nazi concentration camps: scores of emaciated persons huddled against moldy and peeling plaster walls.

These grim depictions of mental hospital life were confirmed by responsible authorities. The remarks of administrators, often in more colorful and brazen language than that found in journalistic exposés, corroborated a widespread professional and lay assumption that mental institutions had reached a nadir. One superintendent asserted that the grass around his hospital received better care and more consideration than the patients inside. Another administrator saw patients "wolfing food like animals." Several mental health authorities used the term "snake pit" to label mental institutions. Dr. Mesrop A. Tarumianz, a Delaware psychiatrist and state mental hygiene official, commented to a group of mental hospital administrators: "Your hospital stinks. My hospital stinks. They all stink."

Tarumianz and other officials worried that the deplorable institutional conditions would discourage young, progressive psychiatrists from embarking on careers in state hospital practice. Their concern reflected a well-established trend. In 1947, a year of serious shortage of institutional psychiatrists, only 60 out of 938 physicians seeking careers in psychiatry accepted positions in state hospitals. Shortages of other types of personnel—notably psychologists, social workers, and nurses—remained a constant in the postwar years. A 1949 estimate of mental health manpower needs cited 20,000 psychiatrists, 14,000 psychologists, 14,000 nurses, and 6,000 social workers. These figures were three or four times the currently available personnel in the state hospitals.

When mental institutions sink to a substandard status, into the depths of apathy, neglect, and custodialism, the ascent out of this quagmire is a painfully difficult and tedious task. The stark fact of chronicity, the most critical issue facing institutional psychiatry, locked mental hospitals to a treadmill. The chronic formed an unusually high proportion of the public mental hospital population. In 1950, U.S. Public Health Service statistics revealed that over half of the first admissions to state institutions suffered from the most severe disorders, including schizophrenia, manic depression, senile psychosis, and cerebral arteriosclerosis. Many remained hospitalized for years. This residue population of first admissions was swelled by large numbers of deteriorated individuals transferred from other psychiatric facilities and correctional agencies. In short, a public hospital accumulated incurables and rejects who occupied the same beds over a long time. In 1950 the hospital age of a patient—the time the patient had been institutionalized—averaged between seven and ten years.

Superintendents viewed with trepidation the growing chronological age of the "incurable" population. About half of the patients in public institutions were over 55 years old. Some of the elderly were cantankerous, confused individuals who could not care for themselves; some had been abandoned to the hospital; a few were physically infirm; others displayed memory impairment. A large number of patients had grown old in the hospital. Superintendents complained that providing custodial care for the chronic aged diverted funds and personnel away from potentially rehabilitative therapeutic programs for the younger psychotics. Older persons kept beds occupied, preventing admission of new and younger patients. One superintendent remarked, with some bitterness, that if this trend continued, he would soon be administering an "old ladies home."

This dreary institutional scene was not without hope. The exposés of state hospitals and the federal government's promotion of mental health activities had generated a milieu receptive to change and innovation. A sizable professional opinion searched for solutions to the many problems plaguing mental institutions, notably how to jolt the chronic patient out of the back ward. In this effort much research and experimentation centered on the interaction between the patient and the institution's social structure. The relevance of this approach to hospital practice had been indicated in numerous studies, beginning with the pioneering work of Dr. Harry Stack Sullivan at the Sheppard and Enoch Pratt Hospital at Towson, Maryland, in 1929-31. Sullivan organized a special ward for treating schizophrenics and worked intensely with the staff and the patients, stimulating an interest in the use of the hospital social environment as a therapeutic tool. Other psychiatrists demonstrated the importance of positive social interaction between patients and between staff and patients.

In the late 1930s, Dr. Abraham Myerson, professor of psychiatry at the Medical School of Tufts College in Boston, developed the "total push" method of treating chronic schizophrenics. Myerson advocated a vitalistic approach to psychiatry, believing that strong appetites and desires enhanced an individual's mental health. The care given a patient at the typical state hospital, he argued, produced "a prison stupor" that complemented and reinforced withdrawal delusions. The patient lost social contacts, became passive, and was absorbed into a demanding routine devoid of either psychological or physiological activity. To counteract such a regimen, Myerson administered a two-year experimental program at Boston State Hospital, where he restored institutional vitality and improved patient health by means of vigorous exercise and recreational activities, intensive use of hydrotherapy, a varied and liberal diet, and a reward-punishment system aimed at encouraging proper behavior. Much of this was reminiscent of nineteenth-century moral treatment. Myerson neither claimed nor believed that the "total push" method cured schizophrenia; indeed, he recorded modest results: it simply slowed the deterioration process and improved patient appearances.

Other studies suggested that behavior was influenced by a particular social setting, that it was more than simply the functioning of a unique personality structure. During World War II military psychiatrists utilized group and social forces in treating combat casualties. Important observations for social psychiatry also emerged from institutions for children. At Hampstead Nursery, a British institution for war-orphaned infants, Anna Freud noted how dramatically children's behavior changed following a reorganization of the ward staff. When all the attendants cared for all of the children, pandemonium prevailed. The division of the nursery into groups of four to six children, each under the supervision of a "substitute mother," greatly diminished disciplinary problems and regressive behavior. This became a classic example of how an institution's social structure could affect its residents. In another study Bruno Bettelheim described how institutionalized children who had few relationships with adults developed a syndrome of psychological institutionalism, a condition of apathy and passivity exhibited by chronic mental patients.

The decade following World War II was a boom period for research on the social milieu of the mental hospital. The institution itself became the object of study; and many nonpsychiatric professionals, notably social scientists, analyzed its characteristics. A sample of research topics included "Institutional Social Hierarchies and Patient Care," "The Social World of the Ward," "Applying the Principles of Social Psychiatry to Ward Settings," "The Administration of Therapy by Ancillary Personnel," "Relationships Among Psychiatrists, Staff, and Patients," "Occupational Strains Within the Hospital," "Values and Beliefs of Attendants and Nurses," "Staff Images of Patients," "Patient Friendship Patterns." This research buttressed a growing conviction among mental health workers that the social-psychological characteristics of a mental hospital community determined the speed and the quality of a patient's recovery.

A few mental hospitals applied this idea and vigorously exploited social factors and interpersonal relationships in managing their patients. The California Department of Mental Hygiene, for example, conducted an 18-month study of 400 psychotic men at Stockton State Hospital. They had languished for years in the back wards, and the project aimed at returning them to the community. To fulfill that objective, a new and dedicated staff created an enriched and permissive social environment. Special attention was given to instruction in personal hygiene and to the preparation of attractive meals. Group activities stimulated the men: they took walks, played catch or volleyball, participated in discussions, poetry recitations, and community singing. Music therapy preceded electric shock treatment. The staff encouraged unresponsive patients to talk about daily events. While many of the men remained mute, the atmosphere of therapeutic optimism prevailed. The staff formed a treatment team, shared responsibilities, maintained its enthusiasm, and claimed significant results. The final report of the Stockton study recorded a high discharge rate and an improved status for the men remaining in the hospital.

Another experiment in transforming an institutional milieu occurred at Boston Psychopathic Hospital under the direction of Dr. Harry C. Solomon. The change began with redecorating patients' rooms. New, attractive furniture, draperies, carpets, and paintings created a pleasant setting in rooms previously furnished with ugly, heavy tables and uncomfortable chairs. Patients kept their own clothing and personal possessions; punitive treatments were eliminated, including the use of the seclusion room, the continuous bath, and the wet-sheet pack. These measures promoted morale and produced a more congenial atmosphere. The most important element in transforming the hospital milieu was developing quality interpersonal relationships. While every employee, including a janitor, was assumed to be capable of influencing patients, the attendant was singled out as a neglected, untapped source of therapeutic potential. Attendants had traditionally held the lowest status and received the least salary, yet they were closest to patients and were the most numerous of all hospital personnel. At Boston Psychopathic the quality of attendants was improved by a careful recruitment and screening process; the hospital sought persons dedicated to helping the mentally ill. Once involved in psychiatric care, they were integrated into a therapeutic team composed of physicians, clinical psychologists, nurses, social workers, and occupational and recreational therapists. Solomon and other hospital innovators maintained that this team approach replaced the rigid, authoritarian hierarchical pattern of institutional relations with more open, democratic procedures that encouraged the growth and development of all staff members.

Training and stimulating the staff remained a constant at Boston Psychopathic, with special emphasis placed on increasing and deepening personnel interrelationships by means of psychodramas, seminars, and group conferences. At these gatherings the staff worked out tensions, discussed the problems of handling difficult patients, and refined and clarified treatment objectives. The whole thrust of this effort aimed at improving patient care on the ward. A variety of activities, including music and game therapy, enriched the ward milieu, promoting resocialization for the many psychologically isolated individuals. Patient government generated interested in ward affairs. As a form of nonstructured group therapy, it permitted the airing of grievances and encouraged patients to make decisions for ward betterment.

Other policies at Boston Psychopathic fostered change. Research on ward life, for example, identified patient leaders, showed the importance of visits by relatives and friends, and revealed the factors contributing to good rapport between patients and staff. The hospital maintained that a good relationship with the community was another element necessary to a therapeutic milieu. Positive associations and contacts between hospital and community generated public interest in mental health care, facilitated patient acceptance of the institution's treatment program, educated family members, and encouraged volunteers to participate in hospital activities, enabling them to join the therapeutic team.

By the early 1950s Boston Psychopathic had a therapeutic climate that produced the desired effects. The hospital statistical reports showed increased patient discharges in all categories of mental illness; within the institution patient behavior improved, even among cases of catatonic schizophrenia. Administrators, however, did not attribute this success solely to the manipulation of the hospital's social milieu. A vigorous employment of shock treatments, they claimed, had beneficial results. For them social measures prepared patients for insulin coma treatment or electroconvulsive therapy. While waiting for treatment, patients engaged in social activities that reduced fear and anxiety, notably in card games, piano playing, and group singing. Psychosurgeons believed that lobotomy also contributed to the creation of a therapeutic milieu. For a time Boston Psychopathic was a statewide center for lobotomy operations, and it received some of Massachusetts' most deteriorated mental cases. While a permissive ward atmosphere apparently did lessen some of the belligerent tendencies of these patients, the staff enthusiastically endorsed surgical intervention to diminish assaultive and aggressive behavior.

In short, the new enthusiasm for creating a therapeutic social milieu did not mean the elimination of shock therapies. Any method deemed productive for enhancing patient recovery was used. In effect, the traditional somatic methods, the many psychotherapeutic procedures, and the utilization of a rich, permissive social environment constituted a three-pronged attack on chronicity, on preventing patients from regressing into the back wards.

Other institutions applied intensive treatment measures, including the VA hospital at New Bedford, Massachusetts, Medfield State Hospital in Massachusetts, Topeka State Hospital and Osawatomie State Hospital in Kansas, Delaware State Hospital, and Warren State Hospital in Pennsylvania. Each hospital produced increased patient discharges. One qualification dampened this achievement: acute cases always had the best results. The appearance and behavior of untidy, withdrawn chronic patients might improve, but only newly admitted psychotics gained significant remission. Those institutions where the prognosis for the acutely ill was good were characterized by improved physical facilities, the upgrading and expansion of the staff, professionals skilled at delivering available therapies, an invigorated social milieu, therapeutic optimism, and an aggressive leadership committed to change and innovation. A distressing fact also remained: most state mental hospitals lacked these ingredients necessary for treatment success.

In the early 1950s the crowded, understaffed, inadequately financed state hospitals still produced bleak conditions in which patients suffering from all types of disorders mingled in an atmosphere reminiscent of Bedlam. Some individuals paced the floor like caged zoo animals. Others sat on the floor, alert only to their delusions and hallucinations. Catatonic individuals stood for weeks, oblivious to their swollen legs. Wild and combative patients required seclusion. Shouts, haunting whines, piercing screams agitated the ward setting, keeping nurses and attendants on the defensive, anticipating abuse. They functioned as guards standing ready to constrain a frenetic person by means of the bath, the wet-sheet pack, the straitjacket, or the seclusion room. These conditions were reported by leading psychiatrists, who lamented the fact that most mental patients received no treatment, only care and custody.

In 1953-54 the introduction of tranquilizing agents, the ataractic drugs, notably chlorpromazine, into mental hospital practice promised relief for institutional psychiatry. A therapeutic revolution began, and the new field of psychopharmacology grew immensely and gained high professional status. Chlorpromazine (CPZ) originated at the Rhone-Poulenc Specia Laboratories in France and became known under different trade names. In England and Canada it was called Largactil; in the United States its manufacturer and promotor, Smith, Kline, and French, named it Thorazine; and others called it R. P. 4560 and Megaphen. CPZ received an enthusiastic reception in American lay and professional circles. The mass media called it a miracle drug. Professional journals devoted special issues to assessing its importance and credited CPZ as a major advance in psychiatric treatment. At state, national, and international psychiatric conferences and symposiums, scientific papers confirmed the drug's dramatic and positive impact on hospital patients. Leading psychiatrists testified to its efficacy. Dr. Winfred Overholser, superintendent of St. Elizabeth's Hospital in Washington, D.C., believed that CPZ had "inagurated a new era in mental hospitals." It "completely revolutionized" the institutional atmosphere by quieting unruly patients. This fact provided an opportunity to reach intractables by means of psychotherapy and other adjunctive treatments.

Some of the most beneficial effects of CPZ occurred in mental hospitals that lacked the human and material resources necessary for effective treatment programs. On the wards of these institutions, Overholser's new era began. Here a tone of enthusiasm, almost exuberance, pervaded the reports that documented how patient behavior changed with the administration of CPZ. Belligerent, abrasive, loud patients became calm, cooperative, and communicative. They attended to their normal physiological needs, remained clothed, paid attention to their personal appearance, and, without incidents, ate meals with silverware in the dining hall, Their hallucinatory states subsided. This transformation in patient behavior seemed remarkable; indeed, it was miraculous to some observers. And it happened without apparent side effects or complications.

Quiet, pacified patients improved staff attitudes and morale. Much of the fear, and anxiety associated with caring for the mentally ill diminished. Attendants and nurses no longer acted solely as guards, and became more optimistic about the chances for rehabilitating patients. This was a major change for an impoverished state hospital: widespread drug therapy brought order to disturbed wards and reoriented the staff away from the custodial outlook. Old treatment patterns were broken and new options emerged. Patients were now more amenable to psychotherapy, and they demanded recreational and occupational programs. The need for shock treatments, physical restraints, and seclusion rooms lessened. In short, drug therapy gave hospitals with deficient staffs and facilities the opportunity to initiate policies that previously had been unthinkable, to develop and sustain intensive treatment programs. On the other hand, any institution unwilling or unable to seize this chance for making positive change used drugs to maintain the status quo. Patients were easily and painlessly pacified and forgotten.

A significant and controversial effect of the rapid application of drug treatment was a reduction in the nation's mental patient population. In 1955 over 550,000 persons resided in American mental hospitals. The resident population had been mounting for decades, a fact that produced critically overcrowded conditions, particularly in such populous states as New York and California. In 1956 this long-term trend was reversed, and every year since has seen a substantial decrease in the numbers of insitutionalized mentally ill. A vigorous debate ensued over determining what factors accounted for the reduction.

Psychopharmacologists easily concluded that the rapid, widespread use of CPZ and other drugs produced the decline. It was a clear cause-effect relationship, and some of the most ardent supporters of drug therapy anticipated final solutions to the problems of institutional psychiatry. Chemical agents, inexpensively administered to large masses of patients, they argued, would soon empty state institutions and transform them into small treatment centers devoted to crisis intervention. Most psychiatrists did not see this millennial future, and remained skeptical optimists. Social psychiatrists active in promoting milieu therapy challenged the assumption that drugs alone had reduced patient populations. For them the introduction of CPZ and related drugs coincided with a well-established trend of increased hospital discharges. Drawing upon evidence accumulated from institutions that experimented with social therapies, notably in Kansas and Massachusetts, they maintained that drugs simply accelerated the existing trend of rising discharge rates. This debate soon became academic. The massive introduction of the ataractics into state hospital practice made drug therapy an established norm, not a passing fad. No one could ignore an unprecedented trend in the history of institutional psychiatry: the continued diminution of the mental patient population.

By the late 1950s hospital reports on the results of drug therapy were extensive and complex. While some of this evidence was contradictory, the accumulated data did permit certain conclusions. Tense, anxious, hostile individuals between 25 and 44 years old benefited most from psychopharmacology. They suffered from the acute psychoses and were frequently new admissions, or readmissions, or persons institutionalized for less than two years. Their symptoms were sufficiently palliated so that they could return to the community and receive treatment at a general hospital or in some other clinical setting. On the other hand, drug treatment did not resolve the problem of chronicity. It did make the chronic more manageable, an achievement of major administrative importance. Combative and destructive persons were subdued, and on occasion long-term mute and withdrawn individuals communicated with staff members. This reduction of severe psychotic manifestations permitted chronics to function better within the hospital and made possible the creation of a more pleasant physical setting, complete with radios and television sets. It did not affect the rate of discharges of chronic patients. The number of residents institutionalized for over five years, especially persons over 65 years of age, remained basically unchanged. Hospital administrators expressed hope that the best prospect for reducing this reservoir of chronics was decreasing the number of acute psychotics, the individuals who responded to drug therapy.

Many patients on a drug regimen lived in the community and required maintenance treatment, the administration of a periodically applied dosage to control stresses and prevent the recurrence of psychotic symptoms. This routine fostered patient dependency upon drugs, a fact that initially aroused little concern. All side effects, including jaundice and Parkinsonism, seemed transient and insignificant. The termination of treatment reversed other complications, including photosensitivity, impotence, and excessive weight gain.

The real risks of drug therapy mounted with lengthy usage. While the role of drugs in causing cardiac disorders was uncertain, the patient under drug treatment for several years could succumb to a neurologic condition known as tardive dyskinesia. This syndrome consisted of bizarre activity of the facial muscles, including involuntary mastication, protrusion of the tongue, smacking of the lips, and blowing of the cheeks. Other parts of the body could exhibit motor disorder, and often the individual had difficulty standing still in an erect position. Such a person constantly shifted weight from one foot to another, and the body rocked backward and forward and from side to side. The actual number of persons afflicted with tardive dyskinesia is unknown. Estimates suggest that 5 percent of all long-term drug therapy patients, both young and old, have suffered from it. Since 1957 over 2,000 cases have been reported and discussed in the professional journals. Most clinicians soft-pedaled this risk, maintaining that the benefits of drug therapy outweighed any potentially undesirable side effect.

Psychotherapists and psychoanalysts made the sharpest and most frequent criticisms of drug therapy. They charged that the pharmaceuticals dulled the patient's capacity for gaining insight into his or her problems, making him or her more dependent upon the physician. To them a drug was "a chemical straitjacket," a tool for "brainwashing" individuals.

The sharpest blows of psychotherapists fell on the practice of pharmaceutical therapy in mental hospitals. Institutional drug treatment, they contended, tranquilized the hospital social environment, the staff, and the physician more than the patient. The institution discharged increasing numbers of persons, thus easing the pressures and tensions associated with living in congested quarters; annoying and belligerent patients were subdued, making them acceptable to the staff; a drug prescription conveniently permitted a physician to abdicate the responsibility of listening to the patient. In effect, psychotherapists held that a drug ritual concealed and ignored patients' behavioral problems. It generated and perpetuated a spurious feeling of security and accomplishment that equated therapeutic success with peaceful wards and the discharge of large numbers of patients. While this critique had merit and validity, it also represented a defense of psychotherapists against the growing power and respectability of psychopharmacology.

Another dimension of the psychotropic drug treatments was the new status and prestige acquired by biological psychiatrists. These clinicians had long worked at a disadvantage when compared with personnel in other areas of medicine. They treated illnesses without knowing causes, recommending procedures whose mechanism of action was not clearly understood. The new drugs offered a possible way out of this dilemma, and established a closer tie and identification with medicine. By the late 1950s psychopharmacology had become a specific medical field complete with professional journals and national and international societies. Within these circles an aura of buoyant confidence prevailed; indeed, there was a zest and arrogance long missing from psychiatry.

Psychopharmacologists anticipated a major breakthrough in psychiatric treatment. They asserted that the new drugs represented opportunities for creating "a truly biologic psychiatry"; research would increase the variety of pharmaceuticals, thereby greatly enlarging the number of persons being helped; and the near future would see the "chemical conquest of mental illness." These bold assertions were accompanied by a disdain for criticism. Any reported complication or negative therapeutic result associated with drug therapy was attributed to the work of a physician improperly trained in psychopharmacology. Drug clinicians also held an antihistorical attitude that minimized all previous psychiatric methods. The predrug era had lacked effective therapies; now, with the advent of pharmaceuticals, "unprecedented advances" in psychiatric treatment had occurred.

"Revolution" is the best term for describing the ramifications of psychopharmacology . During the 1950s its sensational growth and acceptance inaugurated a new era in American mental hospital care. While not curing mental illness, drug therapy reduced the severity of symptoms and calmed patients, providing relief from the harsh tedium of institutional life. Most important, it created new options for the future. The confidence generated by the success of the psychotropic drugs became infectious, spreading to all types of mental health workers. Conditions were opportune for setting a new course for treating the mentally ill: the development of community psychiatry and the establishment of a hierarchy of new community mental health facilities and authorities.

11
COMMUNITY ALTERNATIVES

The 1960s was a tumultuous decade for America. A war on poverty, civil rights agitation and advance, antiwar protests and demonstrations, a student rebellion, the emergence of the "flower people," and numerous liberation fronts sustained an unprecedented level of direct action. These vigorous outbursts of dissent shook confidence in established institutions and traditions, and raised visions of a new society, a community ruled by the ideal of participatory democracy. This social milieu of turmoil, agitation, and rising expectations affected psychiatry and delivery of mental health care. Psychiatry came under attack from both within and outside its ranks. Critics identified it with social repression and an overzealous addiction to the medical model of mental illness. A profusion of mental health fads and activities flourished. Encounter groups multiplied, a community mental health movement developed, and many called for the dismantling of the state hospital system. Throughout the 1960s and 1970s mental health workers searched for alternatives to hospital care. They sought a place where persons would receive respect and humane care while remaining in the community, close to family and friends.

While the radical spirit of the times stimulated change and innovation, many other factors shifted the direction of mental health care into the community. The obvious, basic elements in this thrust were the increased use of tranquilizing drugs and the creation of therapeutic environments within institutions. Drugs and therapeutic milieus ameliorated much disturbed behavior, permitting the release of more patients into the community. Alternatives to hospitalization now became a reality, a fact that encouraged a reassessment of existing institutions and programs.

Throughout this period professional dissatisfaction with state hospitals remained constant, and much of the criticism dealt with the impersonality of the mental institution and its inadequate programs for reintegrating patients into community life. In his 1958 presidential address before the American Psychiatric Association, Dr. Harry Solomon stated that mental hospitals were "bankrupt beyond remedy," and that all large ones should be systematically liquidated. At about the same time Dr. Charles Goshen, director of the General Practitioner Project of the American Psychiatric Association, held that institutional psychiatrists wasted their talents on the routines of custodial care. Both Solomon and Goshen deplored the anonymity of institutional care and called for new approaches to housing mental patients.

Still another critic, Dr. Ernest Klein, superintendent of Peoria State Hospital in Illinois, charged that the mental hospital might be the "worst place" to treat the mentally ill because it banished people from society, divorcing them from home, family, and community living. Concurring on that point in 1961, Dr. Robert M. Felix, a former president of the American Psychiatric Association and director of the National Institute of Mental Health, identified the mental hospital as an antitherapeutic agency where patients lived in an abnormal setting. Improving hospital programs in the community, Felix believed, was the most important requisite for a better mental health care delivery system. He especially recognized the importance of social agencies that attended to the problems of the patient's discharge and return to normal life.

There was awareness that many released patients needed an agency of transition. Discharge from an institution marked only the first step toward getting well. To ease the transition from illness to health, which might be a prolonged process, new types of facilities evolved. The hospital was only one element in a continuum of agencies including the halfway house, the sheltered workshop, and the society for former mental patients.

During the mid- and late 1950s, a number of halfway houses opened throughout the country: Rutland Corners House in Boston; Portals, a facility associated with the VA hospital in Brentwood, California; and the rehabilitation houses at Montpelier and Burlington, Vermont. A foster home cottage was connected with the VA hospital in Brockton, Massachusetts, and two years of planning established a halfway house linked with Modesto State Hospital in California. While each place was unique, they all shared common characteristics. Each guided patients along a sheltered pathway between the protected, over-dependent life of the hospital and the stresses and demands of community life. A former patient might not need the supervised hospital regimen, yet might not be prepared to handle the problems of independent community living. Continued hospitalization could make such a person drift into the role of a permanent patient; a premature return to the community could arouse feelings of inadequacy and lead back to the hospital. The halfway house helped the former patient out of this dilemma, motivating the individual toward recovery and independence. A relaxed, informal supervision governed the house. Usually each person cared for his or her own clothing and room; meals were taken in a common dining room or at nearby restaurants. Men and women were admitted, and the number of residents varied from six to fifteen. Some of these individuals were under medication; all received psychotherapy, either in groups or individually, and were subjected to a vigorous social and recreational program. The atmosphere was communal and familial, militating against patient fears of isolation, loneliness, and anonymity.

At a few mental hospitals sheltered workshops dealt with the problems of employment of former patients. Frequently a discharged patient could not keep a job, an unfortunate fact that aggravated his or her financial and domestic situation. The sheltered workshop was a supportive environment for the individual who needed time and a place to develop skills, recover composure, and regain confidence before entering the competitive labor market. A successful example occurred at the VA hospital in Palo Alto, California, where a "veterans workshop" employed patients. Supervised by a director sensitive to the changing moods, excessive irritability, and irregular work habits of mental patients, the workshop helped them gain ego satisfaction and become self-supporting persons.

A rehabilitation movement of former mental patients helping themselves gained momentum. In 1957 over 40 organizations of former mental patients existed, and many were sponsored by state hospitals. Club 103, for example, was a social outlet for the dischargees of the Massachusetts Mental Health Center. The former-patient organization filled a void in a members's life. A happy homecoming did not necessarily follow discharge from a mental hospital. The former inmate often lived alone in a rented room or in the awkward familial setting of the original illness. Anxious and perhaps ashamed, the discharged patient had difficulty meeting people and finding new friends, a situation that thwarted resocialization, the most important step in the rehabilitation process. Facilitated by the common background of its members, the experience of hospitalization, the former-patient club provided a milieu for making meaningful human contacts. Common behavioral norms and understandings characterized club life: the club allowed a member to act out frustrations; it accepted a member's refusal or inability to work and his or her dependence on the club. Recreational activities, designed to encourage interaction, included informal discussion groups, parties, picnics, and dances.

Recovery, Inc., the largest national association of former patients, had a therapeutic as well as a social purpose. It was established in 1937 by a Chicago psychiatrist, Dr. Abraham Low, author of *Mental Health Through Will Training*, and by the 1950s it had over 200 affiliates in 20 states with about 4,000 members. At meetings panel discussions related an individual's day-to-day problems and experiences to a theme or specific chapter in Low's book. The group and its leader praised and encouraged any member who demonstrated improvement and independence. In short, the society of former mental patients, whether organized for "will training" or recreation, had an objective similar to that of the halfway house or the sheltered workshop: to strengthen the indivi-- dual's self-confidence and adaptive qualities, making possible the move into the mainstream of society.

Other institutional services extended patient life into the community. An arrangement known as the day hospital allowed a patient to participate in morning and afternoon therapy sessions at the institution and to return home before supper. The night hospital complemented this approach: the patient remained employed at a daytime job and returned for group therapy and recreational activities at the institution in the evening. In both programs the patient avoided any abrupt severance of relations with family and community. In effect the day and night hospitals, the halfway house, the sheltered workshop, and the club for former mental patients formed a new network of community-hospital liaisons and reflected the emerging trend of community-based mental health programs.

The activities and policies of state governments and the federal government constituted another major element in the search for new ways of community care. A mental health landmark occurred in 1954, when New York passed the first community mental health act; California followed suit in 1957, and by 1976, 27 states had enacted community mental health legislation. These laws provided state aid to local governments for the operation of outpatient clinics, psychiatric care in general hospitals, and mental health consultation and educational work.

The federal government scrutinized methods of caring for the mentally ill, and in 1961 published *Action for Mental Health*, the final report of the Joint Commission on Mental Illness and Mental Health. Authorized by the Mental Health Study Act of 1955, this commission represented a collective, interdisciplinary enterprise embracing 36 national organizations, including the American Psychiatric Association and the American Medical Association. Other agencies widened the spectrum of viewpoints, notably the American Psychological Association, the American Occupational Therapy Association, the National Association of Social Workers, the National Education Association, the National Institute of Mental Health, and the U. S. Department of Justice.

After six years of deliberations and spending over $1 million, the Joint Commission proclaimed dramatic revelations about the nation's mental health system and issued recommendations for improving it. Perhaps the Joint Commission's most candid observation was the disclosure of extensive public and professional rejection of the mentally ill. Few could empathize with persons who were stereotyped as weak, undesirable beings without appeal or any potentially redeeming qualities. Psychiatrists also confessed difficulty in relating to many patients, notably psychotics. These individuals were seen as a wearisome, ungrateful lot who alienated even the most dedicated, resolute, and humane workers. According to *Action for Mental Health*, this general rejection contributed immensely to the lag in the care and treatment of the mentally ill.

The Joint Commission recommended ways to improve mental health care. The first steps involved the allocation of more funds for basic, long-term research and the establishment of research institutes. A more immediate and concrete demand called for better utilization of present knowledge and experience. On this matter some of the new proposals included the employment of nonmedical personnel to perform short-term psychotherapy; the encouragement of volunteers, notably college students, to work with mental patients; and the inauguration of a national recruitment and training program to encourage more young people to embark on careers in mental health work.

The most important recommendation dealt with the delivery of psychiatric care, namely, the creation of a new outpatient facility, the community mental health clinic, which would provide the institutional framework for a national mental health program. It would function as a center of prevention and would service a population of 50,000. Each clinic would have a mental health team composed of psychiatrists, psychologists, and social workers that would offer treatment and help to adults or children. Other proposals urged the expansion of psychiatric units in community general hospitals and the transformation of small state mental hospitals into intensive treatment centers. A special and controversial recommendation concerned the disposition of large mental hospitals: no institution of more than 1,000 beds should be built, and all existing ones should be transformed into long-term care centers for all kinds of chronic disorders, including physical diseases.

Action for Mental Health asserted that the plight of the chronic insane remained "the unfinished business of the mental health movement," and it strongly supported all forms of aftercare and rehabilitative services. These treatment measures kept patients out of mental institutions and prevented them from sinking into chronicity. Most state hospitals had no therapeutic programs for the increasing number of chronic cases who simply occupied space in the back wards. A hospital might break out of this torpid state of isolation, the report continued, by establishing cooperative programs and activities with the community. In effect this was the basic recommendation of the Joint Commission: the need for increased community involvement in mental health care, a demand that obviously diminished the importance of the state mental hospital.

Institutional psychiatrists gave a guarded response to *Action for Mental Health*. While supporting the recommendations on research and on the need for additional patient facilities in clinics and in general hospitals, they were concerned about two matters: the proposal to use nonmedical personnel as psychotherapists, and the demand for the establishment of hospitals for the chronically ill. The practice of psychotherapy, the critics argued, must remain under the control of psychiatry, lest interprofessional rivalries create disruptive situations and inexperienced, poorly trained persons enter private practice. On the matter of hospitals for chronic patients, administrators held a unanimous opinion: an institution for incurables would mark a setback for mental health care. Few professionals cared to work at a facility where all patients were labeled chronic or incurable. After a time the facility would acquire the stigma of a death house characterized by impersonal custodial routines. Institutional psychiatrists also objected to some of the report's negative descriptions of mental hospitals, notably a statement identifying a mere 20 percent of the nation's 277 state hospitals as therapeutic centers. This, in their opinion, represented a sweeping, inaccurate generalization and harmed the public view of the mental institution.

The recommendations of the Joint Commission were confirmed by other agencies searching for new community resources to cope with mental health care problems. Among these were the 1961 Governors' Conference, the Surgeon General's Ad Hoc Committee on Planning for Mental Health Facilities, and the 1962 Mental Health Conference of the American Medical Association. These agencies recommended that local communities assume more responsibility for treating and rehabilitating patients. This could be accomplished through the establishment of small community facilities that would eventually replace existing large mental hospitals.

Within this context of public and professional scrutiny of mental health delivery systems, President John F. Kennedy, in February 1963, submitted a special message to Congress on mental illness and mental retardation. He condemned the practice of abandoning patients to the "cold custodialism" of institutions and called for a "bold new approach," a program of comprehensive community care. Kennedy raised hopes of a major breakthrough, asserting that by applying "our medical knowledge and social insight fully, all but a small portion of the mentally ill" could achieve "a wholesome and constructive social adjustment." The launching of the new program, he claimed, would permit more patients to remain at home, and within a decade the number of hospitalized would be reduced by 50 percent.

Kennedy's program was initiated in late October 1963, three weeks before his death, when he signed the Mental Retardation Facilities and Community Mental Health Centers Act, popularly known as the Community Mental Health Centers Act of 1963. Under the law a community mental health center received federal funds for construction and staffing if it provided "five essential services": inpatient care, outpatient care, transitional care, emergency care, and community consultation and education. While each center serviced the mentally ill residents in its catchment area, amendments to the original act widened the field of clients to include children, drug addicts, and alcoholics. In 1963, 2,000 centers were projected; but there were only 450 by 1975 and only 603 by 1978.

The new facilities varied enormously, and some state hospitals created confusion by adopting the new name, presumably to receive federal funds. In Michigan, for example, Pontiac State Hospital became the Clinton Valley Mental Health Center. Ideally the community mental health center represented something new and different, divorced from the state hospital. It kept ties with any agency or facility that maximized an individual's treatment program, but engaged in preventive work and provided services largely to outpatients. In the mid-1960s it promised a concrete, dramatic alternative to long-term hospitalization and provided the institutional framework for a growing community psychiatry movement.

Community psychiatry defies precise definition, and might even be viewed as representing a mood or a promise of the seventh decade of twentieth-century America. Nevertheless, it did embrace a number of assumptions. Its basic component was the absolute necessity of supplanting the traditional mental hospital with a community-based mental health facility. Residence in a state mental institution was seen as a negative, punitive experience comparable with imprisonment. It thwarted recovery by superimposing a new institutional psychiatric syndrome on a patient's original disorder, producing serious problems of rehabilitation and readjustment. These difficulties would be averted by maximizing therapeutic facilities within the community. In short, community psychiatrists held that institutional isolation from family and community impaired a mental patient's health; on the other hand, an extensive system of convenient and accessible services would bring a disturbed person back into the mainstream of life at minimum shock and expense to that person and the public.

Community psychiatry required that the psychiatrist accept an expanded professional and public role and move into the arena of social change. It demanded the communitizing of the psychiatrist, who reached out of the clinic and the hospital, and accepted a team approach to mental health care. In the planning and implementing of programs, the psychiatrist sought the contributions of a wide spectrum of professional and lay persons, including clinical psychologists, sociologists, lawyers, teachers, ministers, and business and labor leaders. The community psychiatrist was also a consultant to any business or agency requesting advice and direction on matters of mental health. In this work the psychiatrist went beyond purely educational efforts and supervised the treatment of clients of agencies concerned with the care of the aged, the retarded, the alcoholic, the criminal, and other sociopaths.

Another facet of community psychiatry was an etiological notion that mental illness was rooted in community situations. Within the complex web of social entanglements and institutional relations that constitute a community, there exist pathogenic social environments that produce mentally abnormal individuals. This premise was a good rationale for a vigorous program of psychiatric intervention in community life. Indeed, if mentally disturbed persons emerged from a maze of unhealthy social situations and experiences, psychiatry had a moral mandate to eradicate these sources of community pathology. The community was now the patient, and the psychiatrist became a social engineer, identifying problem areas, designing programs, and setting goals for the building of a mentally healthy society.

Findings from many epidemiological projects justified a program of psychiatric social planning. A high incidence of mental disorder was revealed in communities ranging from rural Nova Scotia to urban Syracuse, Baltimore, New Haven, and New York. This research disclosed that much psychopathology went untreated and ignored. For example, the Midtown Manhattan Study, published in 1962 under the title *Mental Health in the Metropolis*, demonstrated that mental health workers saw only "the top of the iceberg"—that is, those persons who were obviously sick and sought help. The submerged part, the study noted, demanded more professional attention and consisted of a large number of mentally disturbed individuals who neither sought nor found psychiatric help. Eighty percent of the sample population of the Midtown Manhattan Study suffered from some type of psychiatric syndrome.

Mental Health in the Metropolis and a multitude of other research projects identified these mentally distraught persons and the specific demographic circumstances that contributed to their high frequency of psychopathology. The most consistent finding marked poverty or low socioeconomic status as the prime environmental source of mental illness. This was a distressing situation. While the psychoses were most prevalent in lower income groups, the poor received little psychiatric attention, remaining on the periphery of professional interest. The implication for the community psychiatry movement was obvious: mental health delivery systems must be democratized so that services could be brought to people who had never had them.

In the political milieu of the mid-1960s, this need found popular support and became public policy. The federal government, during the Kennedy and Johnson administrations, aggressively supported the civil rights movement and the concerns of minority groups and the poor in an effort to bring them into the mainstream of American life. The same rationale, the need for equity, justified the community mental health center. Indeed, much of the fervor and commitment of civil rights protests spilled over into the community psychiatry movement and generated an evangelistic atmosphere of promise and hope. The moral mandate expressed in the war on poverty and the drive to end racial discrimination ran parallel to an attack on the elitism of American medical and psychiatric practice. Demands arose for the implementation of programs relevant to the disadvantaged and the poor. Scorn was directed at the "cream puff" psychiatrist who operated out of a plush downtown private office, administering psychotherapy to the bored, satiated members of the affluent "jet set." This was the villain, the professional absorbed in self-aggrandizement. In contrast, the ideal mental health worker fought for social change and identified with the most beaten-down members of society.

This radical thrust into the community raised troublesome questions and issues. Indeed, mental health workers are still grappling with the doubts and consequences stemming from the emphasis placed on providing community-based services. One hot issue that emerged from the radical social and political milieu of the late 1960s dealt with the question of community control over mental health facilities. This was an example of the heightened social consciousness and the intensely serious quest of blacks for equality and identity, the passion of antiwar demonstrators, and the militancy of students armed with nonnegotiable demands. Persons inspired by the popular slogan "Power to the People" called for "participatory democracy" and insisted on exercising more control over police, welfare agencies, educational establishments, and health facilities.

Mental health centers, notably in urban areas, were confronted with militant, articulate citizen groups, mostly black and chicano, that identified the centers' programs with racism and psychiatric colonialism. Physicians were told: "You doctors just gotta learn we're not your good little house niggers any more!" "It's a new ball game, baby, and you better learn the rules fast if you still want to play!" In an atmosphere seething with tension and dissension, abrasive relationships developed between community and staff, and all issues became polarized. The community mental health center became fraught with conflict over its goals, hiring policies, allocation of funds, and modes of treatment.

These sources of contention at the community mental health center represented a microcosm of the general state of psychiatry and its relation to society. A professional identity crisis existed, a condition precipitated largely by the intertwining of psychiatry with societal problems. One force of change and conflict came from nonmedical personnel, who formed the majority on the staffs of the expanding facilities of community mental health care. Some of these persons had little or no formal training, and owed their positions to community pressures. Others represented such new areas of public concern as drug abuse, abortion counseling, suicide prevention, and "halfway" programs for legal offenders. The resultant staff mix produced a situation of role ambiguity; individuals from varied backgrounds or disciplines performed functions previously considered the sole domain of a specific profession. While nonmedical personnel accepted this state of affairs with greater ease than physicians did, the psychiatrist, the M.D., still dominated the mental health team, a fact that produced an atmosphere of resentment and disharmony.

Another problem dealt with the aggressive proselytizing of psychiatry as a panacea for resolving community problems, an activity that stirred rancorous debate both within and outside the profession. By accepting this all-encompassing view, a psychiatrist was placed in a vortex of community problem solving, an undefined, vaguely delineated area beyond his or her professional competence and jurisdiction. The psychiatrist required more than the wisdom of Solomon to arbitrate conflict, identify deviancy, and cope with such issues as poverty, racism, crime, abortion, and even pornography. Critics warned that placing serious legal, social, and cultural problems under the domain of mental health put a smoke screen over them. It represented, they said, evasive action, thwarting real problem solving by relegating a controversial matter to psychiatric experts, allowing it to be forgotten by society. This situation may give too much power to psychiatry, and a few critics have forecast a future of "psychiatric fascism," in which dissent and freedom will be quashed in a drive to eradicate mental illness and treat the behaviorally disordered.

Criticism of the medical model of mental illness also has caused professional confusion and malaise. The medical model held that psychiatric disorder was analogous to a bodily illness and followed a pattern of developing that could be categorized, measured, and subjected to specific treatments. This concept was supported by historic tradition. The mental institution had long been identified as a hospital where people came as sick patients in need of treatment from doctors and nurses. Some critics of this tradition were psychotherapists who stressed the importance of environmental or psychosocial factors as causes of mental disturbance. They viewed the mental hospital as a source of pathology. The medical model represented a cold, rigid concept divorced from life and the needs of the masses of the mentally ill.

The attack on the traditional medical view of mental illness emerged from a unique professional and social context. A psychotherapeutic explosion occurred in the 1960s and 1970s, a development that constitutes one of the most revolutionary trends in the history of the care and treatment of the mentally ill. A great proliferation of types of therapists and therapies appeared in an attempt to satisfy what seemed like an insatiable demand for mental health and psychological counseling services. Many interrelated factors were behind this demand: the traditional American quest for health and happiness; the democratization of psychological knowledge; the availability of a vast body of popular self-help or self-discovery literature, including such best sellers as *Peace of Mind, Be Glad You're Neurotic, Games People Play,* and *I'm OK—You're OK.* A social revolution of rising expectations, most noticeable among minority and feminist groups, involved individuals who refused to remain silent and suffer from anxieties; they demanded a better and fuller life here and now.

Some Americans suffered from an alienated life-style and sought professional psychological help. They found little satisfaction in a routinized job, a family milieu of abrasive, destructive relationships, or organized religion. The usual sources of security and support were no longer useful in the quest for meaning in life. A psychotherapist assumed the consoling role formerly assigned to a relative or clergyman. Other persons were influenced by the demoralized state of the country. America in the late 1960s witnessed massive distrust of leaders and institutions, and bitter disapproval of societal goals and priorities. Many felt helpless, isolated, and fearful of a future in a dehumanized and computerized society. Some found relief and inner peace by probing the mystical and cosmic religions of the East: Hare Krishna, Sufism, and Transcendental Meditation.

A panorama of options existed for persons wanting professional guidance and help. This amounted to an amorphous and variegated personal growth movement best typified by the encounter group. Its participants had a common background and shared many characteristics: they were middle-class, upwardly mobile, educated, and articulate, willing to spend money and effort to overcome a condition of general malaise and demoralization. The encounter group offered them open, intimate, and positive interactions with others, and stressed the importance and desirability of communicating one's feelings rather than thoughts. There was no discussion of questions of mental illness or theories of repression or neurosis. The accent was on the "now," the joy of experiencing immediate personal contact with others and with the environment. The encounter group expanded the consciousness, the emotional commitment, the "self-actualization" of its participants, an accomplishment achieved by such diverse procedures and techniques as role-playing, sensory awareness, psychodrama, videotape playback, and body exercise.

With these techniques a teaching-learning process occurred. The group leader, the teacher, was not a physician; indeed, he or she may have had little professional training in mental health. Whatever his or her background, the leader formed personal relationships with the clients. The settings for encounter groups were as diverse as the leadership, and ranged from hotel rooms to the Esalen Institute at Big Sur, California. The basic requirement of the meeting place was its removal from the clients' environment. The sessions varied in length from a few hours to marathon experiences lasting several days. In short, the encounter group offered an educational, retraining experience. It ignored psychiatry and obliterated the boundaries between mental health professionals and the community. It served the needs of a rapidly growing segment of a population of dissatisfied, unhappy, relatively affluent persons who, in their quest for a fuller life, became consumers of psychotherapy.

The community mental health center and the encounter group represent the two most innovative developments in recent mental health history. Both offered short-term group psychotherapy. While the more traditional modes of guidance and counseling were stressed at the community mental health center, the encounter group utilized more innovative, creative therapeutics, stressing warmth and intimacy with others. In either case rigid lines of authority were broken; an egalitarian atmosphere was created; and the distinction between therapist and client was blurred. The therapist was a friend offering guidance without probing the client's distant past for causes of conflict.

Encounter groups and community mental health centers diverged on aims and clientele. The encounter group, a private agency, provided growth experiences to its middle-class participants, who eagerly sought involvement with others. The community mental health center, a public facility, largely served low socioeconomic ranks, including marginal and disadvantaged groups who rarely sought out or were aware of its activities. The community mental health center first had to inform potential clients of the availability and desirability of its services, and then treat a client so that he or she might better adapt to the stresses of the social environment. For the encounter group the concern was expanding the consciousness of its clients; for the mental health center the goal was adjustment—the emotional dilemmas of clients were interpreted as a reflection of some broader social problem.

The growth of community mental health centers and encounter groups demonstrated that many people could avoid the stigma of mental illness by finding solace and treatment outside of the traditional mental institution. Success with these alternatives profoundly affected the state mental hospital, the mainstay in the delivery of mental health care. The most fundamental change was the greatly diminished size of the hospital patient population, with institutions averaging a 33 percent decline between 1955 and 1970; some states measured a 50 percent reduction.

This dramatic drop of inpatients produced a political and professional climate favorable to the closing of state hospitals. There was growing support for institutional shutdowns. Politicians were concerned about the high cost of mental health programs, and recognized the excessive cost of renovating antiquated, dilapidated structures at many mental hospitals. A sizable part of the public was disenchanted with taxes and wasteful government spending, and demanded cuts in allocations to state helping agencies. Considerable professional opinion remained hostile to the state institution, pointing to its negative, anti-therapeutic atmosphere. Two points were emphasized: first, no matter how good a hospital might be, it was still a dehumanizing environment that gratified a patient's dependency wishes and reinforced the sense of failure; second, the mental patient faced a major reentry problem: he or she had a record of psychiatric hospitalization, a stigma that would always affect his or her life.

Citizen groups and legal aid societies, notably the associations concerned with the civil rights of mental patients, favored institutional closings. On this matter a series of legal rulings complicated state mental hospital politics and policies. For example, in a 1972 Federal District Court decision, *Wyatt* v. *Stickney*, Judge Frank M. Johnson in Alabama legally established the "right to treatment," justifying confinement only if an institution could meet basic standards for therapeutic care. Another landmark decision came in 1975, when the U.S. Supreme Court ruled in the case of *O'Conner* v. *Donaldson* that a state may not confine involuntarily, with only custodial care, any mental patient who is not dangerous and is capable of functioning in society.

Involved in both the *Wyatt* and *O'Connor* cases, the Mental Health Legal Project, a group founded in Washington, D.C., in 1972, initiated other legal moves to better define the rights of the emotionally disturbed. Its lawyers and mental health professionals forced a number of issues into the courts: some involved setting institutional standards for staff-patient ratios and nutrition; others dealt with employment rights of patients, the right to refuse treatment, and the right to live in the community. The right to a least restrictive alternative setting demanded the creation of such community services as halfway houses or mental health centers for patients needlessly confined in mental hospitals. These legal pressures and developments stimulated concern and discussion, and produced noticeable effects: conditions improved within mental hospitals. At the same time administrators, sensitive to pressures from legal rights advocates, often discharged patients without adequate preparation or provision for them in the community.

The drive to close mental hospitals produced hot rhetoric and debate, and achieved limited results. A few institutions shut down in California, Illinois, Massachusetts, New York, Ohio, Oklahoma, Washington, and Wisconsin. By the mid-1970s the closing movement had ebbed, and each mental hospital found its own destiny in view of its location, resources, and political and legal conditions. In areas where the community owed its economic existence to a state hospital, strong local pressures, notably from businesses dependent upon the trade of the institution, prevented closing. Also, the hospital system was perpetuated by societal inertia, historic tradition, and simple convenience for both professionals and the public. Mental health workers perferred to gather patients in one physical facility where they could be easily seen and maintained; some professionals had vested in the continuation of their services, positions, and programs. For relatives weary of coping with the difficult behavior of a family member, the institution provided a way out of a stressful situation. It fulfilled a painfully realistic objective of keeping unwanted persons "out of sight, out of mind." In short, the mental institution was a safety valve; it indulged people with a ritual of avoidance by handling one of life's most awkward ambiguities.

A reassessment of the community mental health movement dampened the enthusiasm for phasing out mental hospitals. One of the distressing problems of the community care system was its inability to provide for the needs of many former mental patients, especially the most difficult cases. Part of the problem was not knowing how to treat severely disturbed people: beyond the use of psychotropic drugs, a first step toward ameliorating a serious emotional dysfunction, the resources and methods needed for transforming a back-ward patient into a self-motivated person have remained elusive.

Along with this ignorance there was another factor thwarting aid to the chronic: the programs and services of community mental health aimed at helping persons with acute, treatable disorders. The main activities have centered on prevention, on early diagnosis, and on treatment of symptoms by means of social action, crisis intervention, consultation, and outpatient care. These services have assisted persons with a capacity for helping themselves. Professional bias has favored the acute. Mental health center staffs have preferred working with individuals motivated to get well. The chronic have been seen as a hopeless lot who disregard medication, irresponsibly ignore appointments, and make no progress in psychotherapy. The staffs have gained little sense of accomplishment from dependent, passive, psychotic patients who can be easily ignored, shunted aside, and pacified with heavy doses of drugs.

The lack of support and understanding from professionals reflected the realities and attitudes of the community, where disheartening experiences awaited former mental patients. Ideally a person discharged from the hospital broke from the isolated life of the institution and enjoyed all the amenities of community living. He or she held a tolerable, nondemanding job, spent leisure hours in quiet activities, and lived with family or friends in a congenial, benign social setting. Alas, this characterization represented a fantasy divorced from actual conditions. Most of the chronic were transient, poor, aged, physically and socially unattractive persons without ties to anyone. They could not be easily reintegrated into the community, and thus became a problem to local and state welfare agencies. Insensitive to their surroundings and incapable of protecting themselves from the predatory violence of slum life, some slept in the streets and drifted in and out of the cheap and dirty rooming houses, decayed hotels, and flophouses of the inner city, where they mingled with and fell prey to society's castaways: pimps, prostitutes, drug addicts, and petty criminals.

These circumstances exacerbated their hapless condition and contributed further to their psychological deterioration, sinking them deep into a mire of anonymous degradation. Some of the chronically ill went into nursing homes that had little experience with mental patients. Invariably the untrained personnel, the lack of programs and activities, and the inadequate treatment procedures created disastrous custodial situations. Locked rooms isolated the severely disturbed, and heavy doses of tranquilizers kept patients so apathetic and listless that they could only sit in a stuporous condition and stare blankly at a television set. They were desperate, alone, and without a sense of identity and belonging, just as they would be in the back ward of a state mental hospital.

Public hostility and revulsion toward the mentally ill presented another obstacle to treating and caring for chronic patients in the community. People remained frightened and anxious about unusual behavior. While few admitted prejudice, they showed little sympathy for former mental patients and expected them to create antisocial scenes, such as urinating in public or frightening children. Identified and rejected as derelicts whose presence in a neighborhood reduced property values and lowered the quality of life, former patients were kept out of the mainstream of community life by a variety of formal and informal methods, and were segregated in the most deteriorated sections of the city. They were excluded through the enforcement of fire and safety codes, zoning regulations, and city ordinances designed to prevent the creation of new facilities or the use of existing structures for housing discharged patients.

In places where large numbers of the mentally ill concentrated, local residents erected high fences and displayed security dogs. Middle-class neighborhood groups closed ranks to prevent the opening of treatment centers. Police detained former patients in jail on charges of mischievous behavior, loitering, or simply wandering aimlessly about the community. This inhospitable atmosphere inevitably produced disheartening consequences. Some of the chronic fell to the bottom of society, and remained lost and forgotten. Others returned to the mental hospital for a time and then were dumped back into the community, initiating a revolving-door cycle of continuous admissions and discharges.

The facts of community life for the chronic justified the existence of the mental hospital and confirmed its major role. It remained a welfare agency, an institution of last resort, a depository for society's most unwanted people. Along with the chronic, its clientele sometimes included drug addicts, alcoholics, sex offenders, acting-out adolescents, runaway youths, assaultive belligerent persons requiring involuntary institutionalization, those awaiting trial, and the mentally retarded. These were the types of patients who could not be accommodated at community mental health centers. Viewed as untouchables and rejects, the state mental hospital became their home and community, a place of belonging.

The fact that the hospital could be a home for the unwanted, the infirm, and the psychotic was not necessarily viewed as a liability. Some mental health experts were challenged by the problems confronting institutional psychiatry, and recognized that not all hospitals have remained outmoded places with a deteriorating physical plant, a limited treatment staff, and excessive maintenance personnel. A pragmatic, eclectic spirit pervaded better facilities, which aimed at becoming human service centers. Here a wide spectrum of therapeutic options were offered, ranging from the biomedical to the social learning approaches, and the institution functioned as a place of reprieve, a temporary haven where people could gain strength for purposeful living. Special programs for the chronic persisted, notably in community placement efforts.

The answers to the dilemmas of mental health care may rest in the community, at the contact points between patient and society. Clearly the isolation of an individual in the back ward of a hospital or in the back room of a nursing home has had deleterious, if not tragic, consequences. Better alternatives need to be found. A few do exist. The most positive, encouraging, and hopeful developments in the delivery of mental health care have occurred at places that ease the patient's transition to normal life. In the early 1970s, for example, Philadelphia State Hospital achieved success with a community treatment program for chronics that utilized the talents and the experience of community members called enablers. The average patient was 49 years old, had no relatives, was labeled schizophrenic, and had been hospitalized for over 13 years. After a 12-week preparatory and orientation program, the patient went into the community with an enabler who managed his or her daily activities. An enabler spent long hours with a patient, easing adjustment to community life. The enabler instructed the patient on personal hygiene, took the patient to the dentist, oriented the patient to the library and other community resources. Acting as a model, an arbiter of community standards, and a restraining influence, the enabler prevented the patient from being overwhelmed by confusing social situations and pressures.

The Philadelphia project demonstrated the importance of finding a familial setting for the chronic: a person who lived in the enabler's home achieved a better integration into community life than one living alone in an apartment.

A Colorado program of placing chronic patients in private homes had the same result. Under the auspices of the Southwest Denver Community Mental Health Services, each participating family accepted only two patients, who became involved in its household chores and activities. The intimate setting, unlike the depersonalized routines of a large hospital, provided models of healthy family interaction and encouraged good personal relationships between home sponsors and patients.

In Detroit a warm, familial atmosphere permeates the House of Care, a small, private, nonprofit adult foster home for young, behaviorally disoriented women. Its founder and administrator, Lenore Bombard, a dedicated woman, governs the residence with a unique and positive philosophy. It is best expressed in the verbal agreement each young woman makes when she moves into the House of Care: "It is not OK to be mentally ill. It is OK to grow." Mrs. Bombard believes that an individual grows within the context of a permissive family environment. As mother of the family, she offers her "daughters" love, tolerance, and guidance, with the aim of helping each become a productive and independent person. There are opportunities for self-expression, for learning, for thrashing out problems with family members. The open, intimate, positive atmosphere has produced effective results. Many of her "daughters" live in the community as capable and self-directed persons interested and involved in life, in planning for the future, in helping the family of Mrs. Bombard.

Soteria House, an old, large dwelling in a decaying neighborhood of San Jose, California, has accommodated six psychotic persons at any given time, with a turnover rate of one or two individuals a month. Its founders and directors were Dr. Loren Mosher, an existentialist psychiatrist, and Alma Menn, a creative social worker. They have been assisted by nonprofessional staff members and volunteers. The use of lay people is based on the assumption that untrained persons bring a fresh innocence to the care of the mentally ill. The lay staff has no theories about insanity; they have not learned any set procedures or methods for handling psychotics; they relate to a resident as one friend to another. A relaxed communal atmosphere envelops Soteria. The staff and the residents share responsibilities for maintenance, meals, and cleanup. There are two important rules: no illegal drugs, and no sexual contact between staff and residents. All therapeutic efforts relate to a general view of schizophrenia, a concept that it represents an "altered state of consciousness." Traditionally schizophrenia has been viewed as a manifestation of irrational or mystical or withdrawn behavior entailing loss of identity or personal fragmentation. At Soteria the staff integrates the psychotic experience with the individual's life history, making the patient's psychosis a real and valid psychological growth experience. This therapeutic approach terminates if the individual poses a danger to self, others, or the Soteria project.

From this sample of institutions devoted to transitional care, similar features emerge. The disturbed individual is brought into a small group or family-like setting and encouraged to develop a sense of loyalty and devotion. Professional medical and psychiatric personnel remain in the background; lay persons dominate the care of the person, showing him or her how to start life anew in the community. A strong supportive environment builds confidence and helps to overcome fears of inadequacy and rejection. This kind of rehabilitative work has produced encouraging results; participants have achieved a good adjustment to normal living. The best evidence is their low rate of return to the mental hospital.

The concern and dedication found at the House of Care and the other alternative rehabilitative places touches only a tiny minority of the mentally disturbed. While some have found a community to be an alternative to long-term hospitalization, the masses of mentally troubled persons continue to be feared by the public and locked in a narrow world on the edges of society. It is argued that this fate is a fact of life: there will always be homeless persons who lack volition, seem aberrant, and on occasion commit random acts of violence. They cannot be made into better persons; it is utopian to wish something other than custodial care for them. This is a deterministic view. Indeed, the mentally ill may endure forever, like sickness and taxes. Nevertheless, a brighter vision is needed; the search for a better life for the mentally disturbed persists. It is a quest for human dignity.

12
CONCLUSION

A profound sense of déja vu, a continuum of repetitive events and trends, emerges from a history of American mental health care. The patterns are evident: the persistent societal rejection and fear of the mentally ill; the exposé of the mental institution, a constant journalistic or political outrage occurring in every decade from the 1860s to the present; the discomforting anonymity of patients and their acquiescence to any form of treatment; the isolation of the mentally ill from normal life, a situation popularly expressed and condoned by the phrase "out of sight, out of mind."

There has been another significant historic characteristic: the modes and types of therapy have remained in a state of flux. Indeed, institutional psychiatry has supported a bewildering array of therapeutics that have followed a roller-coaster pattern of fashionability. A new therapy is introduced with great excitement and enthusiasm. Sophisticated, detailed reports verify its effectiveness and show remarkable cure and improvement ratios. This excitement and interest soon fade. Follow-up studies and additional research challenge the initial reports and reveal that the therapy has limited applications, that it should be given only a modest place in psychiatry's armamentarium. Even the most dramatic therapeutics have followed this cycle of hope and disillusionment.

In the early years of the asylum movement, the institution itself became the therapeutic agent. Superintendents published statistics and reports that revealed fantastic recovery rates; in a few instances institutions reported 100 percent cures. A century later exaggerated claims of success accompanied the introduction of shock treatment and drug therapy. Here an exuberant optimism and confidence conveyed an impression that at last something had been found that could strike at the root of the psychosis and offer relief for the emotionally

181

distressed. In each case great hopes and expectations were aroused and then dashed. The asylum became a custodial facility; the limitations of shock and drug treatments were soon revealed. Perhaps mental health workers have expected too much from any therapeutic innovation, for when the results have deflated the promises, a professional and public malaise, even nihilism, has developed. What has been important, however, is the constant groping, the continual search for a way to bring help to the mentally ill. The quest for new therapies in itself signifies hope.

In the confusing and ever-changing world of American mental health care, moral treatment has had perennial interest and represents an anchor of stability, a standard for judging other models of treatment. Efforts to recapture its innocence and simplicity have persisted. While some of this interest represents nostalgia, there has been a professional awareness that the principles and therapeutics understood and practiced by asylum superintendents of the pre-Civil War period represented quality institutional care. The components of this treatment—a retreat to a therapeutic reeducational atmosphere, a sympathetic physician, good rapport between doctor and patient, and, for the disturbed person, an active social and intellectual life complemented with a vigorous work and recreational regimen—have been periodically reincarnated. The most outstanding recent examples were the post-World War II experiments in milieu therapy and the manipulation of the hospital social environment.

If moral treatment set a high standard of care, it also established other trends important to psychiatric practice. It justified the asylum as the place for keeping the mentally ill, a fact that demanded legislation to control and administer to the needs of the insane, notably to determine commitment procedures and give patients a legal identity. Moral treatment sanctified the medical model of mental illness, the view that insanity was a disease that needed a physician's attention and care. It also involved lay and professional people in the management of the insane, and raised hopes that madness could be cured and contained. In effect, moral treatment provided the basic rationale for institutional psychiatry.

Another major trend in the history of the care and treatment of the mentally ill has been the growing power and influence of the mental health community. Throughout the nineteenth century the care of the insane was restricted largely to institutions dominated by paternalistic physicians. While many asylum administrators were talented men who established a high quality of care, psychiatry was a pariah specialty alienated from the mainstream of medical practice, a place for the unsuccessful and the mediocre who had no intellectual nor professional scope beyond the asylum walls. Absorbed in institutional routines, they developed a self-centered attitude that made them insensitive to positive outside criticism.

In the opening decades of the twentieth century, a combination of factors produced a new and expanded mental health community, notably the reforming milieu of Progressivism; the new breakthroughs in science, technology, and medicine; and the experiences of mental health workers in World War I. Psychiatry gained respectability, developed more community services, and acquired supportive personnel. Psychologists, social workers, law enforcement and correctional officials, and educators became part of the mental health community. This diverse and enlarged group charted a new course for mental health care that focused on preventive efforts and the treatment of acute cases of mental disorder. On their agenda the state mental hospital was a low-priority item; it housed the chronic, the failures of psychiatric care; and it was far removed from the more exciting and constructive professional developments in psychotherapy and mental hygiene.

Among mental health workers a new assumption found increasing acceptance: the idea that psychiatry could be used to ameliorate social problems. Clearly this fact, the increased involvement of mental health personnel in community services and problems, fostered an expansive ideology and created new styles of care and practice. Distinct hierarchies of status and service were evolving: institutional psychiatry was absorbed in the problems of administering programs for the chronic; private psychiatrists experimented with psychotherapies and enjoyed a lucrative practice treating both the neurotic and the acutely disordered; a mental health team composed of psychiatrists, psychologists, and social workers operated in the new areas of juvenile delinquency and child guidance.

The growing role of the federal government in psychiatric care added another dimension to the mental health community. This development was most noticeable after World War II, when federal agencies moved into the field in a massive way and established new priorities and programs. The community mental health movement, for example, broadened and deepened the ideology of social psychiatry, and required a new array of facilities and workers to sustain and nurture the increasing number of patients being released from mental hospitals.

Today a powerful and complex mental health community, vigorously supported by the federal government, exercises influence far beyond the realm of institutional care. The purveyors of mental health have greatly multiplied in kind and in number. An imposing group of counselors and mental health technicians assume roles previously reserved for psychiatrists. Treating individual patients represents only one area of interest; their concerns embrace major social problems including war, aggression, prejudice, racism, crime, and other forms of social deviance. Psychiatry itself has been inundated with expanding waves of social subspecialties that move out in all directions. A sample of the wide spectrum of fields might include ethnopsychiatry, ecopsychiatry, forensic, child, industrial, military, student health, public health, transcultural, and family psychiatry. Their existence alone reflects a confident acceptance of the need for a psychiatric perspective on social problems.

There is a touch of irony here. While psychiatry gained status and power, and the problems of the mentally ill received wider public sympathy, the mental institution, the bedrock of American mental health care, diminished in stature. This may be a reflection of its divergent historic roles. Initially the mental institution was a therapeutic center where individuals received treatment and returned to society. It functioned ideally as a retreat that had all the resources necessary for facilitating the recovery of emotionally disturbed persons. Perhaps this role was fulfilled only in the 1830s and the 1840s, when the asylum was first introduced and accepted as a therapeutic haven for the mentally troubled. By the 1870s the typical mental institution could not hide another reality: it had become a custodial facility, a fearful place where patients remained mad, grew old, and died. Treatment efforts remained minimal and the superintendent muted criticism by running a quiet organization, keeping it isolated from the wider society. This quiescence was disturbed occasionally by a prying journalist or politician. Along with the practice and ideology of custodialism, the mental institution assumed a welfare burden. Social outcasts, rejects, and incompetents, as well as the poor, the black, and the immigrant, formed the major part of its clientele.

In short, long before 1900 the mental institution was beset with inner tensions caused by conflicting roles. Its therapeutic, custodial, and welfare functions were at cross purposes. Ostensibly and officially it was a place of solace, a therapeutic center; in fact it was overcrowded with persons no one else wanted. This fact discouraged public support, kept appropriations low, made change and innovation difficult, undercut treatment efforts, and stigmatized the institution as an undesirable place, a snake pit. Once this historic pattern was set, many important developments in mental health care happened outside of the institutional milieu. To be sure, the institution did not remain static. It evolved from an asylum to a hospital to a mental health center, and in each transformation important and positive innovations occurred. Nevertheless, the fact remains that the major twentieth-century movements in mental health care, notably mental hygiene and community mental health, each had a decided anti-institution flavor, yet each enhanced the prestige of psychiatry and sensitized the public to mental health issues and problems. A major consequence has been professional and public ambivalence toward the mental institution.

Disaffection with the institution is also symptomatic of the fervor and controversy existing within the fields of mental health care. What exasperates contemporary workers in dealing with the mentally troubled is still the question of defining mental illness and accounting for its occurrence. Historically this conflict has been between organic and analytic psychiatrists. Today the battle lines extend beyond psychiatry, and many challenge the traditional position that mental disorder is a physical ailment, a genetic-biochemical illness. An influential professional opinion, most notable in the fields of social psychology and sociology, claims that mental illness is a label that society uses to stigmatize individuals who exhibit deviant behavior.

Accordingly, there are no madmen, only violators of social rules and customs. Some people see the mentally ill person as an irresponsible individual in need of moral training and guidance, the condition as caused by improper and inadequate upbringing. Related to this moral assumption is a model of madness that insists that insanity is caused by emotionally painful family dynamics, by an unkind father or mother. Others blame society for shattering minds. A sick community produces sick individuals, and nothing short of a social revolution can stamp out mental illness. There are a few who romanticize insanity and assert that the mad person has achieved a high level of consciousness, a unique state of being, a condition divorced from the workaday world. This individual has gone on "a mind-expanding trip."

The articulation of these viewpoints has been accompanied with extravagant language and self-righteous attitudes. Some of the advocates of the nonmedical models of mental illness have assumed the roles of religious sectarians. They dogmatically advocate a concept of mental illness that becomes a new orthodoxy. In proclaiming their new faith they morally condemn and denounce the traditional practitioners of psychiatric care. One is reminded of the vociferous charges and counter charges between neurologists and asylum administrators in the late nineteenth century. On the other hand, debates over the etiology and the meaning of mental illness have generated more public awareness of the problems inherent in contemporary mental health care. This dialogue has shown a unique intensity and breadth, demonstrating the commitment and the quest of all kinds of mental health workers to find new ways to aid psychiatrically wounded people. There is now, more than at any other time in the history of American mental health care, a recognition that social, familial, experiential, and biological factors can all contribute to an understanding of mental illness, a fact that permits a multiplicity of treatment options.

BIBLIOGRAPHY

The literature on American mental health care is voluminous and has reached proportions so vast as to defy description and synthesis. By necessity, then, this bibliography is selective and subjective, and lists the most important sources consulted in preparing the text. My main aim is to suggest useful further reading to persons interested in pursuing a special topic.

A few reference works provide orientations to recent literature, notably Edwin D. Driver, *The Sociology and Anthropology of Mental Illness—a Reference Guide* (Amherst: University of Massachusetts Press, 1965); Armando R. Favazza and Mary Oman, *Anthropological and Cross-Cultural Themes in Mental Health: An Annotated Bibliography 1925-1971* (Columbia: University of Missouri Press, 1977); Karl A. Menninger, *A Guide to Psychiatric Books in English* (3rd ed.; New York: Grune and Stratton, 1972); Genevieve Miller, ed., *Bibliography of the History of Medicine of the United States and Canada 1939-1960* (Baltimore: Johns Hopkins University Press, 1964); and Richard A. Schermerhorn, ed., *Psychiatric Index for Interdisciplinary Research. A Guide to the Literature. 1950-1961* (Washington, D.C.: U.S. Government Printing Office, 1964).

Some helpful bibliographic essays are Otto M. Marx, "What Is the History of Psychiatry?" *American Journal of Orthopsychiatry* 40 (1970): 593-605; George Mora, "The History of Psychiatry: A Cultural and Bibliographical Survey," *Psychoanalytic Review* 52 (1965): 298-328; and "The Historiography of Psychiatry and Its Development: A Re-evaluation," *Journal of the History of the Behavioral Sciences* 1 (1965): 43-52; and George Mora and Jeanne L. Brand, eds., *Psychiatry and Its History* (Springfield, Ill.: Charles C. Thomas, 1970).

Only a few standard historical works exist: Albert Deutsch, *The Mentally Ill in America* (New York: Columbia University Press, 1949) remains an important book. Deutsch's lifework is evaluated in Jeanne L. Brand, "Albert Deutsch: The Historian as Social Reformer," *Journal of the History of Medicine and Allied Sciences* 18 (1963):149-57. Gerald N. Grob, *Mental Institutions in America: Social Policy to 1875* (New York: Free Press, 1973), is the best study of nineteenth-century American mental health care. J. K. Hall, Gregory Zilboorg, and Henry Alden Bunker, ed., *One Hundred Years of American Psychiatry* (New York: Columbia University Press , 1944), provides general historical articles on topics ranging from mental institutions to psychiatric therapies. Henry M. Hurd, ed., *The Institutional Care of the Insane in the United States and Canada,* 4 vols. (Baltimore: Johns Hopkins University Press, 1916), is a largely descriptive study.

The following abbreviations are used in designating the most frequently cited periodicals:

AJI	*American Journal of Insanity*
AJP	*American Journal of Psychiatry*
Hosp & Comm Psych	*Hospital and Community Psychiatry*
JAMA	*Journal of the American Medical Association*
JCEP	*Journal of Clinical and Experimental Psychopathology and Quarterly Review of Psychiatry and Neurology*
JNMD	*Journal of Nervous and Mental Disease*
MH	*Mental Hygiene*
Ment H	*Mental Hospital*
Mod H	*Modern Hospital*

The bibliography that follows is divided by chapter, with no overlapping citations. Some sources consulted for chapters 2-4, have not been listed. These include the annual asylum reports and the proceedings of annual meetings of the Association of Medical Superintendents of American Institutions for the Insane, published in the *American Journal of Insanity.* Also, the *American Journal of Medical Science* published lengthy excerpts from asylum reports, notably in the 1840s. This is interesting and accessible material that the professional student can easily find.

CHAPTER 1

Bridenbaugh, Carl. *Cities in Revolt: Urban Life in America 1743-1776.* New York: Capricorn Books, 1964.

Bringer, C. *Revolutionary Doctor, Benjamin Rush, 1746-1813.* New York: Norton, 1966.

Buchan, William. *Domestic Medicine, or, A Treatise on the Prevention and Cure of Diseases, by Regimen and Simple Medicines.* London: 1797; A. and R. Spottiswoode, 22nd ed., 1826. This was a very popular book.

Caporael, Linnda R. "Salem's Witches: Was There a Satan in the Rye?" *Horticulture* 14 (1976):12-19. An argument that the rye harvest of 1691 contained a fungus that set off the witchcraft crisis.

Carlson, Eric T., and May F. Chale. "Dr. Rufus Wyman of the McLean Asylum." *AJP* 116 (1960):1034-37.

Cochrane, Hortense S. "Early Treatment of the Mentally Ill in Georgia," *Georgia Historical Quarterly* 32 (1948):103-18.

Croskey, John W., comp. *History of Blockley: A History of the Philadelphia General Hospital from Its Inception, 1731-1928.* Philadelphia: F. A. Davis, 1929.

Dain, Norman. *Disordered Minds. The First Century of Eastern State Hospital in Williamsburg, Virginia, 1766-1866.* Williamsburg, Va.: Colonial Williamsburg Foundation, 1971. An excellent study of America's first mental institution.

_____, "American Psychiatry in the 18th Century." In *American Psychiatry: Past, Present, and Future*, edited by George Kriegman, Robert D. Garner, and D. Wilfred Abse, pp. 15-27. Charlottesville: University of Virginia Press, 1975. A chapter packed with much useful information.

Dain, Norman, and Eric T. Carlson. "Social Class and Psychological Medicine in the United States, 1789-1824." *Bulletin of the History of Medicine* 33 (1959):45-55. A good discussion of an important aspect of early asylum life.

_____. "Milieu Therapy in the Nineteenth Century: Patient Care at the Friends' Asylum, Frankford, Pennsylvania, 1817-1861." *JNMD* 131 (1960): 277-90.

Deutsch, Albert. "The Sick Poor in Colonial Times." *American Historical Review* 46 (1941):560-79.

Duffy, John. *A History of Public Health in New York City 1625-1866.* New York: Russell Sage Foundation, 1968.

Eaton, Leonard. "Eli Todd and the Hartford Retreat." *New England Quarterly* 24 (1953):435-53.

_____. *New England Hospitals, 1790-1833.* Ann Arbor: University of Michigan Press, 1957. An essential source book.

Forster, Robert, and Orest Ranum, eds. *Deviants and the Abandoned in French Society.* Baltimore: Johns Hopkins University Press, 1978.

Foucault, Michel. *Madness and Civilization. A History of Insanity in the Age of Reason.* New York: Vintage Books, 1973. A brilliant and provocative book.

Galdston, Iago. *Historic Derivations of Modern Psychiatry.* New York: McGraw-Hill, 1967.

Goodman, Nathan G. *Benjamin Rush. Physician and Citizen 1746-1813.* Philadelphia: University of Pennsylvania Press, 1934.

Grange, Kathleen M. "Pinel and Eighteenth Century Psychiatry." *Bulletin of the History of Medicine* 35 (1961):442-53.

Hansen, Chadwick. *Witchcraft at Salem.* New York: George Braziller, 1969.

Harris, Johnathan. *The Rise of Medical Science in New York, 1720-1820.* Ann Arbor, Mich.: University Microfilms, 1971.

Hawke, David Freeman. *Benjamin Rush.* New York: Bobbs-Merrill, 1971.

Heale, M. J. "Humanitarianism in the Early Republic: The Moral Reformers of New York 1776-1825." *Journal of American Studies* 2 (1968):161-75.

Hunter, Robert J. *The Origin of the Philadelphia General Hospital. Blockley Division*. Philadelphia: Rittenhouse Press, 1955.

Jones, Kathleen. *Lunacy, Law, and Conscience, 1744-1845: The Social History of the Insane*. London: Routledge and Kegan Paul, 1955. A standard study of English policies that influenced early American practices.

Jordan, W. K. *Philanthropy in England 1480-1660: A Study of the Changing Pattern of English Social Aspirations*. London: George Allen and Unwin, 1959.

Kavka, Jerome. "Pinel's Conception of the Psychopathic State." *Bulletin of the History of Medicine* 23 (1949):461-68.

King, Lester. *The Medical World of the Eighteenth Century*. Chicago: University of Chicago Press, 1958.

Klebaner, Benjamin. "Pauper Auctions: The 'New England Method' of Public Poor Relief." *Essex Institute Historical Collections* 91 (1955):195-210.

————. "Employment of Paupers at Philadelphia's Almshouse Before 1861." *Pennsylvania History* 24 (1957):137-47.

Larrabee, Eric. *The Benevolent and Necessary Institution. The New York Hospital, 1771-1971*. New York: Doubleday, 1971.

Leiby, James. *Charity and Correction in New Jersey. A History of State Welfare Institutions*. New Brunswick, N. J.: Rutgers University Press, 1967.

Levin, David. *What Happened in Salem?* New York: Harcourt, Brace, 1960.

Little, Nina F. *Early Years of the McLean Hospital*. Boston: Francis A. Countway Library of Medicine, 1972.

Meyer, Adolf. "Revaluation of Benjamin Rush." *AJP* 101 (1945):433-42.

Morton, Thomas G. *The History of the Pennsylvania Hospital, 1751-1895*. Philadelphia: Times Printing House, 1895.

Neaman, Judith S. *Suggestion of the Devil. The Origins of Madness*. New York: Anchor, 1975.

Overholser, Winfred. "Cox and Trotter—Two Psychiatric Precursors of Benjamin Rush." *AJP* 110 (1954):825-30.

Packard, Francis R. *Some Account of the Pennsylvania Hospital*. Philadelphia: Eagle Press, 1938.

————. "Medical Case Histories in a Colonial Hospital." *Bulletin of the History of Medicine* 12 (1942):150-51.

Page, Charles Whitney. "Dr. Eli Todd and the Hartford Retreat." *AJI* 69 (1913):761-85.

Parkhurst, Eleanor. "Poor Relief in a Massachusetts Village in the Eighteenth Century." *Social Science Review* 11 (1937):446-64.

Pendleton, O. A. "Poor Relief in Philadelphia, 1790-1840." *Pennsylvania Magazine of History and Biography* 70 (1946):161-72.

Pinel, Philippe. *A Treatise on Insanity*. New York: Hafner, 1962. This facsimile of the edition published at London in 1806 is one of the best sources on "Enlightenment" psychiatry.

Quen, Jacques M. "Early Nineteenth Century Observations on the Insane in the Boston Almshouse." *Journal of the History of Medicine and Allied Sciences* 23 (1968):80-85.

Rosen, George. *Madness in Society. Chapters in the Historical Sociology of Mental Illness*. Chicago: University of Chicago Press, 1968.

Rush, Benjamin. *Medical Inquiries and Observations upon the Diseases of the Mind.* New York: Hafner, 1962. This facsimile of the edition published at Philadelphia in 1812 is the most relevant primary source for the "Father of American Psychiatry."

Russell, William L. *The New York Hospital: A History of the Psychiatric Service, 1771-1936.* New York: Columbia University Press, 1945.

Shryock, Richard H. "The Psychiatry of Benjamin Rush." *AJP* 101 (1945): 429-32.

_____. *Medicine and Society in America 1660-1860.* New York: New York University Press, 1960. An excellent overview of medical history.

Starkey, Marion L. *The Devil in Massachusetts: A Modern Enquiry into the Salem Witch Trials.* New York: Anchor, 1969. A standard for the subject of witchcraft in early colonial America.

Teeters, Negley K. "The Early Days of the Philadelphia House of Refuge." *Pennsylvania History* 32 (1960):165-87.

Tuke, Samuel. *Description of the Retreat.* London: Dawsons of Paul Mall, 1964. This reprint of the edition published at London in 1813 is a delightful book and gives interesting details of institutional life.

Veith, Ilza. *Hysteria. The History of a Disease.* Chicago: University of Chicago Press, 1965.

Viets, Henry R. "A Note from Samuel Tuke to the New York Hospital." *AJP* 78 (1922):425-32.

_____. "Some Features of the History of Medicine in Massachusetts During the Colonial Period (1620-1770)." *Isis* 23 (1935):389-405.

Williams, William H. *America's First Hospital: The Pennsylvania Hospital, 1751-1841.* Wayne, Pa.: Haverford House, 1976.

Wisner, Elizabeth. "The Puritan Background of the New England Poor Laws." *Social Science Review* 19 (1945):381-90.

Wittels, Fritz. "The Contribution of Benjamin Rush to Psychiatry." *Bulletin of the History of Medicine* 20 (1946):157-66.

Woods, Evelyn A., and Eric T. Carlson. "The Psychiatry of Philippe Pinel." *Bulletin of the History of Medicine* 35 (1961):14-25.

CHAPTER 2

Andrews, J. B. "Asylum Periodicals." *AJI* 33 (1876):42-49.

Bockoven, J. Sanbourne. *Moral Treatment in American Psychiatry.* New York: Springer, 1963. A classic for understanding the rise and fall of moral treatment.

Bond, Earl D. *Dr. Kirkbride and His Mental Hospital.* Philadelphia: Lippincott, 1947.

Brigham, Amariah. "Insanity and Insane Hospitals." *North American Review* 44 (1837):91-121.

_____. *An Inquiry Concerning the Diseases and Functions of the Brain, the Spinal Cord, and the Nerves.* New York: George Adlard, 1840.

_____. "Meeting of the Association of the Medical Superintendents of American Institutions for the Insane." *AJI* 2 (1845):253-54.

Buttolph, H. A. "Modern Asylums." *AJI* 3 (1847):364-78.

Caplan, Ruth B. *Psychiatry and the Community in Nineteenth Century America.* New York: Basic Books, 1969. A useful survey enlivened with long quotes from original sources.

Carlson, Eric T. "Amariah Brigham: I. Life and Works." *AJP* 112 (1956): 831-36.

———, "Amariah Brigham: II. Psychiatric Thought and Practice." *AJP* 113 (1957):911-16.

———, "The Influence of Phrenology on Early American Psychiatric Thought." *AJP* 114 (1958):535-38.

Carlson, Eric T., and Norman Dain. "The Psychotherapy That Was Moral Treatment." *AJP* 117 (1960):519-24.

Dain, Norman. *Concepts of Insanity in the United States, 1789-1865.* New Brunswick, N. J.: Rutgers University Press, 1964. An important book with an extensive bibliography.

Davies, J. D. *Phrenology: Fad and Science. A 19th Century American Crusade.* New Haven: Yale University Press, 1955.

Dix, Dorothea L. *On Behalf of the Insane Poor.* New York: Arno Press, 1971. A selection of reprints of her memorials to state legislatures.

Drews, Robert. "A History of the Care of the Sick Poor of the City of Detroit." *Bulletin of the History of Medicine* 7 (1939):770-74.

Ebert, Myrl. "The Rise and Development of the American Medical Periodical, 1797-1850." *Bulletin of the Medical Library Association* 40 (1952):243-76.

Griffin, Clifford. *Their Brothers' Keepers: Moral Stewardship in the United States, 1800-1865.* New Brunswick, N. J.: Rutgers University Press, 1960.

Grob, Gerald N. "Samuel Woodward and the Practice of Psychiatry in Early Nineteenth-Century America." *Bulletin of the History of Medicine* 36 (1962):420-43.

———, "Origins of the State Mental Hospital: A Case Study." *Bulletin of the Menninger Clinic* 29 (1965):1-19.

———, *The State and the Mentally Ill: A History of Worcester State Hospital in Massachusetts 1830-1920.* Chapel Hill: University of North Carolina Press, 1966. A classic in the historical literature of American mental health care. It covers much more ground than the subtitle indicates.

Hooker, Worthington. *Physician and Patient.* New York: Baker and Scribner, 1849.

Howe, Samuel Gridley. "Insanity in Massachusetts." *North American Review* 56 (1843):171-91.

Jones, Robert E. "Correspondence of the APA Founders." *AJP* 119 (1963): 1121-34.

Kirkbride, Thomas S. *On the Construction, Organization, and General Arrangements of Hospitals for the Insane. With Some Remarks on Insanity and Its Treatment.* Philadelphia: Lindsay and Blakiston, 1854. The classic that influenced the construction and administration of nineteenth-century American mental institutions.

Lewis, W. David. *From Newgate to Dannemora: The Rise of the Penitentiary in New York, 1796-1848.* Ithaca, N. Y.: Cornell University Press, 1965.

"Life in the New York State Lunatic Asylum; or, Extracts from the Diary of an

Inmate." *AJI* 6 (1849):289-302.

Marshall, Helen E. *Dorothea Dix Forgotten Samaritan.* Chapel Hill: University of North Carolina Press, 1937.

"The Moral Treatment of Insanity." *AJI* 4 (1847):1-15.

Myers, Marvin. *The Jacksonian Persuasion.* Stanford, Calif.: Stanford University Press. 1957.

Overholser, Winfred. "The Founding and the Founders of the Association." In *One Hundred Years of American Psychiatry*, edited by J. K. Hall et al, pp. 45-72. New York: Columbia University Press, 1944.

————, "Jacksonville 1847–Psychiatry Then and Now." *Journal of the History of Medicine and Allied Sciences* 3 (1948):381-94.

Pessen, Edward. *Jacksonian America.* Homewood, Ill.: Dorsey Press, 1969.

"Progress of the Periodical Literature of Lunatic asylums." *AJI* 2 (1845):77-79.

Ray, Isaac. "American Hospitals for the Insane." *North American Review* 79 (1854):66-90.

————, *Mental Hygiene.* Boston: Ticknor and Fields, 1863.

Riegal, Robert E. "The Introduction of Phrenology to the United States." *American Historical Review* 39 (1933):73-78.

Rosen, George. "Social Stress and Mental Disease from the Eighteenth Century to the Present: Some Origins of Social Psychiatry." *Milbank Memorial Fund Quarterly* 37 (1959):5-32.

Rosenkrantz, Barbara G., and Maris A. Vinovskis. "Caring for the Insane in Ante-Bellum Massachusetts: Family, Community, and State Participation." In *Kin and Community. Families in America*, edited by Allan J. Lichtman and Joan R. Challinor, pp. 187-218. Washington, D.C.: Smithsonian Institution Press, 1979.

Rothman, David J. *The Discovery of the Asylum.* Boston: Little, Brown, 1971.

Schwartz, Harold. *Samuel Gridley Howe, Social Reformer 1801-1876.* Cambridge, Mass.: Harvard University Press, 1956.

Shershow, John C., ed. *Delicate Branch. The Vision of Moral Psychiatry.* Oceanside, N. Y.: Dabor Science Publications, 1977.

Shryock, Richard H. "The Beginnings: From Colonial Days to the Founding of the American Psychiatric Association." In *One Hundred Years of American Psychiatry*, edited by J. K. Hall et al, pp. 1-28. New York: Columbia University Press, 1944.

Thompson, E. Bruce. "Reforms in the Care of the Insane in Tennessee, 1830-1850." *Tennessee Historical Quarterly* 3 (1944):319-34.

Tyler, A. F. *Freedom's Ferment: Phases of American Social History to 1860.* New York: Harper and Row, 1944.

Walk, Alexander. "Some Aspects of the 'Moral Treatment' of the Insane up to 1854." *Journal of Mental Science* 100 (1954):807-37.

CHAPTER 3

Billington, Ray A. *The Protestant Crusade 1800-1860: A Study of the Origins of American Nativism.* Chicago: Quadrangle Books, 1964.

Carlson, Eric T., and Norman Dain. "The Meaning of Moral Insanity." *Bulletin of the History of Medicine* 36 (1962):130-140.

Carlson, Eric T., and Lilian Peters. "Dr. Pliny Earle." *AJP* 116 (1959): 557-58.

Dain, Norman, and Eric T. Carlson. "Moral Insanity in the United States 1835-1866." *AJP* 118 (1962):795-801.

Deutsch, Albert. *The Mentally Ill in America*. New York: Columbia University Press, 1949.

Dewey, R. S. "Differentiation in Institutions for the Insane." *AJI* 39 (1882): 1-21.

Earle, Pliny. *The Curability of Insanity: A Series of Studies*. Philadelphia: J. B. Lippincott, 1887. An indispensable source for understanding the theoretical and administrative changes in mid-nineteenth-century mental health care.

Gish, Lowell. *Reform at Osawatomie State Hospital. Treatment of the Mentally Ill 1866-1970*. Lawrence: University of Kansas Press, 1972.

Gray, John P. "Insanity and Its Relation to Medicine." *AJI* 25 (1868):145-72.

_____, "The Dependence of Insanity on Physical Disease." *AJI* 27 (1871): 377-408.

_____, "Mental Hygiene." *AJI* 34 (1878):307-41.

_____, "Heredity." *AJI* 41 (1884):1-21.

_____, "Insanity: Its Frequency and Some of Its Preventable Causes." *AJI* 41 (1885):1-45.

Grob, Gerald N. *Mental Institutions in America: Social Policy to 1875*. New York: Free Press, 1973.

_____, *Edward Jarvis and the Medical World of 19th Century America*. Knoxville: University of Tennessee Press, 1978. A delightful biography of an important and distinguished mid-nineteenth-century psychiatrist.

"Insanity in the State of New York." *AJI* 13 (1856):39-50.

Jarvis, Edward. "On the Comparative Liability of Males and Females to Insanity and Their Comparative Curability and Mortality When Insane." *AJI* 7 (1850):142-71.

_____, *Insanity and Idiocy in Massachusetts: Report of the Commission of Lunacy 1855*. Cambridge, Mass.: Harvard University Press, 1971.

"Mental and Physical Characteristics of Pauperism." *AJI* 13 (1857):309-20.

Ordronaux, John. "On Expert Testimony in Judicial Proceedings." *AJI* 30 (1874):312-22.

Ranney, M. H. "On Insane Foreigners." *AJI* 7 (1850):53-63.

Robison, Dale W. *Wisconsin and the Mentally Ill. A History of the "Wisconsin Plan" of State and County Care 1860-1915*. Ph.D. dissertation, Marquette University. New York: Arno Press, 1979. An analysis of a successful experience with county care.

Rosenberg, Charles E. *The Trial of the Assassin Guiteau. Psychiatry and Law in the Gilded Age*. Chicago: University of Chicago Press, 1968.

_____, "The Bitter Fruit: Heredity, Disease, and Social Thought in Nineteenth Century America." *Perspectives in American History* 8 (1974):189-235. An essential article for understanding that mid-nineteenth-century concepts of heredity reflected a Lamarckian perspective and were quite different from the stark, pessimistic views of the twentieth century.

Rosenkrantz, Barbara G., and Maris A. Vinovskis. "The 'Invisible Lunatics':

Old Age and Insanity in Mid-Nineteenth Century Massachusetts." In *Aging and the Elderly. Human Perspectives in Gerontology,* edited by Stuart F. Spicker et al, pp. 95-125. Atlantic Highlands, N.J.: Humanities Press, 1978

Sanborn, Franklin B. "The Present Status of Insanity in Massachusetts." *AJI* 52 (1896):551-55.

Savino, Michael T., and Alden B. Mills. "The Rise and Fall of Moral Treatment in California Psychiatry: 1852-1870." *Journal of the History of the Behavioral Sciences* 3 (1967):359-69.

"Separate Institutions for Certain Classes of the Insane." *AJI* 38 (1881):236-52.

"Thoughts on the Causation of Insanity." *AJI* 29 (1872):264-83.

"The Willard Asylum and Provision for the Insane." *AJI* 22 (1965):192-212.

CHAPTER 4

Adams, Evelyn C. "The Growing Concept of Social Responsibility Illustrated by a Study of the State's care of the Insane in Indiana." *Indiana Magazine of History* 32 (1936):1-22.

"Asylum Reform in the State of New York." *JNMD* 6 (1879):530-36.

Bruno, Frank J. *Trends in Social Work as Reflected in the Proceedings of the National Conference of Social Work, 1874-1946.* New York: Columbia University Press, 1948.

Bucknill, John C. *Notes on Asylums for the Insane in America.* London: J. and A. Churchill, 1876.

Callender, John H. "History and Work of the Association of Medical Superintendents of American Institutions for the Insane—President's Address." *AJI* 40 (1883):1-32.

Casamajor, L. "Notes for an Intimate History of Neurology and Psychiatry in America." *JNMD* 98 (1943):600-08.

Chapin, John B. "Public Complaints Against Asylums for the Insane and the Commitment of the Insane." *AJI* 40 (1883):33-49.

Clevenger, S. V. "Treatment of the Insane." *JAMA* 27 (Oct. 24, 1896):894-901.

Dana, C. L. "The Asylum Superintendents of the Needs of the Insane with Statistics of Insanity in the United States." *JNMD* 9 (1882):241-57.

Dewey, Ethel L., ed. *Recollections of Richard Dewey. Pioneer in American Psychiatry.* Chicago: University of Chicago Press, 1936.

Dewey, Richard S. "Present and Prospective Management of the Insane." *JNMD* 5 (1878):60-94.

Eaton, Dorman B. "Despotism in Lunatic Asylums." *North American Review* 132 (1881):263-75. An indignant attack by a reformer on asylum superintendents.

Everts, Orpheus. "The American System of Public Provision for the Insane, and Despotism in Lunatic Asylums." *AJI* 37 (1881):113-39. A superintendent's reply to Dorman Eaton.

———. "Common Errors: Theoretical and Practical, Relating to Insanity," *AJI* 43 (1886):221-42.

Gapin, Clark. "Some Exceptions to the Present Management of Hospitals for the Insane." *JNMD* 6 (1879):441-49.

Godding, W. W. "Progress in Provision for the Insane." *AJI* 41 (1884):129-50.

Grissom, Eugene. "Mechanical Protection for the Violent Insane." *AJI* 34 (1877):27-56.

Hammond, William A. *The Non-Asylum Treatment of the Insane.* New York: Putnam's, 1879.

"Historical Notes: The Word Psychiatry." *AJP* 107 (1951):868-69.

Kittrie, Nicholas N. *The Right to Be Different.* Baltimore: Johns Hopkins University Press, 1971. An excellent historical review and discussion of commitment procedures and policies.

MacDonald, A. E. "The Examination and Commitment of the Insane." *AJI* 32 (1876):502-22.

"Management of the Insane." *JNMD* 6 (1879):341-47.

National Association for the Protection of the Insane and the Prevention of Insanity. Boston: Tolman and White, 1880.

"The New York Neurological Society and the Insane Asylums." *JNMD* 9 (1882):401-03.

An Open Letter to Eugene Grissom from William A. Hammond. New York: Trow's, 1878.

Parigot, J. "Legislation on Lunacy." *AJI* 21 (1864):200-23, 325-42.

"Proceedings of the Conference of Charities." *JNMD* 5 (1878):348-61.

Quen, Jacques M. "Isaac Ray: Have We Learned His Lessons?" *Bulletin of the American Academy of Psychiatry and the Law* 2 (1974):137-47.

"Report of the Committee to Investigate the Affairs and the Management of the State Lunatic Asylum at Utica." *JNMD* 12 (1885):377-82.

"Report of Investigation of the Central Kentucky Lunatic Asylum, Louisville, Kentucky." *JNMD* 11 (1884):99-101.

Report of the Joint Committee of the Michigan Legislature. Lansing: W. S. George, 1879. A massive volume that provides enormous details on late nineteenth-century institutional life.

"Report of State Lunatic Asylum, Utica, New York." *JNMD* 10 (1883):110-20.

"Restraint in British and American Insane Asylums." *AJI* 35 (1878):512-30.

Riggs, C. Eugene. "An Outline of the Progress in the Care and Handling of the Insane in the Last Twenty Years." *JNMD* 18 (1891):620-28.

Robinson, Victor. *The Don Quixote of Psychiatry.* New York: Historico-Medical Press, 1919.

Ruvtz-Rees, Janet E. "Hospitals for the Insane Viewed from the Standpoint of Personal Experience by a Recovered Patient." *Alienist and Neurologist* 9 (1888):51-57.

Sanborn, Franklin B. "Work Accomplished by the State Boards." *Proceedings, National Conference of Charities and Correction* 14 (1887):75-105.

Santos, Elvin H., and Edward Stainbrook. "A History of Psychiatric Nursing in the Nineteenth Century." *Journal of the History of Medicine and Allied Sciences* 4 (1949):48-74.

Scull, Andrew T. *Museums of Madness: The Social Organization of Insanity in Nineteenth Century England.* Ph.D. dissertation, Princeton University, 1974.

Sequin, E. C. "Lunacy Reform—Historical Considerations." *Archives of Medicine* 2 (1879):184-98.

———, "Lunacy Reform II. Insufficiency of the Medical Staff of Asylums." *Archives of Medicine* 2 (1879):310-18.

Shew, A. M. "Progress in the Treatment of the Insane." *AJI* 42 (1886):429-51.

Sicherman, Barbara. *The Quest for Mental Health in America 1880-1917.* Ph.D. dissertation, Columbia University, 1967. New York: Arno Press, 1979. The best single source for the battle between the superintendents and the neurologists and for the general asylum reform movement of the 1870s and 1880s. It is also basic to the study of early twentieth-century mental health care.

Smith, Margaret H. "Psychiatric History and Development in California." *AJP* 94 (1938):1223-36.

Smith, Stephen. "Remarks on the Lunacy Laws of the State of New York, as Regards the Provisions for Commitment and Discharge of the Insane." *AJI* 40 (1883):50-70.

Spitzka, Edward C. "Merits and Motives of the Movement for Asylum Reform." *JNMD* 5 (1878):694-714.

———, "Reform in the Scientific Study of Psychiatry." *JNMD* 5 (1878):201-28.

———, *Insanity. Its Classification, Diagnosis and Treatment.* New York: E. B. Treat, 1887.

Stevenson, Karl W. "A Brief History of Mental Health Care in North Carolina." *North Carolina Medical Journal* 26 (1965):509-15.

"Thoughts on the Causation of Insanity." *AJI* 29 (1872):264-83.

Tourtellot, L. A. "The Senate Committee on the Insane Asylums of New York." *JNMD* 9 (1882):349-58.

"Treatment of the Insane in the United States." *JNMD* 7 (1880):293-302.

Workman, Joseph. "Asylum Management." *AJI* 38 (1881):1-15.

———, "The Public Care of the Insane and the Management of Asylums." *Alienist and Neurologist* 5 (1884):492-501.

CHAPTER 5

"The Alien-Born in Relation to the Cost of State Care." In *The Institutional Care of the Insane in the United States and Canada,* edited by Henry M. Hurd, vol. I, pp. 362-68. Baltimore: Johns Hopkins University Press, 1916.

Babcock, J. W. "The Colored Insane." *Alienist and Neurologist* 16 (1895): 423-47.

Bailey, Pearce. "A Contribution to the Mental Pathology of Races in the United States." *MH* 6 (1922):370-91.

Bancroft, Charles P. "Presidential Address: Hopeful and Discouraging Aspects of the Psychiatric Outlook." *AJI* 65 (1908):1-14.

Bancroft, J. P. "Separate Provision for the Recent, the Curable, and the Appreciative Insane." *AJI* 46 (1889):177-92.

Barr, Martin W. "The Asexualization of the Unfit." *Alienist and Neurologist* 33 (1912):1-9.

———, "The Prevention of the Mental Defect. The Duty of the Hour." *Alienist and Neurologist* 36 (1915):357-64.

Bean, Robert B. "Some Racial Pecularities of the Negro Brain." *American*

Journal of Anatomy 5 (1906):353-432.

Bevis, W. M. "Psychological Traits of the Southern Negro with Observations as to Some of His Psychoses." *AJP* 78 (1921):69-77.

Billings, N. C. "The Medical Application of the Immigration Law." In *Eugenics in Race and State*, vol. II, pp. 397-401. Baltimore: Williams and Wilkins, 1923. Papers of the Second International Congress of Eugenics held at the American Museum of Natural History, New York, September 22-28, 1921.

Blumer, G. Alder. "Presidential Address." *AJI* 60 (1903):1-18.

Boller, Paul F., Jr. *American Thought in Transition: The Impact of Evolutionary Naturalism 1865-1900*. Chicago: Rand McNally, 1969. A good background study.

Brigham, Amariah. "Exemption of the Cherokee Indians and Africans from Insanity." *AJI* 1 (1845):287-88.

Brigham, Carl C. *A Study of American Intelligence*. Princeton: Princeton University Press, 1923.

Burr, Charles W. "The Foreign-Born Insane." *JAMA* 62 (Jan. 3, 1914):25-27.

_____, "The Prevention of Insanity and Degeneracy." *AJI* 75 (1918):409-24.

Cassedy, James H. *Charles V. Chapin and the Public Health Movement*. Cambridge, Mass.: Harvard University Press, 1962.

Davenport, Charles B., and Elizabeth B. Muncey. "Huntington's Chorea in Relation to Heredity and Eugenics." *AJI* 73 (1916):195-222.

Dawes, Spencer L. "The New Immigration Law." *State Hospital Quarterly* 2 (1917):366-70.

_____, "Immigration and the Problem of the Alien Insane." *State Hospital Quarterly* 10 (1925):199-214.

"Delegates from Fifteen States Form an Interstate Immigration Committee." *State Hospital Quarterly* 2 (1917):309-10.

Deutsch, Albert. "The First U.S. Census of the Insane (1840), and Its Use as Pro-Slavery Propaganda." *Bulletin of the History of Medicine* 15 (1944): 469-82.

"Discussion on Immigration Law." *State Hospital Bulletin* 5 (1912):148-53.

East, Edward M. *Mankind at the Crossroads*. New York: Scribner's, 1926.

Foster, Robert H. "Paresis in the Negro." *AJP* 82 (1926):631-40.

Fox, Richard W. *So Far Disordered in Mind. Insanity in California 1870-1930*. Berkeley: University of California Press, 1978.

Goodell, William. "Clinical Notes on the Extirpation of the Ovaries for Insanity." *AJI* 38 (1882):294-302.

Green, E. M. "Psychoses Among Negroes—a Comparative Study." *JNMD* 41 (1914):697-708.

Grob, Gerald N. "Class, Ethnicity, and Race in American Mental Hospitals, 1830-1875." *Journal of the History of Medicine and Allied Sciences* 28 (1973):207-29.

Grossett, Thomas F. *Race: The History of an Idea in America*. New York: Schocken Books, 1965.

Hall, G. Stanley. "The Negro in Africa and America." *Pedagogical Seminary* 12 (1905):350-68.

Haller, John S., Jr. "The Physician Versus the Negro: Medical and Anthropological Concepts of Race in the Late 19th Century." *Bulletin of the History of Medicine* 44 (1970):154-67. This study shows that medical opinion anticipated the extinction of blacks in America and that segregation was preparing them for that fate.

————, *Outcasts from Evolution: Scientific Attitudes of Racial Inferiority, 1859-1900*. Urbana: University of Illinois Press, 1971.

Haller, Mark H., Jr. *Eugenics: Hereditarian Attitudes in American Thought*. New Brunswick, N.J.: Rutgers University Press, 1963. A central book on the eugenics movement.

Higham, John. *Strangers in the Land. Patterns of American Nativism 1860-1925*. New York: Altheneum, 1963. The standard book on anti-immigration prejudice and campaigns to restrict immigration.

Hodges, J. Allison. "The Effect of Freedom upon the Physical and Psychological Development of the Negro." *Proceedings, American Medico-Psychological Association* (1900): 88-98.

Hofstadter, Richard. *Social Darwinism in American Thought*. Boston: Beacon Press, 1955. An essential background source.

Holmer, Samuel J. *The Trend of the Race*. New York: Harcourt, Brace, 1921.

"Immigration and the Care of the Insane." In *The Institutional Care of the Insane in the United States and Canada*, edited by Henry M. Hurd, vol. I, pp. 355-61. Baltimore: Johns Hopkins University Press, 1916.

"Immigration from a Mental Hygiene Standpoint." *JNMD* 52 (1920):501-07.

"Insanity Among the Negroes." In *The Institutional Care of the Insane in the United States and Canada*, edited by Henry M. Hurd, vol. I, pp. 371-80. Baltimore: Johns Hopkins University Press, 1916.

"Interstate Conference on Immigration." *State Hospital Quarterly* 9 (1923): 88-103.

Jarvis, Edward. "Insanity Among the Colored Population of the Free States." *American Journal of Medical Science* 7 (1844):71-83.

Kiernan, J. G. "Race and Insanity. The Negro Race." *JNMD* 12 (1885):290-93.

Kindred, John L. "Eugenics: Its Relation to Mental Diseases." *Proceedings, American Medico-Psychological Association* (1917): 425-45.

Kirby, George H. "A Study of Race Psychopathology." In *Studies in Psychiatry*. vol. I, pp. 9-15. New York: Journal of Nervous and Mental Disease Publishing Co., 1912.

Krauss, William. "Heredity—with a Study of the Statistics of the New York State Hospitals." *AJI* 58 (1902):607-23.

Laughlin, Harry H. "Nativity of Institutional Inmates." In *Eugenics in Race and State*, vol. II, pp. 402-06. Baltimore: Williams and Wilkins, 1923.

Ludmerer, Kenneth M. *Genetics and American Society*. Baltimore: Johns Hopkins University Press, 1972. A valuable study.

————, "Genetics, Eugenics, and the Immigration Restriction Act of 1924." *Bulletin of the History of Medicine* 46 (1972):59-81.

May, James V. "Immigration as a Problem in the State Care of the Insane." *AJI* 69 (1912):313-22.

Morton, Thomas G. "Removal of the Ovaries as a Cure for Insanity." *AJI* 49 (1893):397-401.

Newby, I. A. *Jim Crow's Defense: Anti-Negro Thought in America, 1900-1930*. Baton Rouge: Louisiana State University Press, 1965. An important history of race prejudice in America.

O'Malley, Mary. "Psychoses in the Colored Race. A Study in Comparative Psychiatry." *AJI* 71 (1914):307-37.

Pollock, Horatio M. "Eugenics as a Factor in the Prevention of Mental Disease." *State Hospital Quarterly* 7 (1921):13-19.

_____, "Mental Disease Among Negroes in the United States." *State Hospital Quarterly* II (1925):47-66.

_____, "Mental Disease in the United States as Shown by the Federal Census of 1923." *State Hospital Quarterly* 10 (1925):460-86.

Pollock, Horatio M., and William J. Nolan. "Sex, Age, and Nativity of Dementia Praecox First Admissions to New York State Hospitals, 1912 to 1918." *State Hospital Quarterly* 4 (1919):498-508.

Popenoe, Paul, and Roswell H. Johnson. *Applied Eugenics*. New York: Macmillan, 1918.

Postell, William D. *The Health of Slaves on Southern Plantations*. Baton Rouge: Louisiana State University Press, 1951.

_____, "Mental Health Among the Slave Population in Southern Plantations." *AJP* 110 (1953):52-54.

Powell, Theophilus O. "The Increase of Insanity and Tuberculosis in the Southern Negro Since 1860." *JAMA* 27 (Sept. 5, 1896):1185-88.

Report of the Board of Trustees of the Eastern Michigan Asylum at Pontiac. Lansing: W. S. George and Co., 1884.

Rice, Thurman B. *Racial Hygiene. A Practical Discussion of Eugenics and Race Culture*. New York: Macmillan, 1929.

Russell, James. "Is the Anglo-Saxon Race Degenerating?" *Proceedings, American Medico-Psychological Association* (1900): 106-17.

Salmon, Thomas W. "The Diagnosis of Insanity in Immigrants." In *Annual Report of the Surgeon-General of the Public Health and Marine Hospital Service of the United States*, pp. 271-78. 59th Cong., 1st sess. House Documents vol. 84, Document no. 320. Washington, D.C.: U.S. Government Printing Office, 1906.

_____, "The Relation of Immigration to the Prevalence of Insanity." *AJI* 64 (1907):53-71.

_____, "Insanity and the Immigration Law." *State Hospital Bulletin* 3 (1910): 379-98.

Savitt, Todd L. *Medicine and Slavery*. Urbana: University of Illinois Press, 1978.

Solis-Cohen, Rosebud T. "The Exclusion of Aliens from the United States for Physical Defects." *Bulletin of the History of Medicine* 21 (1947):33-50.

Spitzka, Edward C. "Race and Insanity." *JNMD* 7 (1880):613-30.

Stampp, Kenneth M. *The Peculiar Institution*. New York: Random House, 1956.

Stanton, William. *The Leopard's Spots. Scientific Attitudes Toward Race in America, 1815-1859*. Chicago: University of Chicago Press, 1960.

"Startling Facts from the Census." *AJI* 8 (1851):150-55.

Strong, Jamin. "Education as a Factor in the Prevention and Cure of Insanity." *AJI* 42 (1885):114-39.

Swados, Felice. "Negro Health on the Ante-Bellum Plantations." *Bulletin of the History of Medicine* 10 (1941):460-72.

Sweeney, Arthur. "Mental Tests for Immigrants." *North American Review* 215 (1922):600-12.

Swift, H. M. "Insanity and Race." *AJI* 70 (1913):143-54.

U.S. Public Health Service. *Manual of the Mental Examination of Aliens 1918.* Miscellaneous Publication no. 18. Washington, D.C.: U.S. Government Printing Office, 1918.

————, *Mental Hygiene with Special Reference to the Migration of People.* Public Health Bulletin no. 148. Washington, D.C.: U.S. Government Printing Office, 1925.

Ward, Robert. "Some Thoughts on Immigration Restriction." *Scientific Monthly* 15 (1922):13-19.

White, William A. "The Geographical Distribution of Insanity in the United States." *JNMD* 30 (1903):257-79.

Wilgus, Sidney D. "The Problem of Immigration." *State Hospital Bulletin* 3 (1910):117-37.

Williams, L. L. "The Medical Examination of Mentally Defective Aliens: Its Scope and Limitations." *AJI* 71 (1914):257-68.

Willie, Charles V., Bernard M. Kramer, and Bertram S. Brown. *Racism and Mental Health.* Pittsburgh: University of Pittsburgh Press, 1973.

Witmer, A. H. "Insanity in the Colored Race in the United States." *Alienist and Neurologist* 12 (1891):19-30.

Woodruff, Charles E. "An Anthropological Study of the Small Brain of Civilized Man and Its Evolution." *AJI* 58 (1901):1-77.

Young, Kimball. "Intelligence Tests of Certain Immigrant Groups." *Scientific Monthly* 15 (1922):417-34.

CHAPTER 6

Abbot, E. Stanley. "Out Patient or Dispensary Clinics for Mental Cases." *AJI* 77 (1920):217-25.

Alford, Leland B. "Dr. E. E. Southard's Scientific Contributions to Psychiatry. An Appreciation After Twenty Years." *AJP* 92 (1935):675-94.

Bardeen, C. R. "Scientific Work in Public Institutions for the Care of the Insane." *AJI* 55 (1899):465-79.

Barker, L. F. "Some Experiences with the Simpler Methods of Psychotherapy and Re-education." *American Journal of Modern Science* 132 (1906):499-522.

Barrett, Albert M. "The Psychopathic Hospital." *AJI* 77 (1921):309-20.

————, "The Broadened Interests of Psychiatry." *AJP* 79 (1922):1-13.

Braceland, Francis J. "Kraepelin, His System and His Influence." *AJP* 113 (1957):871-76.

Briggs, L. Vernon. "Observation Hospital for Mental Disease." *Boston Medical and Surgical Journal* 154 (1906):696-702.

Briggs, L. Vernon, and A. Warren Stearns. "Recent Extension of Out-Patient Work in Massachusetts State Hospitals for the Insane and Feeble-Minded." *AJI* 72 (1915):35-43.

Briggs, L. Vernon, et al. *History of the Psychopathic Hospital, Boston, Massachusetts*. Boston: Wright and Potter, 1922.

Burnham, John C. "Psychiatry, Psychology, and the Progressive Movement." *American Quarterly* 12 (1960):457-65. A seminal article.

Burns, Chester R. "Richard Clarke Cabot (1868-1939) and the Reformation in American Medical Ethics." *Bulletin of the History of Medicine* 51 (1977): 353-68.

Campbell, C. Macfie. "Adolf Meyer." *Archives of Neurology and Psychiatry* 37 (Apr. 1937):715-24.

Channing, Walter. "Some Remarks on the Address Delivered to the American Medico-Psychological Association, by S. Weir Mitchell, M.D., May 16, 1894." *AJI* 51 (1894):171-81.

Cowles, Edward. "The Advancement of Psychiatry in America." *AJI* 52 (1896): 364-84.

Cunningham, Raymond J. "The Emmanuel Movement: A Variety of American Religious Experience." *American Quarterly* 14 (1962):48-63.

Dana, Charles L. "The Future of Neurology." *JNMD* 40 (1913):753-57.

Earnest, Ernest. *S. Weir Mitchell: Novelist and Physician*. Philadelphia: University of Pennsylvania Press, 1950.

Fifth Biennial Report of the Board of Trustees of the State Psychopathic Hospital at the University of Michigan. Lansing, 1917.

First Biennial Report of the Board of Trustees of the State Psychopathic Hospital at the University of Michigan. Lansing, 1909.

Fourth Biennial Report of the Board of Trustees of the State Psychopathic Hospital at the University of Michigan. Lansing, 1915.

Fox, Richard W. *So Far Disordered in Mind. Insanity in California 1870-1930*. Berkeley: University of California Press, 1978.

Grob, Gerald N. "Adolf Meyer on American Psychiatry in 1895." *AJP* 119 (1963):1135-42.

Hall, G. Stanley. *Adolescence. Its Psychology and Its Relation to Physiology, Anthropology, Sociology, Sex, Crime, Religion and Education*. New York: Appleton, 1904.

Healy, William. *The Individual Delinquent: A Text-book of Diagnosis and Prognosis for all Concerned in Understanding Offenders*. Boston: Little, Brown, 1915.

———, "The Newer Psychiatry." *AJP* 82 (1926):391-401.

Hill, Charles G. "Presidential Address." *AJI* 64 (1907):1-8.

Hinkle, Beatrice. "Psychotherapy, with Some of Its Results." *JAMA* 50 (May 9, 1908):1495-98.

Hurd, Henry H. "The Care of Cases of Mental Disease in General Hospitals." *Mod H* 5 (1915):33-35.

Jarrett, Mary C. "The Psychiatric Thread Running Through All Social Case Work." *Proceedings, National Conference of Social Work* 46 (1919):587-93.

Kline, George M. "Social Service in the State Hospital." *AJI* 73 (1917):567-81.

Lief, Alfred, ed. *The Commonsense Psychiatry of Dr. Adolf Meyer*. New York: McGraw-Hill, 1948.

Lubove, Roy. *The Professional Altruist: The Emergence of Social Work as a Career 1880-1930*. Cambridge, Mass.: Harvard University Press, 1965.

MacDonald, Carlos F. "President's Address." *AJI* 71 (1914):1-12.

May, James V. "Some of the More Recent Problems Connected with the State Care of the Insane." *AJI* 72 (1915):315-23.

_____, "The Functions of the Psychopathic Hospital." *AJI* 76 (1919):21-34.

Meyer, Adolf. "After-Care and Prophylaxis and the Hospital Physician." *JNMD* 34 (1907):113-16.

_____, "Reception Hospitals, Psychopathic Wards and Psychopathic Hospitals." *AJI* 64 (1907):221-30.

Mitchell, S. Weir. *Wear and Tear, or Hints for the Overworked.* Philadelphia: Lippincott, 1871.

_____, *Fat and Blood: An Essay on the Treatment of Certain Forms of Neurasthenia and Hysteria.* Philadelphia: Lippincott, 1884.

_____, "Address Before the Fiftieth Annual Meeting of the American Medico-Psychological Association, Held in Philadelphia, May 16, 1894." *JNMD* 21 (1894):413-37.

Mosher, J. Montgomery. "A Consideration of the Need of Better Provision for the Treatment of Mental Disease in Its Early Stage." *AJI* 45 (1909): 499-508.

_____, "The Treatment of Mental Disease in a General Hospital." *Mod H* 5 (1915):327-32.

Page, Charles W. "The Adverse Consequences of Repression." *AJI* 20 (1893): 373-90.

Prince, Morton, ed. *Psychotherapeutics.* Boston: Richard G. Badger, 1912.

_____, "The Subconscious Settings of Ideas in Relation to the Pathology of the Psychoneuroses." *Journal of Abnormal Psychology* 11 (1916):1-18.

Pumphrey, Ralph E. "Social Work and Mental Illness, 1890-1919." In *Transactions. Conference Group for Social and Administrative History* edited by, Werner Braatz. vol. III, pp. 15-27. Madison: State Historical Society of Wisconsin, 1973.

Riese, Walther. "History and Principles of Classification of Nervous Disease." *Bulletin of the History of Medicine* 18 (1945): 465-512.

_____, "An Outline of a History of Ideas in Psychotherapy." *Bulletin of the History of Medicine* 25 (1951):442-56.

Ross, Dorothy. *G. Stanley Hall. The Psychologist as Prophet.* Chicago: University of Chicago Press, 1972.

Rowe, J. T. W. "Is Dementia Praecox the 'New Peril' in Psychiatry?" *AJI* 63 (1907):385-93.

Russell, William L. "The Widening Field of Practical Psychiatry." *AJI* 70 (1913):459-66.

Salmon, Thomas W. "Some New Fields in Neurology and Psychiatry." *JNMD* 46 (1917):90-99.

Schneck, Jerome M. "William Osler, S. Weir Mitchell, and the Origin of the Rest Cure." *AJP* 119 (1963):894-95.

Second Biennial Report of the Board of Trustees of the State Psychopathic Hospital at the University of Michigan. Lansing, 1911.

Sicherman, Barbara. "From Asylum to Community: Changing Psychiatric Goals, 1880-1921." In *Transactions. Conference Group for Social and Administrative History*, edited by Werner Braatz. vol.III, Madison: State

Historical Society of Wisconsin, 1973.

Sixth Biennial Report of the Board of Trustees of the State Psychopathic Hospital at the University of Michigan. Lansing, 1919.

Southard, Elmer E. "The Psychopathic Hospital Idea." *JAMA* 61 (Nov. 29, 1913):1972-75.

Sweeney, George H. "Pioneering General Hospital Psychiatry." *Psychiatric Quarterly Supplement* 36 (1962):209-68.

Taylor, Edward W. "The Attitude of the Medical Profession Toward the Psychotherapeutic Movement." *Boston Medical and Surgical Journal* 157 (Dec. 5, 1907):843-50.

Third Biennial Report of the Board of Trustees of the State Psychopathic Hospital at the University of Michigan. Lansing, 1912.

Tilney, Frederick. "Opportunities in Neurology." *JNMD* 46 (1917):81-89.

Veith, Ilza. "S. Weir Mitchell, Psychiatrist of Women." *Modern Medicine* 30 (1962):234-50.

Walter, Richard D. *S. Weir Mitchell, M.D.-Neurologist.* Springfield, Ill.: Charles C. Thomas, 1970.

White, William A. "The Problem of the Individual Patient in Large Hospitals." *AJI* 75 (1917):405-07.

Winters, Eunice E., ed. *The Collected Papers of Adolf Meyer.* 4 vols. Baltimore: Johns Hopkins University Press, 1950-52.

_____, "Adolf Meyer's Two and a Half Years at Kankakee." *Bulletin of the History of Medicine* 40 (1966):441-58.

CHAPTER 7

Abbott, E. Stanley. "Program for Mental Hygiene in the Public Schools." *MH* 4 (1920):320-30.

Auer, E. M. "Some of the Nervous and Mental Conditions Arising in the Present War." *MH* 1 (1917):383-88.

Bailey, Pearce. "Care of Disabled Returned Soldiers." *MH* 1 (1917):345-54.

_____, "Efficiency and Inefficiency—a Problem in Medicine." *MH* 1 (1917): 196-210.

_____, "Care and Disposition of the Military Insane." *MH* 2 (1918):345-58.

Bailey, Pearce, and Thomas W. Salmon. *Neuropsychiatry. The Military.* Department of the United States Army in the World War, vol. 10. Washington, D.C.: U.S. Government Printing Office, 1929. This is an important mine of information and contains an extensive bibliography on "American contributions to war neuropsychiatry."

Barker, C. F. "How to Avoid Spoiling the Child." *MH* 3 (1919):240-52.

Barker, Lewellys F. "The Wider Field of Work of the National Committee for Mental Hygiene." *MH* 1 (1917):4-6.

_____, The First Ten Years of the National Committee For Mental Hygiene, with Some Comments on Its Future." *MH* 2 (1918):557-81.

Beers, Clifford W. *A Mind That Found Itself.* New York: Doubleday, 1937. This Edition of the 1908 original publication contains articles that provide a historical perspective on the mental hygiene movement.

Bernard, Harold W. "College Mental Hygiene—a Decade of Growth." *MH* 24 (1940):413-18.

Bingham, Anne T. "The Application of Psychiatry to High School Problems." *MH* 9 (1925):1-27.

Bingham, W. V. "Achievements of Industrial Psychology." *MH* 14 (1930): 369-83.

Bliss, Malcolm A. "What the Mental Hygiene Movement Has Meant in Missouri." *AJP* 82 (1926):625-29.

Bond, E. D. *Thomas W. Salmon: Psychiatrist.* New York: W. W. Norton, 1950. A general biography of an important mental hygiene leader.

Bromberg, Walter. *The Mind of Man: A History of Psychotherapy and Psychoanalysis.* New York: Harper and Brothers, 1959. A popular account.

Brown, Sanger. "Nervous and Mental Disorders of Soldiers." *MH* 2 (1920):404-33.

————. "Community Work in Mental Hygiene." *Psychiatric Quarterly* 7 (1933):547-62.

Burnham, John C. "The Beginnings of Psychoanalysis in the United States." *American Imago* 13 (Spring 1956):65-68.

————. *Psychoanalysis and Medicine: 1894-1918. Medicine, Science, and Culture.* New York: International Universities Press, 1967. An indispensable and exhaustive study.

————. "The Struggle Between Physicians and Paramedical Personnel in American Psychiatry, 1917-41." *Journal of the History of Medicine and Allied Sciences* 29 (1974):93-106.

————. "The Influence of Psychoanalysis upon American Culture." In *American Psychoanalysis: Origins and Development*, edited by Jacques M. Quen and Eric T. Carlson, pp. 52-72. New York: Brunner Mazel, 1978.

Burnham, W. H. "Mental Health for Children." *MH* 2 (1918):19-22.

Campbell, C. Macfie. "Educational Methods and the Fundamental Causes of Dependency." *MH* 1 (1917):235-40.

————. "Education and Mental Hygiene." *MH* 3 (1919):398-408.

———— "The Responsibilities of the Universities in Promoting Mental Hygiene." *MH* 3 (1919):199-209.

————. "Mental Hygiene in Industry." *MH* 5 (1921):468-96.

Davies, Stanley P. "Mental Hygiene and Social Progress." *MH* 13 (1929):225-49.

Davis, Kingsley. "Mental Hygiene and the Class Structure." *Psychiatry* 1 (Feb. 1938):55-65.

Deutsch, Albert. "The History of Mental Hygiene." In *One Hundred Years of American Psychiatry*, edited by J. K. Hall, et al., pp. 325-66. New York: Columbia University Press, 1944.

Fisher, B. "Has Mental Hygiene a Practical Use in Industry." *MH* 5 (1921):479-96.

Gesell, Arnold. "Mental Hygiene and the Public School." *MH* 3 (1919):4-10.

————. "The Kindergarten as a Mental Hygiene Agency." *MH* 10 (1926):27-37.

Gifford, George E., Jr., ed. *Psychoanalysis, Psychotherapy, and the New England Medical Scene, 1894-1944.* New York: Science History Publications, 1978.

Glueck, Bernard. "Psychiatric Aims in the Field of Criminology." *MH* 2 (1918):

546-56.

_____, "Constructive Possibilities of a Mental Hygiene of Childhood." *MH* 8 (1924):648-67.

Gursslin, O., R. Hunt, and J. Roach. "Social Class, Mental Hygiene, and Psychiatric Practice." *Social Science Review* 33 (Sept. 1959):237-44. A study relating mental hygiene themes and activities to a middle-class value system.

Hale, Nathan G., Jr. *Freud and the Americans. The Beginnings of Psychoanalysis in the United States, 1876-1917.* New York: Oxford University Press, 1971. A carefully researched study.

Jarrett, Mary C. "The Educational Value of Psychiatric Social Work." *MH* 5 (1921):509-18.

Kindred, John Joseph. "The Neuro-Psychiatric and Disabled Wards of the United States Government. The Present Status of Their Medical Care, Hospitalization, Rehabilitation, and Compensation Disability." *AJP* 83 (1927):711-24.

Kline, George F. "The Function of the Social Worker in Relation to a State Program." *MH* 3 (1919):618-26.

Lord, John R. "The Human Factor in International Relations." *MH* 18 (1934): 177-88.

Meyer, Adolf. "The Birth and Development of the Mental Hygiene Movement." *MH* 19 (1935):29-37.

Oberndorf, C. P. *A History of Psychoanalysis in America.* New York: Grune and Stratton, 1953.

Powers, Margaret J. "The Industrial Cost of the Psychopathic Employee." *MH* 4 (1920):932-39.

Pratt, George K. "The Problem of the Mental Misfit in Industry." *MH* 6 (1922): 526-78.

_____, "Twenty Years of the National Committee for Mental Hygiene." *MH* 14 (1930):417-28.

"Progress in Mental Hygiene 1919." *Mod H* 14 (Mar. 1920):197-203.

Richards, Esther Loring. "What Has Mental Hygiene to Offer Childhood at the End of 1926?" *MH* 11 (1927):1-14.

Rivers, W. H. R. "War Neurosis and Military Training." *MH* 2 (1918):513-33.

Russell, William L. "What the State Hospital Can Do in Mental Hygiene." *MH* 1 (1917):88-95.

_____, "Community Responsibilities in the Treatment of Mental Disorders." *MH* 2 (1918):416-25.

Salmon, Thomas W. "Insane in a County Poor Farm." *MH* 1 (1917):16-24.

_____, "Use of Institutions for the Insane as Military Hospitals." *MH* 1 (1917): 354-63.

"Schoolroom Hazards and the Mental Health of Children." *MH* 12 (1928):18-24.

Schwab, Sidney I. "Influence of War upon Concepts of Mental Diseases and Neuroses." *MH* 4 (1920):654-69.

Seely, John R. ."Social Values, the Mental Hygiene Movement and Mental Health." *Annals of the American Academy of Political and Social Science* 286 (Mar. 1953):15-25.

Singer, H. D. "The Function of the Social Worker in Relation to the State

Hospital." *MH* 3 (1919):609-17.

Southard, E. E. "Mental Hygiene and Social Work." *MH* 2 (1918):388-406.

———, "The Modern Specialist in Unrest: A Place for the Psychiatrist in Industry." *MH* (1920):550-63.

———, "Trade Unionism and Temperament." *MH* 4 (1920):281-300.

Spaulding, Edith. "The Training of the Psychiatric Social Worker." *MH* 3 (1919):420-35.

"Spirtual Values and Mental Hygiene." *MH* 14 (1930):779-90.

Stevenson, George. "Role of Community Clinics in Mental Hygiene." *JAMA* 96 (Mar. 28, 1931):997-99.

Strecker, E. A. "Military Psychiatry: World War I." In *One Hundred Years of American Psychiatry,* edited by J. K. Hall et al., pp. 385-418. New York: Columbia University Press, 1944.

Swile, Ira. "Laziness in School Children." *MH* 6 (1922):68-82.

Taft, J. "Qualifications of the Psychiatric Social Worker." *MH* 3 (1919):427-35.

Thompson, C. Mildred. "The Value of Mental Hygiene in the College." *MH* 11 (1927):225-40.

Truitt, Ralph P. "Mental Hygiene and the Public Schools." *MH* 11 (1927):261-71.

"Twenty-Fifth Anniversary Celebration of the National Committee for Mental Hygiene." *MH* 19 (1935):1-37.

Viteles, M. S. "Psychology and Psychiatry in Industry." *MH* 13 (1929):367-77.

White, William A. "The State Hospital and the War." *MH* 1 (1917):377-82.

———, "Underlying Concepts in Mental Hygiene." *MH* 1 (1917):7-15.

———, "Childhood: The Golden Period for Mental Hygiene." *MH* 4 (1920): 257-67.

Williams, Frankwood E. "Mental Hygiene: An Attempt at a Definition." *MH* 11 (1927):482-88.

Winters, Eunice E. "Adolf Meyer and Clifford Beers, 1907-1910." *Bulletin of the History of Medicine* 36 (1962):414-43.

Yerkes, Robert. "How We May Discover the Children Who Need Special Care." *MH* 1 (1917):252-59.

CHAPTER 8

Allison, Wilmer L. "What Texas Has not Done for Her Insane." *Texas State Journal of Medicine* 2 (1925):479-83.

Anderson, C. H. "Methods of Limiting Changes in Hospital Personnel." *AJP* 82 (1926):641-46.

"Annual Congress on Medical Education, Medical Licensure, and Hospitals." *JAMA* 9 (Apr. 11, 1931):1235.

"Arguments for More Teaching of Psychiatry." *New England Journal of Medicine* 211 (Oct. 18, 1934):739-40.

Ashworth, W. C. "The Recognition, Diagnosis, and Treatment of Mental Disorders." *Southern Medical Journal* 16 (1923):754-56.

Barber, T. M. "Some Responsibilities of the General Practitioner in the Care of Mental Patients." *Nebraska Surgical and Medical Journal* 18 (May 1932):

175-78.

Baskett, George T. "The Depression and Mental Health." *Mental Health Bulletin* 13 (Apr. 15, 1935):5-7.

Bell, J. H. "Mental Diseases from the Standpoint of the General Practitioner." *Virginia Medical Monthly* 58 (1931):283-86.

Berman, Harold H. "Treatment of Psychoneurosis in State Hospitals." *Psychiatric Quarterly* 9 (1935):105-15.

Biscoe, Maurice B. "Colorado Plans State Psychopathic Hospital." *Mod H* 22 (Apr. 1924):367-70.

Blalock, Joseph R. "A Program for Adequate Prevention and Better Treatment of Mental Illness." *Virginia Medical Monthly* 65 (1938):467-71.

Bliss, M. A. "Nutrition in Mental Hospitals." *AJP* 90 (1934):1175-81.

Bock, Arlie V. "Psychiatry in Private Practice." *New England Journal of Medicine* 208 (May 25, 1933):1092-94.

Bond, Mabel A. M. "How Occupational Therapy Is Used in the Mental Hospital." *Mod H* 30 (June 1928):81-82.

Bonsteel, Ruth M. "A Recreation-Occupational-Therapy Project at a State Hospital Under WPA Auspices." *MH* 24 (1940):552-65.

Bowen, A. L. "Recreation Is an Asset in the Care of the Mental Patient." *Mod H* 30 (Jan. 1928):69-72.

Brenner, M. Harvey. *Mental Illness and the Economy*. Cambridge, Mass.: Harvard University Press, 1973.

Brewster, George F. "Physical Features, Administration, and Work of a US Veterans' Psychiatric Hospital." *Psychiatric Quarterly* 3 (1929):40-48.

Briggs, L. Vernon. "Occupational and Industrial Therapy. How Can This Important Branch of Treatment of Our Mentally Ill Be Extended and Improved?" *AJI* 74 (1918):459-79.

_____. *Occupation as a Substitute for Restraint in the Treatment of the Mentally Ill*. Boston: Wright and Potter, 1923.

Brown, Frederick W. "General Hospital Facilities for Mental Patients." *MH* 15 (1931):378-84.

Brown, Sanger. "Specialism Within the Field of Psychiatry." *AJP* 84 (1928): 583-90.

Burlingame, C. C., and C. P. Wagner. "The Psychiatric Hospital as an Institute of Learning." *JAMA* 105 (Nov. 9, 1935):1509-11.

Burnham, John C. "The New Psychology: From Narcissism to Social Control." In *Change and Continuity in Twentieth Century America: The 1920's* edited by John Braeman, Robert H. Bremner, and David Brody, pp. 351-98. Columbus: Ohio State University Press, 1968.

Campbell, John D. "Psychiatry and General Practice." *JAMA* 112 (June 24, 1939):2578-81.

Carter, F. G. "Should the General Hospital Treat Mental and Contagious Cases?" *Mod H* 39 (July 1932):45-48.

Chapman, Ross. "Psychoanalysis in Psychiatric Hospitals." *AJP* 91 (1935): 1093-1101.

Colomb, H. O. "The Utilization of the State Hospital in the Training of Psychiatrists." *MH* (1940):390-412.

Crabtree, Walter P., and Roy L. Leak. "Connecticut's New Mental Hospital

Strives for Home Touch." *Mod H* 42 (May 1934):45-52.

Cumming, Hugh S. "Mental Disorders and the Public Health." *Public Health Reports* 45 (Apr. 4, 1930):726-734.

Daspit, Henry. "What the State Is not Doing for Its Mentally Diseased." *New Orleans Medical and Surgical Journal* 76 (Sept. 1923):144-48.

Davis, John Eisele. "Supervised Exercise as an Aid to the Mentally Ill." *Mod H* 32 (June 1929):81-82.

――――. "The Value of Physical Education for the Mentally Ill." *Mod H* 35 (Nov. 1930):79-84.

Dorn, Harold F. "The Incidence and Future Expectancy of Mental Disease." *Public Health Reports* 53 (Nov. 11, 1939):1991-2004.

Duncan, Dean H. "Psychoneuroses in General Practice." *New Orleans Medical and Surgical Journal* 83 (Dec. 1930):379-82.

Dunn, Miriam. "Psychiatric Treatment of the Effects of the Depression: Its Possibilities and Limitations." *MH* 18 (1934):279-86.

"Duty of the General Hospital to the Mentally Ill." *Mod H* 53 (Sept. 1939):93.

"The Duty of the General Hospital Toward Mental Cases." *Mod H* 34 (Feb. 1930):20.

Dynes, John B. "Mental Disorders in the CCC Camps." *MH* 23 (1939):363-70.

Ebaugh, Franklin G. "The Crisis in Psychiatric Education." *JAMA* 99 (Aug. 27, 1932):703-07.

――――. "The Mental Hospital Educates Its Staff." *Mod H* 46 (Mar. 1936):71-74.

Ebaugh, Franklin G., and Charles A. Rymer. "Teaching and Research in State Hospitals." *AJP* 96 (1939):535-49.

"Economic Conditions Blamed for Increase of Mental Patients." *Mod H* 36 (Feb. 1931):74.

"The Effect of the Depression on Health." *Psychiatric Quarterly Supplement* 7 (Apr. 1933):160-61.

Emch, Minna. "The Role of Occupational Therapy in Modern Psychiatry." *AJP* 92 (1935):207-14.

Erickson, Milton H., and R. G. Hoskins. "Grading of Patients in Mental Hospitals as a Therapeutic Measure." *AJP* 88 (1931):103-09.

Erikson, Carl A. "The Psychiatric Department of Christ Hospital, Topeka, Kansas." *Mod H* 23 (July 1924):5-7.

Farrar, C. B. "Ways to Remove the Stigma Attached to Mental Illness." *Mod H* 37 (Aug. 1931):75-78.

Frost, Henry P. "Occupation of Patients in State Hospitals for the Insane." *Mod H* 5 (Sept. 1915):151-55.

Furbush, Edith M. "General Paralysis in State Hospitals for Mental Disease." *MH* 7 (1923):565-78.

Gardner, W. E. "A Decade of Transition in American Psychiatry." *Southern Medical Journal* 22 (1920):31-35.

Garvin, William C. "The Veterans Memorial Hospital at the Kings Park State Hospital, Kings Park, New York." *MH* 9 (1925):387-400.

――――. "Treatment of Mental Patients in New York State Hospitals." *New York State Journal of Medicine* 30 (Jan. 1, 1930);16-19.

――――. "How a Mental Hospital Disseminates Mental Hygiene Knowledge." *Mod H* 38 (Jan. 1932):89-92.

Gayle, R. Finley. "The Problem in Caring for the Mentally Sick in Virginia." *Virginia Medical Monthly* 66 (1939):6-12.

Ginsburg, Sol Wiener. "What Unemployment Does to People." *AJP* 99 (1942): 439-46.

Gosline, Harold I. "The Laboratory Service in State Hospitals for Mental Diseases." *AJP* 79 (1922):409-23.

Grimes, John M. *Institutional Care of Mental Patients in the United States.* Chicago: John M. Grimes, 1934.

Haas, Louis J. "Occupational Therapy—a Field of Endeavor for Men." *Mod H* 25 (July 1925):357-59.

Hall, Roscoe W. "The Organization of Psychotherapy." *AJP* 90 (1933):671-77.

Hamilton, Samuel W. "Psychopathic Building of the Gallinger Municipal Hospital, Washington, D.C." *Mod H* 22 (Feb. 1924):134-140.

_____. "Common Errors in Planning Mental Hospitals." *Mod H* 24 (May 1925):420-25.

_____. "Psychiatry Before World War II." *JNMD* 101 (1945):416-28.

Hamilton, Samuel W., and Grover A. Kempf. "Trends in the Activities of Mental Hospitals." *AJP* 96 (1939):551-74.

Harris, Isham G. "Some Principles Applicable to the Planning of Hospitals for Mental Disease." *Mod H* 22 (Mar. 1924):228-30.

Harrison, I. C. "The General Practititoner in Relation to Mental Hygiene." *Virginia Medical Monthly* 59 (1933):592-94.

Hart-Stone, Esther. "Selecting Nurses for Mental Hospitals." *Mod H* 30 (Apr. 1928):85-86.

Haskell, Robert H. "Present Needs in Michigan for the Care of the Insane and Feebleminded." *Journal of the Michigan State Medical Society* 27 (Dec. 1928):793-98.

Heldt, Thomas J. "The Functioning of a Division of Neuropsychiatry in a General Hospital." *AJP* 84 (1927):460-81.

_____. "Psychiatric Services in General Hospitals." *AJP* 95 (1939):865-71.

"Helping the Mentally Ill to Become Self-Supporting." *Mod H* 25 (Nov. 1925): 383-85.

Henry, H. C. "Current Methods of Treating Mental Cases in Virginia." *Virginia Medical Monthly* 65 (1938):664-67.

Heyman, M. B. "Some Problems of Hospital Personnel." *AJP* 80 (1923):199-210.

Hill, E. L. "Patient Labor In Hospitals for the Insane." *Mod H* 10 (Jan. 1918): 1-4.

Hill, Lewis B. "Obstacles to Psychotherapy." *AJP* 90 (1933):679-83.

Hincks, C. M. "What Mental and General Hospitals Can Learn from Each Other." *Mod H* 37 (Sept. 1931):57-60.

Hinsie, Leland E. "The Treatment of Schizophrenia. A Survey of the Literature." *Psychiatric Quarterly* 3 (1929):5-39.

Hoffman, Harry F. "Physical Therapy." *AJP* 91 (1934):59-71.

Holland, John A. "Physical Treatment of Mental Illness." *New England Journal of Medicine* 205 (Aug. 20, 1931):371-73.

Hollingworth, H. L. *Vocational Psychology and Character Analysis.* New York: Appleton, 1929.

"The Hospital Farm." *Mental Health Bulletin* 8 (Jan. 15, 1931):12.
"Hospitals for Nervous and Mental Patients." *JAMA* 100 (Mar. 25, 1933):895, 901-10.
"How a Famous Hospital Is Curing Paresis." *Mod H* 39 (July 1932):82.
"How Shall Research Be Promoted in the Mental Hospital." *Mod H* 30 (Apr. 1928):146.
Hunt, Clement W. "Pennsylvania's Mental Hospital Farms." *Mental Health Bulletin* 8 (Jan. 15, 1931):5-7.
Hutchings, Richard H. "Psychotherapy in Public Mental Hospitals." *AJP* 90 (1933):659-65.
"Incidence and Future Expectancy of Mental Disease." *JAMA* 112 (Jan. 14, 1939):146-47.
Ireland, G. O. "Bibliotherapy as an Aid in Treating Mental Cases." *Mod H* 34 (June 1930):87-91.
Jackson, J. Allen. "Modern Methods Alleviate the Lot of the Mentally Ill." *Mod H* 29 (Dec. 1927):73-75.
_____, "Outlining the Staff Functions in a Mental Hospital." *Mod H* 30 (Feb. 1928):60-62.
_____, "The Role of the State Hospital in Mental Hygiene." *JAMA* 96 (Mar. 28, 1931):1000-02.
_____, "Where Science and Sympathy Join to Prevent Mental Ills." *Mod H* 36 (May 1931):77-80.
Jackson, J. Allen, and H. V. Pike. "Community Service Activities of the Danville State Hospital." *MH* 10 (1926):130-42.
Jaffary, Stewart K. *The Mentally Ill and Public Provision for Their Care in Illinois.* Chicago: University of Chicago Press, 1942.
Jones, Sullivan, and Howard Scott. "Functional Planning of Hospitals for Mental Disease." *AJP* 81 (1924):317-31.
Jones, W. A. "Care and Treatment of the Psychoneurotic." *Minnesota Medicine* 8 (Sept. 1925):577-83.
Kamm, Alfred. "Physical Education in a State Hospital for the Mentally Disturbed." *Mental Health Bulletin* 10 (Jan. 15, 1933):15-23.
Kasanin, J. "The Problem of Research in Mental Hospitals." *AJP* 92 (1935):397-405.
Kindwall, Josef A., and George W. Henry. "Wet Packs and Prolonged Baths." *AJP* 91 (1934):72-94.
Komora, Paul O., and Mary Augusta Clark. "Mental Disease in the Crisis." *MH* 19 (1935):289-301.
Kopeloff, N., and C. O. Cheney. "Studies in Focal Infection: Its Presence and Elimination in the Functional Psychoses." *AJP* 79 (1922):139-56.
LaRue, F. G. "Justice for the Insane! Are the Hospitals for the Insane in Kentucky Mere Custodial Institutions." *Kentucky Medical Journal* 27 (1929):573-75.
Leahy, Sylvester R. "How Mental Problems Are Solved in the General Hospital." *Mod H* 27 (Oct. 1926):63-67.
Lewis, Nolan D. C. "A Brief Review of the Research and Teaching Functions of the New York State Psychiatric Institute and Hospital for the Ten Year Period 1930-1940." *Psychiatric Quarterly* 14 (1940):360-81.

Lunt, Lawrence K. "The Psychoneuroses in General Practice." *New England Journal of Medicine* 203 (Aug. 14, 1930):301-06.

Lutgens, Harry. "Administrative Conditions and Problems of the California Mental Hospitals." *AJP* 95 (1939):1103-18.

Luther, Jessie. "Occupational Treatment in Nervous Disorders." *Mod H* 11 (July 1918):11-15.

Lyday, June F., and Maida H. Solomon. "The Problem of the Supply of Psychiatric Social Workers for State Hospitals." *AJP* 84 (1928):629-38.

MacPherson, Donald J. "Psychiatry in Relation to Hospital Practice." *New England Journal of Medicine* 208 (May 25, 1933):1091-92.

Marsh, L. Cody. "Practical Aspects of Psychiatry for the General Practitioner." *New England Journal of Medicine* 206 (June 30, 1932):1337-42.

_____. "An Experiment in the Group Treatment of Patients at the Worcester State Hospital." *MH* 17 (1933):396-416.

McDougall, George B. "Special Housing for Psychopathic Patients." *Mod H* 50 (Mar. 1938):58-61.

McGarr, T. E. "Fifty Years of Development in the Care of the Insane in New York State, 1878-1928." *Psychiatric Quarterly* 3 (1929):98-112.

McGraw, Robert B., and Agnes Conrad. "Occupational Therapy—Wise and Unwise." *Mod H* 48 (Jan. 1937):77-80.

McKinnis, C. R. "The Mental Hospital Farm from the Superintendent's Viewpoint." *Mental Health Bulletin* 8 (Jan. 15, 1931):8-9.

Menninger, Karl A. "The Place of the Psychiatric Department in the General Hospital." *Mod H* 22 (July 1924):1-4.

Menninger, William C. "Doing Right by the Neurotic Patient." *Mod H* 48 (Jan. 1937):81-83.

Menninger, William C., and Leona Chidester. "The Role of Financial Losses in the Precipitation of Mental Illness." *JAMA* 100 (May 6, 1933):1398-1400.

"Mental Health in Hard Times." *American Journal of Public Health* 22 (June 1932):634-37.

"Mental Hospital Survey." *AJP* 93 (1936):470-73.

"A Mental Hospital That Has Been Planned Along Strictly Modern Lines." *Mod H* 44 (Jan. 1935):40-48.

"Mental Hygiene and the Depression." *American Journal of Public Health* 22 (Apr. 1932):393.

Meyers, Garry Cleveland. "The Present Crisis and the Mental Health of the School Child." *MH* 18 (1934):294-98.

Michael, J. C. "Mental Hygiene and the General Practitioner." *Minnesota Medicine* 5 (Apr. 1922):240-42.

Mitchell, H. W. "Diagnostic and Therapeutic Requirements in Hospitals for Mental Illness." *Mental Health Bulletin* 8 (Apr. 30, 1930):6-11.

"More Patients in Mental Than in General Hospitals." *Mod H* 36 (Mar. 1931):62.

Myers, Harry J. "Providing Dental Health for Mental Patients." *Mental Health Bulletin* 9 (Oct. 15, 1931):7-9.

Newer, Bernard. "The Need of a Personnel Program for State Institutions." *MH* 20 (1936):55-61.

Noyles, Arthur P. "Psychotherapy in State Hospitals." *AJP* 91 (1935):1353-66.

O'Hara, J. A. "Insanity Responsibility." *New Orleans Medical and Surgical*

Journal 79 (July 1926):43-46.

O'Malley, Mary. "Hydrotherapy in the Treatment of the Insane." *Mod H* 1 (Nov. 1913):143-54.

"Overcrowding in State Mental Hospitals." *JAMA* 110 (Mar. 26, 1938):969.

Overholser, M. P. "The Problem of State Care of the Mentally Sick." *Journal of the Missouri Medical Association* 29 (Feb. 1932):69-74.

Overholser, Winfred. "The Early Treatment of Mental Disorders." *Journal of the Michigan State Medical Society* 37 (Oct. 1938):883-93.

Parsons, Frederick W. "The Pilgrim State Hospital." *Psychiatric Quarterly* 7 (1933):5-15.

_____, "That New Mental Hospital." *Mod H* 45 (Nov. 1935):41-44.

Partlow, W. D. "Problems of a State Mental Hospital." *Southern Medical Journal* 33 (1940):863-69.

Plant, J. S. "Some Psychiatric Aspects of Crowded Living Conditions." *AJP* 86 (1930):849-60.

Pollock, Horatio M. "Personnel Relations in State Hospitals." *MH* 6 (1922): 592-97.

_____, "Organization of Occupational Therapy in a State Hospital." *MH* 7 (1923):149-53.

_____, "The Future of Mental Disease from a Statistical Viewpoint." *AJP* 80 (1924):423-34.

_____, "Mental Disease in the United States in Relation to Environment, Sex, and Age, 1922." *AJP* 82 (1925):219-32.

_____, "Outcome of Mental Diseases in the United States." *MH* 9 (1925):783-804.

_____, "State Institution Population Still Increasing." *MH* 12 (1928):103-12.

_____, "Economic Loss to New York State and the United States on Account of Mental Disease, 1931." *MH* 16 (1932):289-99.

_____, "The Depression and Mental Disease in New York State." *AJP* 91 (1935):763-71.

Pollock, Horatio M., and Benjamin Malzberg. "Trends in Mental Disease." *MH* 21 (1937):456-65.

Polon, Albert. "The Relation of the General Practitioner to the Neurotic Patient." *MH* (1920):670-78.

Pratt, George K. "Psychiatric Departments in General Hospitals." *AJP* 82 (1926):403-10.

_____, "Professional Opportunities in Psychiatry." *JAMA* 97 (Sept. 26, 1931):910-13.

_____, "What the Community Expects of the State Hospital." *AJP* 89 (1933): 823-30.

Preston, George H. "Financing Adequate Psychotherapy." *AJP* 90 (1933):685-89.

"Professional Service in the Mental Hospital." *Mod H* 30 (Feb. 1928):96.

"Psychiatry, Past and Present." *New England Journal of Medicine* 211 (Sept. 27, 1934):598.

Randall, Edward, and Lucius Wilson. "Solving a Difficult Problem for the Psychiatric Department." *Mod H* 44 (June 1935):56-58.

Read, Charles F., and John T. Nerancy. "Modern State Hospital Treatment of the Psychotic." *JAMA* 104 (Jan. 26, 1935):292-97.

"Recognizing the Needs of the Mentally Ill," *Mod H* (Apr. 1930):100.

"Report of the Committee on the Survey of State Mental Hospitals of Pennsylvania." *Mental Health Bulletin* 11 (Oct. 15, 1933):3-19.

"Report of the Special Medical Advisers on St. Elizabeths Hospital." *AJP* 83 (1927):545-602.

Richardson, Horace K. "Psychopathy and the General Practitioner." *New England Journal of Medicine* 213 (Oct. 24, 1935):787-95.

Ridgway, R. F. L. "Recreation for Mental Cases." *AJP* 78 (1921):87-95.

Riley, W. H. "Progress in the Care and Treatment of Mental Diseases." *Journal of the Michigan State Medical Society* 33 (June 1934):285-90.

Russell, William L. "Is It to the Advantage of the Mental Hospital to Maintain a School of Nursing?" *MH* 16 (1932):56-62.

_____, "Whitney Clinic Offers Complete Care for Mental Patients." *Mod H* 40 (June 1933):51-57.

Sands, Irving J. "The Psychiatric Clinic in the General Hospital." *JAMA* 85 (Sept. 5, 1925):725-29.

_____, "What We Owe the Mental Patient." *Mod H* 27 (Sept. 1926): 45-47.

Sandy, William C. "The Standardization of Hospitals for the Insane." *Mod H* 11 (July 1918):6-11.

_____, "What the General Hospital Owes to the Psychiatric Patient." *Mod H* 25 (Sept, 1925):189-91.

_____, "The Role of the State Hospital in Mental Health." *Mental Health Bulletin* 10 (Apr. 15, 1932):3-6.

_____, "Progress in the Hospital Care of the Mentally Ill During Twenty-Five Years." *Mental Health Bulletin* 15 (Jan. 19, 1938):9-12.

Sargent, Cora McCabe. "Training School Organizations and Work in Mental Hospitals." *Mod H* 5 (Oct. 1915):228-30.

Sawyer, Carl W. "Occupation for Mental Cases During Institutional Care." *Mod H* 5 (Aug. 1915):85-87.

Schumaker, Henry C. "The Depression and Its Effects on the Mental Health of the Child." *MH* 19 (1934):287-93.

Shields, Eloise. "Normal Living. An Interpretation from the Mental Hospital." *Mental Health Bulletin* 17 (July 17, 1939):6-9.

Sleyster, Rock. "The Mind of Man and His Security." *JAMA* 112 (May 20, 1939):2003-06.

Smith, Philip. "Food Service in Institutions of the New York State Department of Mental Hygiene." *AJP* 91 (1935):1367-77.

Spaulding, E. R. "The Importance of Endocrine Therapy in Combination with Mental Analyses in the Treatment of Certain Cases of Personality Deviation." *AJP* 78 (1922):373-84.

Stein, Calvert. "The Role of Mental Hygiene in General Practice." *New England Journal of Medicine* 214 (Apr. 2, 1936):665-71.

Stevenson, G. H. "Ward Personnel in Mental Hospitals." *AJP* 91 (1935):791-98.

_____, "Clinical Facilities in Mental Hospitals." *Mod H* 46 (Jan. 1936):75-79.

Storchheim, Frederic. "On Utilizing Institutionalized Mental Patients to Influence Other Patients Psychotherapeutically." *AJP* 92 (1935):69-73.

Swint, R. C. "The Mental Disease Problem in Georgia." *Journal of the Medical*

Association of Georgia 20 (June 1931):216-19.
Thom, Douglas, "Mental Hygiene and the Depression." *MH* 16 (1932):564-76.
Thomas, Jackson M. "Medical Progress 1935." *New England Journal of Medicine* 210 (June 25, 1936):1309-13.
_____, "Progress in Psychiatry in 1936." *New England Journal of Medicine* 217 (Aug. 26, 1937):356-64.
Thomas, John R. "What Louisiana Is Doing for Her Insane." *New Orleans Medical and Surgical Journal* 76 (Sept. 1923):148-50.
Thompson, Charles E. "How to Secure Public Support of a State Hospital." *AJP* 80 (1924):309-16.
Thompson, Lloyd D. "Psychiatry in Southern Regions." *Southern Medical Journal* 30 (1937):880-86.
Tillotson, Kenneth J. "Mental Hospital Clinics in General Hospitals." *New England Journal of Medicine* 206 (July 23, 1931):195-98.
_____, "Some Newer Trends in Psychiatry." *New England Journal of Medicine* 207 (July 7, 1932):8-12.
Treadway, Walter L. "Federal Activities in the Care of the Mentally Ill." *JAMA* 96 (Apr. 11, 1931):1233-34.
Tuckerrn, Katherine. "The Nursing Care of the Insane in the United States." *Mod H* 6 (May 1916):357-59.
"Two Mental Hospitals Where Occupational and Diversional Therapy are Used." *Mod H* 11 (Dec. 1918):458-59.
Unsworth, H. R. "The Status of Psychiatry in Louisiana." *New Orleans Medical and Surgical Journal* 94 (Jan. 1942):318-42.
Vogel, Victor. "Our Inadequate Treatment of the Mentally Ill as Compared with Treatment of Other Sick People." *Public Health Reports* 56 (Oct. 3, 1941): 1941-47.
Wagner-Jauregg, Julius. "The History of the Malaria Treatment of General Paralysis." *AJP* 102 (1946):577-82.
Wharton, Howard. "Dressing up Mental Hospitals." *Mod H* 49 (Oct. 1937):60-63.
White, William A. "The New Saint Elizabeth's Hospital." *AJP* 80 (1924):503-13.
_____, "Some Suggestions for the Future." *AJP* 90 (1933):227-34.
White, William A., and Monie Sanger. "Modern Housing of Mental Patients." *Mod H* 45 (July 1935):42-47.
Whitehorn, J. C., and Gregory Zilboorg. "Present Trends in American Psychiatric Research." *AJP* 90 (1933):303-12.
Williams, Frankwood E. "The State Hospital in Relation to Public Health." *MH* 4 (1920):885-96.
_____, "Psychiatry and Its Relation to the Teaching of Medicine." *AJP* 84 (1928):689-700.
Winslow, Walker. *The Menninger Story*. New York: Doubleday, 1956.
Winston, Ellen Black. "Age, a Factor in the Increase of Mental Disease." *MH* 16 (1932):650-52.
Witzel, August E. "Treatment of the Manic-Depressive Psychoses." *Psychiatric Quarterly* 2 (1928):405-21.
Young, W. W. "Mental Hygiene in Changing Times." *Southern Medical Journal*

30 (1937:844-46.

CHAPTER 9

Aldrich, C. Knight. "Problems of Social Adjustment Following Lobotomy." *AJP* 107 (1950):459-62.

Ball, Josephine, C. James Klett, and Clement J. Gresock. "The Veterans Administration Study of Prefrontal Lobotomy." *JCEP* 20 (Sept. 1959):205-17.

Bateman, J. F., and Nicholas Michael. "Pharmacological Shock Treatment of Schizophrenia. A Statistical Study of Results in the Ohio State Hospitals." *AJP* 97 (1940):59-67.

Berkwitz, Nathaniel J. "Treatment of Mental Disorders with Shock Methods." *Minnesota Medicine* 23 (Jan. 1941):25-30.

Billing, Otto, and D. J. Sullivan. "The Therapeutic Value of Protracted Insulin Shock." *Psychiatric Quarterly* 16 (1942):549-64.

Binzley, Richard F., and James L. Anderson. "Prolonged Coma in the Insulin Treatment of Dementia Praecox." *Psychiatric Quarterly* 12 (July 1938): 477-88.

Bond, Earl, Joseph Hughes, and James A. Flaherty. "Results and Observations on the Insulin Shock Treatment of Schizophrenia." *AJP* 96 (1939):317-26.

Bond, Earl, and T. D. Rivers. "Further Follow-up Results in Insulin-Shock Therapy." *AJP* 99 (1942):201-02.

Bond, Earl, and Jay T. Shurley. "Insulin Therapy and Its Future." *AJP* 103 (1946):338-41.

Bowman, Karl M., Joseph Wortis, Hyman Fingert, and Julia Kagan. "Results to Date with the Pharmacological Shock Treatment of Schizophrenia." *AJP* 95 (1939):787-91.

Braceland, Francis J. "Changes in the Treatment of Involutional Melancholia." *Hosp & Comm Psych* 20 (May 1969):136-40.

Bryan, L. Laramour. "The Technique of the Insulin Shock and Metrazol Treatments." *Psychiatric Quarterly* 13 (1939):96-105. A good description of procedural matters.

Cerletti, Ugo. "Electroshock Therapy." *JCEP* 15 (Sept. 1954):191-217. A statement by the "founder" of ECT.

Crowley, Ralph M. "Use of Insulin in Certain Psychiatric Disorders." *Virginia Medical Monthly* 65 (1938):678-82.

Delgado, José M. R. *Evolution of Physical Control of the Brain.* New York: American Museum of Natural History, 1965.

Erickson, Isabel, and Mary Ramsey. "Nursing Care in Shock Therapy." *Bulletin of the Menninger Clinic* 2 (1938):155-60.

Evans, Vernon L. "Convulsive Shock Therapy in Elderly Patients—Risks and Results." *AJP* 99 (1943):531-33.

Feldman, Fred, Samuel Susselman, and S. Eugene Barrer. "Socio-Economic Aspects of the Shock Therapies in Schizophrenia." *AJP* 104 (1947):402-09.

Fink, Max, Robert L. Kahn, and Glen Oaks. "Behavioral Patterns in Convulsive Therapy." *Archives of General Psychiatry* 5 (July 1961):30-36.

Flor-Henry, P. "Psychiatric Surgery 1935-1973. Evolution and Current Perspectives." *Canadian Psychiatric Association Journal* 20 (Mar. 1975):157-67.

Freeman, Walter. "Psychosurgery." *AJP* 105 (1949):581-84.

_____, "Transorbital Lobotomy." *AJP* 105 (1949):734-40.

Freeman, Walter, and James W. Watts. "Prefrontal Lobotomy in the Treatment of Mental Disorders." *Southern Medical Journal* 30 (1937):23-31.

_____, "Prefrontal Lobotomy." *AJP* 99 (1943):798-806.

_____, "Psychosurgery During 1936-1946." *Archives of Neurology and Psychiatry* 58 (Oct. 1947):417-425.

_____, *Psychosurgery in the Treatment of Mental Disorders and Intractable Pain*. Springfield, Ill.: Charles C. Thomas, 1950.

"Frontal Lobotomy." *JAMA* 117 (Aug. 16, 1941):534-35.

Frosch, John, David Impastato, Lilly Ottenheimer, and S. Bernard Wortis. "Some Reactions Seen After Electric Shock Treatment." *AJP* 102 (1945): 311-15.

Frostig, Jacob. "Clinical Observations in the Insulin Treatment of Schizophrenia." *AJP* 96 (1940):1167-90.

Fulton, John F. *Frontal Lobotomy and Affective Behavior. A Neurophysiological Analysis*. New York: W. W. Norton, 1951.

Gaylin, Willard, Joel Meister, and Robert Neville. *Operating on the Mind. The Psychosurgery Conflict*. New York: Basic Books, 1975.

Geeslin, Lawrence E., and Hervey Cleckley. "Anomalies and Dangers in the Metrazol Therapy of Schizophrenia." *AJP* 96 (1939):183-91.

Glueck, Bernard. "The Effect of the Hypoglycemic Therapy on the Psychotic Process." *AJP* 94 (1937):171-73.

Gralnick, Alexander. "A Three Year Survey of Electroshock Therapy." *AJP* 102 (1946):583-93.

Graves, C. C., and F. P. Pignataro. "Injuries Sustained During the Course of Metrazol Shock Therapy." *Psychiatric Quarterly* 14 (1940):128-34.

Greenberg, Joel. "Psychosurgery at the Crossroads." *Science News* 111 (May 14, 1977):314-15, 317.

Greenblatt, M., R. E. Arnot, J. L. Poppen, and W. P. Chapman. "Report on Lobotomy Studies at the Boston Psychopathic Hospital." *AJP* 104 (1947): 361-68.

Greenblatt, M., R. E. Arnot, and H. C. Solomon, eds. *Studies in Lobotomy*. New York: Grune and Stratton, 1950. A classic analysis.

Greenblatt, M., and H. C. Solomon, eds. *Frontal Lobes and Schizophrenia*. New York: Springer-Verlag, 1953.

Grosh, L. C. "Report of Observations of the Insulin Hypoglycemic Shock Treatment on Psychotic Patients." *Journal of the Michigan State Medical Society* 37 (Mar. 1938):238-49.

Grotjahn, Martin. "Psychiatric Observation of Schizophrenic Patients." *Bulletin of the Menninger Clinic* 2 (1938):142-50.

_____, *Research on Prefrontal Lobotomy*. Topeka, Kan.: Group for the Advancement of Psychiatry, 1948.

_____, *Revised Electro-Shock Therapy Report*. Topeka, Kan.: Group for the Advancement of Psychiatry, 1950.

Group for the Advancement of Psychiatry. *Shock Therapy*. Topeka, Kan.:

Group for the Advancement of Psychiatry. 1947.

Halstead, Ward C., Hugh T. Carmichael, and Paul C. Bucy. "Prefrontal Lobotomy." *AJP* 103 (1946):217-28.

Hamilton, Donald M. "The Use of Electric Shock Therapy in Psychoneurosis." *AJP* 103 (1947):665-68.

Heilbrunn, Gert, and Paul Hletko. "Disappointing Results with Bilateral Prefrontal Lobotomy in Chronic Schizophrenia." *AJP* 99 (1943):569-70.

Heilbrunn, Gert, and Ruth Sternlieb. "Insulin Therapy of Schizophrenia in the Elgin State Hospital (with Special Reference to Relapses and Failures). *AJP* 96 (1940):1203-11.

Henry, J. John. "The Problem of Insulin Shock." *AJP* 94 (1937):175-82.

Himwich, Harold E. "Electroshock. A Round Table Discussion." *AJP* 100 (1943):361-64.

Hinko, Edward N., and Louis S. Lipschutz. "Five Years After Shock Therapy." *AJP* 104 (1947):387-90.

Horwitz, William A., Joseph R. Blalock, and Meyer M. Harris. "Protracted Comas Occurring During Insulin Hypoglycemic Therapy." *Psychiatric Quarterly* 12 (1938):466-76.

Hurwitz, Thomas D. "Electroconvulsive Therapy: A Review." *Comprehensive Psychiatry* 15 (July-Aug. 1974):303-13.

Jacobsen, C. F., J. B. Wolfe, and T. A. Jackson. "An Experimental Analysis of the Functions of the Frontal Association Areas in Primates." *JNMD* 82 (1935):1-14.

Jones, Charles H. "Transorbital Lobotomy in Institutional Practice." *AJP* 107 (1950):120-27.

Kalinowsky, Lothar B. "Present Status of Electric Shock Therapy." *Bulletin of the New York Academy of Medicine* 25 (Sept. 1949):541-43.

Kalinowsky, L., and S. Eugene Barrera. "Electric Convulsion Therapy in Mental Disorders." *Psychiatric Quarterly* 14 (1940):719-30.

Kalinowsky, L., N. Bigelow, and P. Brikates. "Electric Shock Therapy in State Hospital Practice. *Psychiatric Quarterly* 15 (1941):450-59.

Kalinowsky, Lothar B., and Paul H. Hoch. *Shock Treatments, Psychosurgery and Other Somatic Treatments in Psychiatry.* 2nd revised and enlarged edition. New York: Grune and Stratton, 1952. A standard text with an extensive bibliography.

Kalinowsky, Lothar B., and John E. Scarff. "The Selection of Psychiatric Cases for Prefrontal Lobotomy." *AJP* 105 (1948):81-85.

Katzenelbogen, S., and Herbert E. Harms. "The Insulin Treatment of Schizophrenic Patients." *AJP* 95 (1939):793-97.

Katzenelbogen, S., H. Harms, and D. A. Clark. "Hypoglycemic Treatment of Schizophrenia." *AJP* 94 (1937):135-52.

Kepler, Edwin J., and Frederick P. Moersch. "The Psychiatric Manifestations of Hypoglycemia." *AJP* 94 (1937):89-110.

Kisker, George W. "Remarks on the Problem of Psychosurgery." *AJP* 100 (1943):180-84.

Kolb, Lawrence, and Victor H. Vogel. "The Use of Shock Therapy in 305 Mental Hospitals." *AJP* 99 (1942):90-100.

Leksell, L. *Stereotaxis and Radiosurgery: An Operative System.* Springfield,

Ill.: Charles C. Thomas, 1971.

Lester, David. "A Study of Prolonged Coma Following Insulin Shock." *AJP* 95 (1939):1083-93.

Libertson, William. "A Critical Analysis of Insulin Therapy at Rochester State Hospital." *Psychiatric Quarterly* 15 (1941):635-47.

Lowinger, Louis, and James Huddleson. "Complications in Electric Shock Therapy." *AJP* 102 (1946):594-98.

Mark, V. H., and F. R. Ervin. *Violence and the Brain.* New York: Harper and Row, 1970. An Argument for the use of amygdalotomy to control violent behavior.

Martin, Peter A. "Convulsive Therapies." *JNMD* 109 (1949):142-57.

McKendree, Oswald J. "Insulin Therapy and Its Complications in the Treatment of the Psychoses." *Psychiatric Quarterly* 12 (1938):444-54.

Medina, R. F., J. S. Pearson, and H. F. Buchstein. "The Long Term Evaluation of Prefrontal Lobotomy in Chronic Psychotics." *JNMD* 119 (1954):23-30.

Meduna, L. J. "The Convulsive Treatment." *JCEP* 15 (Sept. 1954):219-33. A statement by the "founder" of Metrazol shock treatment.

Mermelstein, Matthew D. "Evaluative Study of One Hundred Transorbital Leucotomies." *Journal of Clinical Psychology* 12 (July 1956):271-76.

Mettler, Fred A. "A Comparison Between Various Forms of Psychosurgery." *New York State Journal of Medicine* 49 (Oct. 1, 1949):2283-86.

_____. *Selective Partial Ablation of the Frontal Cortex. A Correlative Study of Its Effects on Human Psychotic Subjects.* New York: Paul Hoeber, 1949.

_____. *Psychosurgical Problems.* New York: Blakiston, 1952.

Mezer, Robert R., and Harry C. Solomon. "Value of Electric-Shock Treatment on Outpatients." *New England Journal of Medicine* 250 (Apr. 1954):721-22.

Moniz, Egas. "Pre-Frontal Leucotomy in the Treatment of Mental Disorders." *AJP* 93 (1937):1379-85.

Muncie, Wendell. "The Present Status of Psychiatry and Psychiatric Treatment with Special Attention to Coma and Convulsive Treatment." *Southern Medical Journal* 34 (1941):968-76.

Murphy, James M. "Fatality Following Insulin Therapy." *Psychiatric Quarterly* 13 (1939):361-68.

Myerson, Abraham. "Borderline Cases Treated by Electric Shock." *AJP* 11 (1943):355-57.

"Neurosurgical Treatment of Certain Abnormal Mental States." *JAMA* 117 (Aug. 16, 1941):517-27.

Oltman, Jane E., Bernard S. Brody, Samuel Friedman, and William F. Green. "Frontal Lobotomy." *AJP* 105 (1949):742-51.

O'Neill, Francis J. "Serious Complications of Insulin Shock Therapy." *Psychiatric Quarterly* 12 (1938):455-65.

Pacella, B. L., and S. E. Barrera. "Follow-up Study of a Series of Patients Treated by Electrically Induced Convulsions and by Metrazol Convulsions." *AJP* 99 (1943):513-24.

Palmer, Dwight M., Harry E. Sprang, and Clarence L. Hans. "Electroshock Therapy in Schizophrenia: A Statistical Survey of 455 Cases." *JNMD* 114 (1951):162-71.

Paster, Samuel, and Saul C. Holtzman. "A Study of One Thousand Psychotic Veterans Treated with Insulin and Electric Shock." *AJP* 105 (1949):811-20.

Peterson, Magnus C., and Harold F. Buchstein. "Prefrontal Lobotomy in Chronic Psychoses." *AJP* 99 (1942):426-30.

Peyton, W. T., H. H. Noran, and E. W. Miller. "Prefrontal Lobotomy. A New Form of Psychosurgery." *AJP* 104 (1948):513-23.

Phillips, S. J. "Observations on Insulin and Metrazol Therapy at Central Louisiana State Hospital." *New Orleans Medical and Surgical Journal* 91 (Sept. 1938):135-44.

Polatin, Phillip, Murray M. Friedman, Meyer M. Harris, and William A. Horwitz. "Vertebrae Fractures Produced by Metrazol Induced Convulsions." *JAMA* 112 (Apr. 29, 1939):1684.

Psychosurgery. A Multidisciplinary Symposium. Lexington, Mass.: D. C. Heath, 1974.

Psychosurgery. Perspective on a Current Problem. Washington D.C.: U.S. Government Printing Office, 1973. A discussion and excellent bibliography.

Read, Charles F. "Consequences of Metrazol Shock Therapy." *AJP* 97 (1940): 667-76.

Read, Charles F., D. Louis Steinberg, Erich Liebert, and Isidore Finkelman. "Use of Metrazol in the Functional Psychoses." *AJP* 95 (1939):781-86.

Redlich, Frederick C. "Metrazol Shock Treatment. Pharmacological and Biochemical Studies." *AJP* 96 (1939):193-203.

Riddell, Sylvia A. "The Therapeutic Efficacy of ECT." *Archives of General Psychiatry* 8 (June 1963):546-56.

Rinkel, M., and H. E. Himwich. *Insulin Treatment in Psychiatry.* New York: Philosophical Library, 1959.

Rivers, T. D., and E. D. Bond. "Follow-up Results in Insulin Shock Therapy After One to Three Years." *AJP* 98 (1941):382-84.

Robie, Theodore R. "Is Shock Therapy on Trial?" *AJP* 106 (1950):902-10.

Rosenberg, Edward F., Frederick P. Moersch, Russell M. Wilder, and Benjamin F. Smith. "The Present Status of the Insulin Hypoglycemia Treatment of Schizophrenia." *Minnesota Medicine* 21 (Mar. 1938):155-62.

Ross, J. R. "Report of the Hypoglycemic Treatment in New York State Hospitals." *AJP* 94 (1937):131-34.

_____. "The Pharmacological Shock Treatment of Schizophrenia: A Statistical Study of Results in the New York State Hospitals." *AJP* 95 (1939):769-79.

Ross, J. R., and Benjamin Malzberg. "A Review of the Results of the Pharmacological Shock Therapy and the Metrazol Convulsive Therapy in New York State." *AJP* 96 (1939):297-316.

Rossman, I. Murray, and William B. Cline, Jr. "The Pharmacological 'Shock' Treatment of Chronic Schizophrenia." *AJP* 94 (1938):1323-36.

Rothschild, David, and Abraham Kaye. "The Effects of Prefrontal Lobotomy on the Symptomatology of Schizophrenic Patients." *AJP* 105 (1949):752-59.

Sackler, A. M., R. R. Sackler, M. D. Sackler, and F. Marti-Ibanez, eds. *The Great Physiodynamic Therapies in Psychiatry.* New York: Paul B. Hoeber, 1956. A good introduction to shock treatments and lobotomy.

Sakel, Manfred. "The Methodical Use of Hypoglycemia in the Treatment of

Psychoses." *AJP* 94 (1937):111-29.

———, "A New Treatment of Schizophrenia." *AJP* 93 (1937):829-41.

———, "The Classical Sakel Shock Treatment." *JCEP* 13 (Sept. 1954):255-316. A statement by the "founder" of the insulin shock method.

Salzman, Leon. "An Evaluation of Shock Therapy." *AJP* 103 (1947):669-79.

Schoolar, Joseph C., and Charles M. Gaitz. *Research and the Psychiatric Patient.* New York: Brunner/Mazel, 1975.

Shuman, Samuel. *Psychosurgery and the Medical Control of Violence.* Detroit: Wayne State University Press, 1977.

Smith, Lawren H., Donald W. Hastings, and Joseph Hughes. "Immediate and Follow-up Results of Electroshock Therapy." *AJP* 100 (1943):351-54.

Smith, L. H., J. Hughes, D. W. Hastings, and B. J. Alpers. "Electroshock Treatment in the Psychoses." *AJP* 98 (1942):558-61.

Snodgrass, Virginia. "Debate over Benefits and Ethics of Psychosurgery Involves the Public." *JAMA* 225 (Aug. 20, 1973):913-20.

Snyder, S. H. *Madness and the Brain.* New York: McGraw-Hill, 1974.

Spiegel, E. A., H. T. Wycis, M. Marks, and A. J. Lee. "Stereotaxic Apparatus for Operations on the Human Brain." *Science* 106 (1947):349-50.

Stainbrook, Edward. "The Use of Electricity in Psychiatric Treatment During the Nineteenth Century." *Bulletin of the History of Medicine* 22 (1948): 156-77.

Steward, Bryon. "Present Status of Shock Therapy in Neuropsychiatry with Special Reference to Prevention of Complications." *Bulletin of the Menninger Clinic* 6 (1942):15-27.

Strecker, Edward A., Harold D. Palmer, and Francis C. Grant. "A Study of Frontal Lobotomy." *AJP* 98 (1942):524-32.

Strickler, Frank A., and James King. "Insulin Shock Treatment of Dementia Praecox." *Virginia Medical Monthly* 65 (1938):407-13.

"The Surgical Treatment of Certain Psychoses." *New England Journal of Medicine* 215 (Dec. 3, 1936):1088.

"Survey of Shock Therapy Practices." *AJP* 106 (1950):708-09.

Tillim, Sidney, and Mildred Squires. "A Clinical Evaluation of Hypoglycemic and Convulsive Therapy." *Psychiatric Quarterly* 16 (1942):469-79.

Tompkins, J. Butler. "A Summary of Thirty-Six Cases of Lobotomy." *AJP* 105 (1948):443-44.

Tow, P. M. *Personality Changes Following Frontal Leucotomy.* London: Oxford University Press, 1955.

Valenstein, Elliot S. *Brain Control.* New York: John Wiley and Sons, 1973. An excellent, balanced study.

Wilcox, Paul H. "Electroshock Therapy. A Review of over 23,000 Treatments." *AJP* 104 (1947):100-12.

Winter, A., ed. *The Surgical Control of Behavior. A Symposium.* Springfield, Ill.: Charles C. Thomas, 1971.

Worthing, Harry J., Newton Bigelow, Richard Binzley, and Henry Brill. "The Organization and Administration of a State Hospital Insulin-Metrazol-Electric Shock Therapy Unit." *AJP* 99 (1943):692-97.

Worthing, Harry J., Henry Brill, and Henry Wigderson. "350 Cases of Prefrontal Lobotomy." *Psychiatric Quarterly* 23 (1949):617-56.

Wortis, Joseph, Karl M. Bowman, Leo L. Orenstein, and Irving J. Rosenbaum. "Further Experience at Bellevue Hospital with the Hypoglycemic Insulin Treatment of Schizophrenia." *AJP* 94 (1937):153-58.

Young, G. Alexander, Richard H. Young, and L. Roucek. "Experiences with the Hypoglycemic Shock Treatment of Schizophrenia." *AJP* 94 (1937):159-70.

CHAPTER 10

Abrams, Julian. "Chlorpromazine in the Treatment of Chronic Schizophrenia." *Diseases of the Nervous System* 19 (Jan. 1958):20-28.

Alexander, Leo. *Treatment of Mental Disorder.* Philadelphia: W. B. Saunders, 1953. An exceptionally good textbook that has comprehensive bibliographies. It is a synthesis of treatment theories and procedures on the eve of the drug era.

Appel, John W. "Incidence of Neuropsychiatric Disorders in the United States Army in World War II." *AJP* 102 (1946):433-36.

Appel, John W., Gilbert W. Beebe, and David W. Hilger. "Comparative Incidence of Neuropsychiatric Casualties in World War I and World War II." *AJP* 103 (1946):196-99.

Armor, D., and G. L. Klerman. "Psychiatric Treatment Orientations and Professional Ideology." *Journal of Health and Social Behavior* 9 (1968):243-55.

Artiss, Kenneth L. *Milieu Therapy in Schizophrenia.* New York: Grune and Stratton, 1962.

Ayd, Frank J., Jr., and Barry Blackwell, eds. *Discoveries in Biological Psychiatry.* Philadelphia: Lippincott, 1970.

Belknap, Ivan. *Human Problems of a State Mental Hospital.* New York: McGraw-Hill, 1956. An important hospital milieu study.

Blackman, Nathan. "Ward Therapy—a New Method of Group Psychotherapy." *Psychiatric Quarterly* 16 (1942):660-67.

Blain, Daniel, and John H. Baird. "The Neuropsychiatric Program of the Veterans Administration." *AJP* 103 (1947):463-66.

Bloomberg, Wilfred, and Robert W. Hyde. "A Summary of Neuropsychiatric Work at the Boston Induction Station." *AJP* 99 (1942):23-28.

Bonn, Ethel M. "Use of Drugs in a Mental Hospital. Please Pass the Pills." *Ment H* 13 (Apr. 1962):208-09.

Bonner, C. A. "Mental Hospital Employees. Their Importance in Future Mental Hospital Betterment." *AJP* 105 (1949):669-72.

Boshes, Benjamin. "The Status of Tranquilizing Drugs, 1959." *Annals of Internal Medicine* 52 (Jan. 1960):182-94.

Bowman, Karl M. "Presidential Address." *AJP* 103 (1946):1-17.

Boyd, David A. "Problems of Institutional Care of the Aged." *AJP* 106 (1950): 616-20.

Braceland, Francis J. "Psychiatric Lessons from World War II." *AJP* 103 (1947):587-93.

Brill, H., and R. E. Patton. "Analysis of 1955-56 Population Fall in New York State Mental Hospitals in First Year of Large Scale Use of Tranquilizing

Drugs." *AJP* 114 (1957):509-14.

_____, "Analysis of Population Reduction in New York State Mental Hospitals During the First Four Years of Large Scale Therapy with Psychotropic Drugs." *AJP* 116 (1959):495-508.

Buel, H., and R. E. Patton. *Evaluation of Psychiatric Treatment*. New York: Grune and Stratton, 1964.

Caldwell, A. E. *Origins of Psychopharmacology from CPZ to LSD*. Springfield, Ill.: Charles C. Thomas, 1970.

Caudill, W. *The Psychiatric Hospital as a Small Society*. Cambridge, Mass.: Harvard University Press, 1958. A study of the hospital milieu.

Chambers, Ralph H. "Inspection and Rating for Mental Hospitals." *AJP* 106 (1949):250-54.

Chisholm, Brock. "The Future of Psychiatry." *AJP* 104 (1948):543-47.

Chlorpromazine and Mental Health. Philadelphia: Lea and Febiger, 1955. A symposium held under the auspices of Smith, Kline, and French.

Clark, Lincoln D. "Evaluation of the Therapeutic Effects of Drugs in Psychiatric Patients." *Diseases of the Nervous System* 17 (Sept. 1956):282-86.

Clarke, Eric Kent. "The Challenge to Psychiatry in the Postwar Period." *Minnesota Medicine* 27 (May 1944):367-72.

Cleckley, Hervey. "Common Sources of Confusion in Psychiatric Matters." *Southern Medical Journal* 42 (1949):341-43.

Cohen, Irvin M. "Complications of Chlorpromazine." *AJP* 113 (1956):115-21.

Crane, George E. "Clinical Psychopharmacology in Its 20th Year." *Science* 181 (July 1973):124-28.

Cumming, John, and Elaine Cumming. *Ego and Milieu. Theory and Practice of Environmental Theory*. New York: Atherton, 1963.

Delay, Jean, and Pierre Deniker. "Chlorpromazine and Neuroleptic Treatments in Psychiatry." *JCEP* 17 (Mar. 1956):19-24.

Denber, Herman C. B., editor, *Research Conference on the Therapeutic Community*. Springfield, Ill.: Charles C. Thomas, 1960.

deRopp, Robert S. *Drugs and the Mind*. New York: Grove Press, 1960.

Deutsch, Albert. "Military Psychiatry: World War II 1941-1943." In *One Hundred Years of American Psychiatry*, edited by J. K. Hall et al, pp. 419-41. New York: Columbia University Press, 1944.

_____. *The Shame of the States*. New York: Harcourt, Brace, 1948.

_____, *The Story of GAP*. New York: Group for the Advancement of Psychiatry, 1959.

Dewitt, Henrietta B. "The Function of the Social Worker in the Total Treatment Program in a State Mental Hospital." *AJP* 105 (1948):298-303.

Dickel, Herman A., and Henry H. Dixon. "Inherent Dangers in the Use of Tranquilizing Drugs in Anxiety States." *JAMA* 163 (Feb. 9, 1957):422-26.

Donnelly, John, and William Zeller. "Clinical Research on Chlorpromazine and Reserpine in State and Private Psychiatric Hospitals." *JCEP* 17 (June 1956):180-88.

Dunham, H. Warren. *Sociological Theory and Mental Disorder*. Detroit: Wayne State University Press, 1959.

Eyres, Alfred E. "Mental Illness. Administrative, Preventive, and Therapeutic Considerations." *Journal of the Michigan State Medical Society* 49 (Jan.

1950):69-74.

Feldman, Paul E. "Clinical Evaluation of Chlorpromazine Theory for Mental Illness: Analysis of One Year's Experience." *JCEP* 18 (Mar. 1957):1-26.

_____, "A Comparative Study of Various Ataractic Drugs." *AJP* 113 (1957): 589-94.

Felix, Robert H. "Psychiatry in Prospect." *AJP* 103 (1947):600-06.

_____, "The National Mental Health Program." *Public Health Reports* 63 (June 25, 1948):837-47.

_____, "Mental Disorders as a Public Health Problem." *AJP* 106 (1949):401-06.

Frankel, Emil. "Outcome of Mental Hospital Treatment in New Jersey." *MH* 32 (1948):459-64.

Galioni, E. F., F. H. Adams, and F. F. Tallman. "Intensive Treatment of Back-Ward Patients—a Controlled Pilot Study." *AJP* 109 (1953):576-83.

Gibbs, James J., Bernard Wilkens, and Carl G. Lauterbach. "A Controlled Clinical Psychiatric Study of Chlorpromazine." *JCEP* 18 (Sept. 1957):269-83.

Goldman, Douglas. "Treatment of Psychotic States with Chlorpromazine." *JAMA* 157 (1955):1274-78.

_____, "Chlorpromazine Treatment of Hospitalized Psychotic Patients." *JCEP* 17 (Mar. 1956):45-56.

Goldstein, H. H. "Neuropsychiatric Evaluation of the Potential Soldier." *AJP* 99 (1942):29-32.

Gordon, H. L. *New Chemotherapy in Mental Illness.* New York: Philosophical Library, 1958.

Gorman, Mike. *Every Other Bed.* New York: World Publishing, 1954.

Greenblatt, Milton, Daniel Levinson, and Gerald Klerman. *Mental Patients in Transition.* Springfield, Ill.: Charles C. Thomas, 1961. An evaluation of drug treatment.

Greenblatt, Milton, Daniel J. Levinson, and Richard H. Williams, editors. *The Patient and the Mental Hospital.* Glencoe, Ill.: The Free Press, 1957. Papers on hospital treatment.

Greenblatt, Milton, Maida H. Solomon, Anne S. Evans, and George W. Brooks, editors. *Drugs and Social Therapy in Chronic Schizophrenia.* Springfield, Ill.: Charles C. Thomas, 1965. A series of good papers with excellent bibliographies.

Greenblatt, Milton, Richard H. York, Esther L. Brown, and Robert W. Hyde. *From Custodial to Therapeutic Patient Care in Mental Hospitals.* New York: Russell Sage Foundation, 1955. A classic study.

Gregg, Alan. "Lessons to Learn. Psychiatry in World War II." *AJP* 104 (1947): 217-20.

_____, "The Limitations of Psychiatry." *AJP* 104 (1948):513-22.

Gross, M. "The Impact of Ataractic Drugs on a Mental Hospital Outpatient Clinic." *AJP* 117 (1960):444-47.

Group for the Advancement of Psychiatry. *Public Psychiatric Hospitals.* Topeka, Kan.: Group for the Advancement of Psychiatry, 1948.

_____, *Statistics Pertinent to Psychiatry in the United States.* Topeka, Kan.: Group for the Advancement of Psychiatry, 1949.

_____, The Problem of the Aged Patient in the Public Psychiatric Hospital. Topeka, Kan.: Group for the Advancement of Psychiatry, 1950.

_____, Pharmacotherapy and Psychotherapy: Paradoxes, Problems, and Progress. New York: Group for the Advancement of Psychiatry, 1975.

Hall, Robert A., and Dorothy J. Dunlap. "A Study of Chlorpromazine: Methodology and Results with Chronic Semidisturbed Schizophrenics." JNMD 122 (1955):301-14.

Haun, Paul, and Z. M. Lebensohn. "New Trends in Hospital Design." AJP 104 (1948):555-64.

Hecker, Arthur, Marvie R. Plesset, and Philip C. Grana. "Psychiatric Problems in Military Service During the Training Period." AJP 99 (1942):33-41.

Hoch, Paul H., ed. Failures in Psychiatric Treatment. New York: Grune and Stratton, 1948.

Hunt, M. M. Mental Hospital. New York: Pyramid Books, 1962.

Hurst, L. C. "The Unlocking of Wards in Mental Hospitals." AJP 114 (1957): 306-08.

Hutchings, Richard H. "Psychoneuroses and Our Changing Times." JNMD 106 (1947):283-91.

"International Symposium on Chlorpromazine." JCEP 17 (1956):15-76, 129-88.

Israel, Robert H., and Nelson A. Johnson. "New Facts on Prognosis in Mental Disease." AJP 104 (1948):540-45.

Jarvik, Murray E. "The Psychopharmacological Revolution." Psychology Today 1 (May 1967):51-59.

Johnson, Nelson. "The Growing Problems of Old-Age Psychoses: An Analysis of the Trend in One State Hospital from 1910 to 1944." MH 30 (1946): 431-50.

Jones, Maxwell. The Therapeutic Community. A New Treatment Method in Psychiatry. New York: Basic Books, 1953. A classic on milieu treatment.

Karczmar, A. G., and W. P. Koella. Neurophysiological and Behavioral Aspects of Psychotropic Drugs. Springfield, Ill.: Charles C. Thomas, 1969.

Kilgore, James M., Jr. "Follow-up Evaluation on a Controlled, Blind Study of Effects of Chlorpromazine on Psychotic Behavior." JCEP 20 (June 1959): 147-61.

Klerman, Gerald L. "Assessing the Influence of the Hospital Milieu upon the Effectiveness of Psychiatric Drug Therapy." JNMD 137 (1963):143-154.

Kline, Nathan S., ed. Psychopharmacology. Washington, D.C.: American Association for the Advancement of Science, 1956. A major conference on chlorpromazine.

Koegler, Ronald R., and Norman Q. Brill. Treatment of Psychiatric Outpatients. New York: Appleton-Century-Crofts, 1967.

Kohn, M. L., and J. A. Clausen. "Social Isolation and Schizophrenia." American Sociological Review 20 (June 1955):265-73.

Kovitz, R., J. T. Carter, and W. P. Addison. "A Comparison of Chlorpromazine and Reserpine in Chronic Psychosis." Archives of Neurology and Psychiatry 74 (Nov. 1955):467-71.

Kramer, M., and E. S. Pollack. "Problems in the Interpretation of Trends in the Population Movement of the Public Mental Hospital." American Journal of Public Health 48 (Aug. 1958):1003-19.

Kris, E. B. "Five-Year Community Follow-up of Patients Discharged from a Mental Hospital." *Current Therapy Research* 5 (1963):451-62.

Kris, E. B., and Donald M. Carmichael. "Follow-up Study on Thorazine Treated Patients." *AJP* 114 (1957):449-52.

Kurtz, Philip L. "The Current Status of the Tranquilizing Drugs." *Canadian Medical Association Journal* 78 (Feb. 1, 1958):209-15.

London, Perry. *Behavior Control*. New York: Harper and Row, 1969.

Lowry, James V. "How the National Mental Health Act Works." *Public Health Reports* 64 (Mar. 11, 1949):303-12.

Malamud, William, Sr., and William Malamud, Jr. "Somatic Therapy in Psychiatry." *JCEP* 19 (Sept. 1958):181-94.

Mandelbrote, B. "An Experiment in the Rapid Conversion of a Closed Mental Hospital into an Open Door Hospital." *MH* 42 (1958):3-16.

Mandell, A. J., and M. P. Mandell. *Psychochemical Research in Man*. New York: Academic Press, 1969.

Marks J., and C. M. B. Pare. *The Scientific Basis of Drug Therapy in Psychiatry*. New York: Pergamon Press, 1965.

McNeel, B. H. "War Psychiatry in Retrospect." *AJP* 102 (1946):500-06.

Meerloo, J. A. "Medication into Submission: The Danger of Therapeutic Coercion." *JNMD* 122 (1955):353-60.

Menninger, William C. "Psychiatric Objectives in the Army." *AJP* 102 (1945): 102-07.

_____, "Psychiatric Experience in the War, 1941-1946." *AJP* 103 (1947):577-86.

_____, "The Role of Psychiatry in the World Today." *AJP* 104 (1947):155-63.

_____, "Facts and Statistics of Significance for Psychiatry." *Bulletin of the Menninger Clinic* 12 (1948):1-12.

_____, *Psychiatry in a Troubled World*. New York: Macmillan, 1948.

_____, "Presidential Address." *AJP* 106 (1949):1-12.

"Mental Hygiene and the National Defense." *MH* 26 (1942):1-38.

"Mental Hygiene in the Emergency." *MH* (1941):1-29.

von Mering, O., and S. H. King. *Remotivating the Mental Patient*. New York: Russell Sage, 1957.

Myerson, Abraham. "Theory and Principles of the 'Total Push' Method in the Treatment of Chronic Schizophrenia." *AJP* 95 (193):1197-1204.

"The National Mental Health Act." *AJP* 103 (1946):417-20.

Newbold, H. L., and W. David Steed. "The Use of Chlorpromazine in Psychotherapy." *JNMD* 123 (1956):270-74.

Overholser, Winfred. "Presidential Address." *AJP* 105 (1948):1-9.

_____, "Has Chlorpromazine Inaugurated a New Era in Mental Hospitals?" *JCEP* 17 (June 1956):197-201.

Ozarin, Lucy D. "The Community and Rehabilitation of the Hospitalized Psychiatric Patient." *JAMA* 161 (July 7, 1956):940-44.

Pauncz, Arpad. "Theory of the 'Total Push' Program in Psychiatry." *American Journal of Psychotherapy* 8 (1954):11-20.

Polatin, Phillip. *A Guide to Treatment in Psychiatry*. Philadelphia: Lippincott, 1966.

Porter, William C. "The Military Psychiatrist at Work." *AJP* 98 (1941):317-23.

_____, "What Has Psychiatry Learned During the Present War?" *AJP* 99 (1943):850-55.

Rennie, Thomas A. C., and Luther E. Woodward. *Mental Health in Modern Society.* New York: Commonwealth Fund, 1948.

Rinkel, Max. *Biological Treatment of Mental Illness.* New York: Farrar, Straus, and Giroux, 1966.

Robinson, Robert L. "The First APA Mental Hospital Institute: A Reminiscence." *Hosp & Comm Psych* 21 (Oct. 1970):317-19.

Rothman, Theodore, ed. *Changing Patterns in Psychiatric Care.* New York: Crown, 1970.

Ruggles, Arthur H. "Presidential Address." *AJP* 100 (1943):1-8.

Russell, William L. " 'Comment' the National Mental Health Act." *AJP* 103 (1946):417-20.

Seale, Arthur L., Marvin Miller, Charles Watkins, and Cecil Wurster. "Changing Nature of State Hospital Populations." *Diseases of the Nervous System* 20 (Nov. 1959):530-34.

Selling, Lowell S. "A Clinical Study of Miltown, a New Tranquilizing Agent." *JCEP* 17 (Mar. 1956):7-14.

Snow, H. B. "The Hospital We Opened: Some Comments in Retrospect." *Ment H* 13 (Nov. 1962):573-79.

Snyder, Howard. "Observations of Psychiatry in World War II." *AJP* 104 (1947):221-25.

Spadoni, Alex J., and Jackson A. Smith. "Milieu Therapy in Schizophrenia. A Negative Result." *Archives of General Psychiatry* 20 (May 1969):547-51.

Stainbrook, Edward. "Hospital Atmosphere Is a Definite Treatment Measure." *Ment H* 8 (Feb. 1957):8-11.

"Standards for Psychiatric Hospitals and Out-Patient Clinics Approved by the American Psychiatric Association." *AJP* 102 (1945):264-69.

Stanton, Alfred, and Morris Schwartz. *The Mental Hospital: A Study of Institutional Participation in Psychiatric Illness and Treatment.* New York: Basic Books, 1954. A classic hospital milieu study.

Stevenson, George S. "Contributions of War Experience to Our Knowledge of Mental Hygiene." *American Journal of Public Health* 36 (Oct.1946):1129-32.

Stotsky, Bernard A. "Positive and Negative Factors in the Therapeutic Community." *Diseases of the Nervous System* 33 (Jan. 1967):19-25.

Strauss, Anselm, and Melvin Sabshin. "Large State Mental Hospitals." *Archives of General Psychiatry* 5 (Dec. 1961):75-87.

Sullivan, Harry Stack. "Socio-Psychiatric Research. Its Implications for the Schizophrenia Problem and for Mental Hygiene." *AJP* 87 (1931):977-92.

Swazey, Judith P. *Chlorpromazine in Psychiatry. A Study of Therapeutic Innovation.* Cambridge, Mass.: MIT Press, 1974. A stimulating historical analysis.

Szasz, Thomas S. "Some Observations on the Use of Tranquilizing Drugs." *AMA Archives of Neurology and Psychiatry* 77 (1957):86-92.

Tenenblatt, Sarah S., and Anthony Spagno. "A Controlled Study of Chlorpromazine Therapy in Chronic Psychotic Patients." *JCEP* 17 (Mar. 1956):82-92.

Terhune, William B., and James R. Dickenson. "Progress in Group Psychotherapy. A Summary of the Literature." *New England Journal of Medicine* 239 (Dec. 2, 1948):854-57.

Tillotson, Kenneth J. "The Practice of the 'Total Push' Method in the Treatment of Chronic Schizophrenia." *AJP* 95 (1939):1205-13.

Tompkins, Harvey J., and Alfred W. Snedeker. "Care and Treatment of the Psychiatric Patient in the Veterans Administration." *AJP* 103 (1947):467-69.

Tourney, Garfield. "A History of Therapeutic Fashions in Psychiatry, 1800-1966." *AJP* 124 (1967):784-95.

Tuteur, Werner, Rochus Stiller, and Jacob Glotzer. "The Discharged Mental Hospital Chlorpromazine Patient." *Diseases of the Nervous System* 20 (Nov. 1959):512-17.

Vail, David J. "Facets of Institutional Living." *Ment H* 15 (Nov. 1964):599-605.

Wessen, Albert F., ed. *The Psychiatric Hospital as a Social System.* Springfield, Ill.: Charles C. Thomas, 1964.

Williams, Vernon P. "Psychiatry: The Neuroses in War." *New England Journal of Medicine* 226 (Feb. 19, 1942):302-06.

Winkelman, N. William, Jr. "Chlorpromazine in the Treatment of Neuropsychiatric Disorders." *JAMA* 155 (May 1, 1954):18-21.

———, An Appraisal of Chlorpromazine Based on Experience with 1090 Patients." *AJP* 113 (1957):967-71.

———, "A Long Term Investigation of Chlorpromazine. A Study of Constant and Inconstant Chlorpromazine Administration over a Period of Six Years with a Discussion of the Evolution of Our Theoretical Thinking." *AJP* 116 (1960):865-69.

Woolley, D. W. *The Biochemical Bases of Psychoses.* New York: John Wiley, 1962.

Wright, Frank, Jr. *Out of Sight, out of Mind.* Philadelphia: National Mental Health Foundation, 1947.

Yoder, O. R. "Care and Treatment of the Psychotic Patient." *Journal of the Michigan State Medical Society* 48 (Sept. 1949):1166-68.

Zeller, William W., Paul N. Graffagnino, Chester F. Cullen, and H. Jerome Rietman. "Use of Chlorpromazine and Reserpine in the Treatment of Emotional Disorders." *JAMA* 160 (Jan. 21, 1956):179-84.

Zusman, Jack. "Some Explanations of the Changing Appearance of Psychotic Patients." *Milbank Memorial Fund Quarterly* 44 (Jan. 1966):363-94.

CHAPTER 11

Abrams, Gene M., and Norman S. Greenfield. *The New Hospital Psychiatry.* New York: Academic Press, 1971.

Ahmed, Paul I., and Stanley C. Plog, eds. *State Mental Hospitals. What Happens When They Close.* New York: Plenum Medical Book Co., 1976.

Anthony, W. A., G. J. Buell, S. Sharrett, and M. E. Althoff. "Efficacy of Psychiatric Rehabilitation." *Psychological Bulletin* 78 (1972):447-56.

Appel, Kenneth. "The Why and How of a Preventive Program in Mental Health."

JCEP 16 (Dec. 1954):405-12.

Arthur, G., R. B. Ellsworth, and D. Kroeker. "Readmission of Released Mental Patients: A Research Study." *Social Work* 13 (1968):78-84.

Aviram, Uri, and Steven P. Segal. "Exclusion of the Mentally Ill: Reflection on an Old Problem in a New Context." *Archives of General Psychiatry* 29 (July 1973):126-31.

Ayd, F., ed. *Medical, Moral, and Legal Issues in Mental Health Care.* Baltimore: Williams and Wilkins, 1974.

Barton, Walter E. "The Future of the Mental Hospital." *Ment H* 13 (July 1962):368-75.

_____, "Vanishing Americans—Mental Hospital Administrators and Commissioners." *Ment H* 13 (Jan. 1962):55-61.

_____, "Trends in Community Mental Health Programs." *Hosp & Comm Psych* 17 (Sept. 1966):253-58.

Becker, A., and H. C. Schulberg. "Phasing out State Hospitals—a Psychiatric Dilemma." *New England Journal of Medicine* 296 (1976):255-61.

Bellak, Leopold, ed. *Handbook of Community Psychiatry and Community Mental Health.* New York: Grune and Stratton, 1964.

Berne, Eric. *Transactional Analysis in Psychotherapy.* New York: Grove Press, 1961.

_____, *Games People Play.* New York: Grove Press, 1964.

Birnbaum, M. "The Right to Treatment." *American Bar Association Journal* 46 (1960):499-505.

Blain, Daniel. "Twenty-Five Years of Hospital and Community Psychiatry, 1945-1970." *Hosp & Comm Psych* 26 (Sept. 1975):605-09.

Blasko, John H. "Action for Intensive Treatment." *Ment H* 12 (July 1961):24-26.

Bockoven, J. Sanbourne. "Community Psychiatry: A Growing Source of Social Confusion." *Psychiatry Digest* 29 (Mar.1968):51-60.

Bockoven, J. Sanbourne, Anna R. Pandiscio, and Harry C. Solomon. "Social Adjustments of Patients in the Community Three Years After Commitment to the Boston Psychopathic Hospital." *MH* 40 (1956):353-74.

Bolman, William M. "Theoretical and Empirical Bases of Community Mental Health." *AJP* 124 (Oct. 1967):8-13.

_____, "Community Control of the Community Mental Health Center." *AJP* 129 (Aug. 1972):173-86.

Bolman, William M., and J. C. Westman. "Prevention of Mental Disorder: An Overview of Current Programs." *AJP* 123 (Mar. 1967):1058-68.

Bombard, Lenore. "House of Care." Detroit: Bombard Lenore, 1977. Mimeographed.

Braceland, Francis L. "The Relationship of Psychiatry to Medicine." *Psychiatry Digest* 29 (Apr. 1969):12-16.

Brady, John Paul, and H. K. H. Brodie. *Controversy in Psychiatry.* Philadelphia: W. B. Saunders, 1978. A massive volume that updates research on the major problems of contemporary psychiatric practice.

Braginsky, Benjamin M., Dorothea D. Braginsky, and Kenneth Ring. *Methods of Madness: The Mental Hospital as a Last Resort.* New York: Holt, Rinehart and Winston. 1969.

Brand, Jeanne L. "The National Mental Health Act of 1946: A Retrospect." *Bulletin of the History of Medicine* 39 (1965):231-45.

Brickman, Harry R. "Community Mental Health—Means or Ends?" *Psychiatry Digest* 27 (June 1967):43-50.

Brill, H. "The Future of the Mental Hospital and Its Patients." *Psychiatric Annals* 5 (1975):352-59.

Buell, G. J., and W. A. Anthony. "Demographic Characteristics as Predictors of Recidivism and Posthospital Employment." *Journal of Counseling Psychology* 20 (July 1973):361-65.

Bullough, B., and V. A. Bullough. *Poverty, Ethnic Identity, and Health Care.* New York: Meredith, 1972.

Caplan, Gerald. *An Approach to Community Mental Health.* New York: Grune and Stratton, 1961.

———. *Principles of Preventive Psychiatry.* New York: Basic Books, 1964. An application of public health principles to psychiatry.

"The Changing Mental Hospital: Emerging Alternatives." *Hosp & Comm Psych* 25 (June 1974):386-92.

Chase, Janet. "Where Have All the Patients Gone?" *Human Behavior* (Oct. 1973):14-21.

Chu, Franklin D., and Sharland Trotter. *The Madness Establishment.* New York: Grossman, 1974.

Clow, Hollis E. "Individualizing the Care of the Aging." *AJP* 110 (1953):460-64.

Cochran, B. "Where Is My Home? The Closing of State Mental Hospitals." *Hosp & Comm Psych* 25 (June 1974):393-401.

Cohen, Leon. "How to Reverse Chronic Behavior." *Ment H* 15 (Jan. 1964):39-41.

Cumming, Elaine. "Three Issues Affecting Partnership Among Mental Health Agencies." *Hosp & Comm Psych* 22 (Feb. 1971):33-37.

Cunningham, M. K., W. Botwinik, J. Dolson, and A. A. Weickert. "Community Placement of Released Mental Patients: A Five Year Study." *Social Work* 14 (1969):54-61.

Deane, William N. "Democracy and Rehabilitation of the Mentally Ill." *Archives of General Psychiatry* 9 (July 1963):1-7.

"The Discharged Chronic Mental Patient." *Medical World* 15 (Apr. 12, 1974): 47-58.

Dohrenwend, B. P. *Social Status and Psychological Disorder.* New York: John Wiley, 1969.

Donaldson, Kenneth. *Insanity Inside out.* New York: Crown, 1976.

Doniger, Joan, Naomi D. Rothwell, and Robert Cohen. "Case Study of a Halfway House." *Ment H* 14 (Apr. 1963):193-99.

Drubin, Lester. "Current Practices and Possible Pitfalls." *Ment H* 11 (Jan. 1960):26-28.

Dunham, H. Warren. "Community Psychiatry—the Newest Therapeutic Bandwagon." *Archives of General Psychiatry* 12 (Mar. 1965):303-13.

Dunham, H. W., and S. K. Weinberg. *The Culture of a State Mental Hospital.* Detroit: Wayne State University Press, 1960.

Ebaugh, Franklin. "Mental Illness—Reversible and Irreversible." *JAMA* 171

(Sept. 26, 1959):377-80.

Ehrlich, D., and M. A. Sabshin. "A Study of Sociotherapeutically Oriented Psychiatrists." *American Journal of Orthopsychiatry* 34 (Apr. 1964):469-80.

Erickson, R. C. "Outcome Studies in Mental Hospitals: A Review." *Psychological Bulletin* 82 (1975):519-40.

Ewalt, Jack R. "Needs of the Mentally Ill." *Ment H* 12 (Feb. 1961):12-15.

_____. "Organizing to Achieve Progressive Treatment." *Ment H* 15 (Jan. 1964): 5-7.

_____. "Presidential Address: Services for the Mentally Ill—Rational or Irrational." *Ment H* 15 (Feb. 1964):63-66.

"The Expanding Vistas of Mental Health Services." *Hosp & Comm Psych* 17 (Jan. 1966):13-15.

Fairweather, George W., ed. *Social Psychology in Treating Mental Illness: An Experimental Approach.* New York: John Wiley, 1964.

Fairweather, George W., David H. Sanders, Hugo Maynard, and David L. Cressler, with Dorothy S. Bleck. *Community Life for the Mentally Ill: An Alternative to Institutional Care.* Chicago: Aldine, 1969.

Faris, Robert E. L., and H. Warren Dunham. *Mental Disorders in Urban Areas.* Chicago: University of Chicago Press, 1939.

Feibleman, J. *Biosocial Factors in Mental Illness.* Springfield, Ill.: Charles C. Thomas, 1962.

Feldman, Saul. "Ideas and Issues in Community Mental Health." *Hosp & Comm Psych* 22 (Nov. 1971):325-29.

Felix, Robert H. "Evolution of Community Mental Health Concepts." *AJP* 113 (1957):673-79.

_____. "Community Mental Health: A Federal Perspective." *AJP* 121 (1964): 428-32.

Fischer, Ames, and Morton Weinstein. "Mental Hospitals, Prestige, and the Image of Enlightenment." *Archives of General Psychiatry* 25 (July 1971): 41-48.

Fleishman, Martin. "Will the Real Third Revolution Please Stand up?" *AJP* 124 (1968):1260-62.

"Former Mental Patients a Source of Pity and Anger on Long Island." *New York Times.* Jan. 1, 1978, p. 22.

Forsyth, R. P., and G. W. Fairweather. "Psychotherapeutic and Other Hospital Treatment Criteria: The Dilemma." *Journal of Abnormal and Social Psychology* 62 (1961):598-604.

Fowlkes, Martha R. "Business as Usual at the State Mental Hospital." *Psychiatry* 38 (Feb. 1975):55-64.

Freedman, Alfred M. "Historical and Political Roots of the Community Mental Health Centers Act." *American Journal of Orthopsychiatry* 37 (Apr. 1967):487-94.

Freeman, H. E., and O. G. Simmons. *The Mental Patient Comes Home.* New York: John Wiley, 1963.

"From Peonage to Pay." *Behavior Today* 9 (1974):331-32, 337-39.

Funkhouser, J., and E. Lantz. "Mental Health: A Glimmer of Statistical Encouragement." *Virginia Medical Monthly* 89 (1962):702-04.

"The Future of the Public Mental Hospital." *Hosp & Comm Psych* 27 (Jan. 1976):15-17.

"The Future Role of the State Hospital." *Hosp & Comm Psych* 25 (June 1974):383-85.

Garber, Robert S. "The Relationship of Psychiatry to Medicine." *Psychiatry Digest* 29 (Aug. 1969):11-15.

Ginzberg, Raphael. "Geriatric Ward Psychiatry." *AJP* 110 (1953):296-300.

Goffman, Erving. *Asylums.* Garden City, N. Y.: Anchor Books, 1961. A classic sociological study of the mental hospital milieu.

Gordon, Hiram, and Clarence Groth. "Mental Patients Wanting to Stay in the Hospital." *Archives of General Psychiatry* 4 (Feb. 1961):124-30.

Goshen, Charles E. "Current Status of Mental Health Manpower." *Archives of General Psychiatry* 5 (Sept. 1961):266-75.

Graham, Thomas F., and James W. Zingery. "Turnover of Psychiatric Attendants." *JCEP* 22 (July 1961):95-105.

Greco, Joseph T. "Action for Community Facilities." *Ment H* 12 (May 1961): 13-15.

Greenberg, Joel. "How Accurate Is Psychiatry?" *Science News* 112 (July 9, 1977):28-29.

_____, "Preventing Emotional Illness." *Science News* 112 (Sept. 24, 1977): 202-03.

_____, "Is Schizophrenia in the Blood?" *Science News* 114 (July 8, 1978):29.

Greenblatt, M., and E. Glazier. "Phasing out of Mental Hospitals in the United States." *AJP* 132 (1975):1135-40.

Greenblatt, M., R. F. Moore, R. S. Albert, and M. H. Solomon. *The Prevention of Hospitalization.* New York: Grune and Stratton, 1963.

Grinker, Roy R., Sr. "Psychiatry Rides Madly in All Directions." *Archives of General Psychiatry* 10 (Mar. 1964):228-37.

Group for the Advancement of Psychiatry. *The Social Responsibility of Psychiatry, a Statement of Orientation.* Topeka, Kan.: Group for the Advancement of Psychiatry, 1950.

_____, *The Dimensions of Community Psychiatry.* New York: Group for the Advancement of Psychiatry, 1968.

_____, *Crisis in Psychiatric Hospitalization.* New York: Group for the Advancement of Psychiatry, 1969.

Gruenberg, E. M. "The Social Breakdown Syndrome—Some Origins." *AJP* 123 (1967):12-20.

Grunebaum, Henry, ed. *The Practice of Community Mental Health.* Boston: Little, Brown, 1970.

Gurel, Lee. "Dimensions of the Therapeutic Milieu: A Study of Mental Hospital Atmosphere." *AJP* 131 (1974):409-14.

Haas, Adolf. "Toward Social Psychiatry." *Ment H* 10 (Apr. 1959):13-15.

Hall, William. "Realistic Goals of Hospitalization—Today and Tomorrow." *Ment H* 15 (Feb. 1964):78-90.

Hammersley, Donald W., and Pat Vosburgh. "Iowa's Shrinking Mental Hospital Population." *Hosp & Comm Psych* 18 (Apr. 1967):106-16.

Harris, Thomas A. *I'm OK—You're OK; A Practical Guide to Transactional Analysis.* New York: Harper and Row, 1969.

Heckel, R., C. Perry, and P. G. Reeves. *The Discharged Mental Patient*. Columbia: University of South Carolina Press, 1973.

Heckel, R. V., and H. C. Salzberg. "How to Make Your Patients Chronic'" *Ment H* 15 (Jan. 1964):37-38.

Hecker, Arthur O. "The Demise of Large State Hospitals." *Hosp & Comm Psych* 21 (Aug. 1970):261-63.

Hersh, Charles. "Mental Health Services and the Poor." *Psychiatry* 29 (1966): 236-45.

_____, "The Discontent Explosion in Mental Health." *American Psychologist* 23 (1968):497-506.

_____, "From Mental Health to Social Action: Clinical Psychology in Historical Perspective." *American Psychologist* 24 (1969):909-16.

_____, "Social History, Mental Health, and Community Control." *American Psychologist* 27 (Aug. 1972):749-54.

Herz, Marvin I. "The Therapeutic Community: A Critique." *Hosp & Comm Psych* 23 (Mar. 1972):69-72.

Hoch, Paul H., and Joseph Zubin. *The Evaluation of Psychiatric Treatment*. New York: Grune and Stratton, 1964.

Hollingshead, A. B., and F. C. Redlich. *Social Class and Mental Illness: A Community Study*. New York: John Wiley and Sons, 1958. A well-known classic analysis.

Honigfeld, G., and R. Gillis. "The Role of Institutionalization in the Natural History of Schizophrenia." *Diseases of the Nervous System* 28 (Oct. 1967):660-63.

Hubbs, Roy S. "Rehabilitation Means Restoration. The Sheltered Workshop." *Ment H* 11 (Apr. 1960):7-12.

Hunt, Raymond. "Social Class and Mental Illness: Some Implications for Clinical Theory and Practice." *AJP* 116 (1960):1065-69.

Hunt, Robert C., and Hyman M. Forstenzer. "The New York State Community Mental Health Services Act: Its Birth and Early Development." *AJP* 114 (1957):680-85.

"Influx of Ex-Mental Patients Upsetting Long Beach." *New York Times*. Dec. 9, 1973, p. 50.

Jackson, Jay. "Consensus and Conflict in Treatment Organizations." *Hosp & Comm Psych* 19 (June 1968):161-67.

Jacobson, A. "A Critical Look at the Community Psychiatric Clinic." *AJP* 124 (1967):14-20.

Janov, Arthur. *Primal Scream; Primal Therapy. The Cure for Neurosis*. New York: Dell, 1970.

Joint Commission on Mental Illness and Health. *Action for Mental Health*. New York: Basic Books, 1961. The summarizing report of the Commission, with emphasis on the need for community-based services.

Jones, Maxwell. "Community Care for Chronic Mental Patients: The Need for Reassessment." *Hosp & Comm Psych* 26 (Feb. 1975):94-98.

Jones, M., and E. M. Bonn. "From Therapeutic Community to Self-Sufficient Community." *Hosp & Comm Psych* 24 (Oct. 1973):675-80.

Kellert, Stephen. "The Lost Community in Community Psychiatry." *Psychiatry* 34 (May 1971):168-79.

Keniston, Kenneth. "How Community Mental Health Stamped out the Riots (1968-1978)." *Transaction* 5 (July-Aug. 1968):21-29.

Kennedy, J. F. "Message from the President of the United States Relative to Mental Illness and Mental Retardation: February 3, 1963." *AJP* 120 (1964):729-37.

Kirk, Stuart A., and Mark E. Therrien. "Community Mental Health Myths and the Fate of Former Hospitalized Patients." *Psychiatry* 38 (Aug. 1975):209-17.

Klerman, G. L. "Psychotropic Hedonism vs Pharmacological Calvinism." *Hastings Center Report* 2 (1972):1-3.

Kolb, L. C. "Community Mental Health Centers: Some Issues in Their Transition from Concept to Reality." *Hosp & Comm Psych* 19 (Nov. 1968):335-40.

Korson, S. M. "Evolution of State Mental Hospital from Custodial Care to Intensive Psychiatric Treatment." *Journal of the Iowa Medical Society* 62 (1972):421-24.

Kraft, A. M., P. R. Binner, and B. A. Dickey. "The Community Mental Health Program and the Longer-Stay Patient." *Archives of General Psychiatry* 16 (Jan. 1967):64-70.

Kramer, B. M. *Day Hospital: A Study of Partial Hospitalization in Psychiatry.* New York: Grune and Stratton, 1962.

Kubie, L. "Pitfalls of Community Psychiatry." *Archives of General Psychiatry* 18 (Mar. 1968):251-66.

Kuehn, J. L., and F. M. Crinella. "Sensitivity Training: Interpersonal Overkill and Other Problems." *AJP* 126 (1969):840-45.

Laing, R. D. *The Divided Self.* London: Tavistock, 1959.

Lamb, H. Richard. "Chronic Psychiatric Patients in the Day Hospital." *Archives of General Psychiatry* 17 (Nov. 1967):615-21.

———, "Release of Chronic Psychiatric Patients into the Community." *Archives of General Psychiatry* 19 (July 1968):38-44.

Lamb, H. Richard, and Victor Goertzel. "Discharged Mental Patients—Are they Really in the Community?" *Archives of General Psychiatry* 24 (Jan. 1971):29-34.

———, "The Demise of the State Hospital—a Premature Obituary?" *Archives of General Psychiatry* 26 (June 1972):489-95.

Lapenna, Lino M. "Delineating the Therapeutic Community." *Ment H* 14 (July 1963):369-74.

"Laying the Foundations for an Open Mental Hospital." *Ment H* 9 (Feb. 1958):10-12.

Lehrman, N. S. "Do Our Hospitals Help Make Acute Schizophrenia Chronic?" *Diseases of the Nervous System* 22 (Sept. 1961):489-93.

———, "Follow-up of Brief and Prolonged Hospitalization." *Comprehensive Psychiatry* 4 (1961):227-40.

Levinson, D. J., and E. B. Gallagher. *Patienthood in the Mental Hospital.* Boston: Houghton Mifflin, 1964.

Levy, Leo. "The State Mental Hospital in Transition: A Review of Principles." *Community Mental Health Journal* 1 (Winter 1965):353-56.

Levy, Leo, and Robert Blachly. "Counteracting Hospital Habituation." *Ment H*

16 (Mar. 1965):114-16.

Lieberman, M. A., I. D. Yalom, and M. B. Miles. *Encounter Groups: First Facts*. New York: Basic Books, 1973.

Linder, Marjorie P., and David Landy. "Post-Discharge Experience and Vocational Rehabilitation Needs of Psychiatric Patients." *MH* 42 (1958):29-44.

Linn, L. "The Fourth Psychiatric Revolution." *AJP* 124 (1968):1043-48.

Low, Abraham. *Mental Health Through Will Training*. 16th edition. Boston: Christopher Publishing House, 1950.

Ludwig, Arnold. *Treating the Treatment Failures. The Challenge of Chronic Schizophrenia*. New York: Grune and Stratton, 1971.

―――, "The Proper Domain of Psychiatry." *Psychiatry Digest* 36 (Jan. 1976): 15-18, 23-24.

Ludwig, A., and F. Farrelly. "The Code of Chronicity." *Archives of General Psychiatry* 15 (Dec. 1966):562-68.

Lynch, M. Gardner. "Some Issues Raised in the Training of Paraprofessional Personnel as Clinic Therapists." *AJP* 126 (1970):1473-79.

Masserman, J., ed. *Current Psychiatric Therapies*. New York: Grune and Stratton, 1966.

May, Rollo. *Existence*. New York: Basic Books, 1958.

McGarry, A. L., and H. A. Kaplan. "Overview: Current Trends in Mental Health Law." *AJP* 130 (1973):621-30.

McPartland, T. S., and R. H. Richart. "Social and Clinical Outcomes of Psychiatric Treatment." *Archives of General Psychiatry* 14 (Feb. 1966):179-84.

Mechanic, David. "Some Factors in Identifying and Defining Mental Illness." *MH* 46 (1962):66-74.

―――, *Mental Health and Social Policy*. Englewood Cliffs, N. J.: Prentice-Hall, 1969.

Meisel, A. "Rights of the Mentally Ill: The Gulf Between Theory and Reality." *Hosp & Comm Psych* 26 (June 1975):349-53.

Meislin, Jack. "The Psychiatric Sheltered Workshop in the Rehabilitation of the Mentally Ill." *Archives of Physical Medicine and Rehabilitation* 35 (Apr. 1954):224-27.

Mendell, W. M., and G. A. Green. *The Therapeutic Management of Psychological Illness*. New York: Basic Books, 1967.

Mental Health Programs of the Forty-Eight States. A Report to the Governors Conference. Chicago: Council of State Governments, 1950.

Michaux, W. W., M. M. Katz, A. A. Kurland, and K. H. Gansereit. *The First Year Out*. Baltimore: Johns Hopkins University Press, 1969.

Mosher, Loren R. "Recent Trends in Psychosocial Treatment of Schizophrenia." *American Journal of Psychoanalysis* 32 (1972):9-15.

Mosher, Loren R., and Alma Z. Menn. "Community Residential Treatment for Schizophrenia: Two Year Followup Data." San Jose, Ca.: Loren and Menn, Oct. 17, 1977. Mimeographed.

Mosher, Loren R., Alma Menn, and Susan M. Matthews. "Soteria: Evaluation of a Home-based Treatment for Schizophremia." *American Journal of Orthopsychiatry* 45 (Apr. 1975):455-67.

Mosher, L., A. Reifman, and A. Menn. "Characteristics of Non-Professionals Serving as Primary Therapists for Acute Schizophrenics." *Hosp & Comm*

Psych 24 (June 1973):391-95.

"My Dog, the Therapist." *Newsweek.* Apr. 22, 1974, p. 80.

"New Horizons in Psychiatric Treatment." *Hosp & Comm Psych* 19 (Jan. 1968):1-8.

"The New Snake Pits." *Newsweek.* May 15, 1978, pp. 93-94.

"New State Policy to Slow Mental Patients' Release." *New York Times.* Apr. 28, 1974, pp. 1, 32.

Nunnally, J. C. *Popular Conceptions of Mental Health.* New York: Holt, Rinehart and Winston, 1961.

Offer, D., and M. Sabshin. *Normality: Theoretical and Clinical Concepts of Mental Health.* New York: Basic Books, 1964.

O'Neill, Francis J. "The Public Mental Hospital in Transition." *Psychiatry Digest* 29 (Apr. 1968):25-33.

Osmond, Humphrey. "The Medical Model in Psychiatry." *Hosp & Comm Psych* 21 (Sept. 1970): 275-81.

Overholser, Winfred. "The Recommendations of the Governors' Conference." *JCEP* 15 (June 1954):135-50.

Ozarin, L. D., and A. I. Levenson. "The Future of the Public Mental Hospital." *AJP* 125 (1969):1647-52.

Palmer, Mary B. "Social Rehabilitation for Mental Patients." *MH* 42 (1958):24-28.

Pasamanick, Benjamin. "A Survey of Mental Disease in an Urban Population." *Archives of General Psychiatry* 5 (Aug. 1961):151-55.

Pasamanick. B., F. R. Scarpitti, and S. Dinitz. *Schizophrenics in the Community.* New York: Appleton-Century-Crofts, 1967.

"The Patient in the Hospital." *Ment H* 13 (Feb. 1962):73-89.

"Patients on Long Island Against Move to Community." *New York Times.* Jan. 1. 1978, p. 22.

Pattison, E. M., and J. R. Eplers. "A Developmental View of Mental Health Manpower Trends." *Hosp & Comm Psych* 23 (Nov. 1972):325-28.

Paul, Gordon L. "Chronic Mental Patient: Current Status—Future Directions." *Psychological Bulletin* 71 (1969):81-94.

Paul, Gordon L., and Robert J. Lentz. *Psychosocial Treatment of Chronic Mental Patients.* Cambridge, Mass.: Harvard University Press, 1977.

Plog, Stanley C., and Robert B. Edgerton, eds. *Changing Perspectives in Mental Illness.* New York: Holt, Rinehart and Winston, 1969.

Polak, Paul. "The Irrelevance of Hospital Treatment to the Patient's Social System." *Hosp & Comm Psych* 22 (Aug. 1971):255-56.

Polak, Paul, and Maxwell Jones. "The Psychiatric Nonhospital: A Model for Change." *Community Mental Health Journal* 9 (Summer 1973):123-32.

Price, R., and B. Denner, eds. *The Making of a Mental Patient.* New York: Holt, Rinehart and Winston, 1973.

Prigmore, C. S., and P. R. Davis. "Wyatt v Stickney: Rights of the Committed." *Social Work* 18 (1973):10-18.

Rakusin, John M., and Louis B. Fierman, "Five Assumptions for Treating Chronic Psychotics." *Ment H* 14 (Mar. 1963):140-48.

Raush, Harold L., and Charlotte L. Raush. *The Halfway House Movement. A Search for Sanity.* New York: Appleton-Century-Crofts, 1968.

Reich, Robert. "Care of the Chronically Mentally Ill—a National Disgrace." *AJP* 130 (1973):911-12.

Reich, Robert, and Lloyd Siegel. "Psychiatry Under Siege: The Chronically Mentally Ill Shuffle to Oblivion." *Psychiatric Annals* 3 (Nov. 11, 1973):38-55.

Rennie, Thomas A. C., Temple Burling, and Luther E. Woodward. *Vocational Rehabilitation of Psychiatric Patients*. New York: Commonwealth Fund, 1950.

Research in the Service of Mental Health. Report of the Research Task Force of the National Institute of Mental Health. Washington, D. C.: U. S. Government Printing Office, 1975.

Riessman, F., J. Cogen, and A. Pearl, eds. *Mental Health of the Poor*. New York: The Free Press, 1964.

Riessman, F., and E. Hollowitz. "The Neighborhood Service Center: An Innovation in Preventive Psychiatry." *AJP* 123 (1967):1408-12.

Roberts, Leigh M., Seymour L. Halleck, and Martin B. Loeb. *Community Psychiatry*. Madison: University of Wisconsin Press, 1966.

Robinson, Robert L. "New Perspectives on Mental Patient Care." *Ment H* 12 (Apr. 1961):11-14.

_____. "The First Mental Hospital Institute: A Reminiscence." *Hosp & Comm Psych* 21 (Oct. 1970):317-19.

Rome, Howard P. "Psychiatry and Changing Social Values." *Ment H* 16 (Nov. 1965):295-300.

Rosenbaum, C. Peter. *The Meaning of Madness. Symptomatology, Sociology, Biology, and Therapy of the Schizophrenias*. New York: Science House, 1970.

Rosenhan, D. L. "On Being Sane in Insane Places." *Science* 179 (Jan. 19, 1973):250-58.

Rothwell, N. D., and J. M. Doniger. *The Psychiatric Half-Way House*. Springfield, Ill.: Charles C. Thomas, 1966.

Rubin, Bernard, and Arnold Goldberg. "An Investigation of Openness in the Psychiatric Hospital." *Archives of General Psychiatry* 8 (Mar. 1963):269-76.

Ryan, William. "Emotional Disorders as a Social Problem: Implications for Mental Health Programs." *American Journal of Orthopsychiatry* 41 (July 1971):638-45.

Sabshin, M. "The Boundaries of Community Psychiatry." *Social Science Review* 40 (Sept. 1966):246-54.

Sandall, H., T. T. Hawley, and G. C. Gordon. "St Louis Community Homes Program: Graduated Support for Long-Term Care." *AJP* 132 (1975):617-22.

Sanders, D. H. "Innovative Environments in the Community: A Life for the Chronic Patient." *Schizophrenia Bulletin* 6 (Fall 1972):49-59.

Saper, B. "Current Trends in Comprehensive Community Mental Health Services." *MH* 51 (1967):270-74.

Schleff, Thomas J. *Being Mentally Ill: A Sociological Theory*. Chicago: Aldine, 1966.

Scherl, Donald J. "Changing Influences on the Delivery of Mental Health

Services and the Role of the State Mental Hospital." *Hosp & Comm Psych* 25 (June 1974):375-78.

Schroeder, Sarah F. "The Place of Social Work in the Treatment of the Hospitalized Mental Patient." *JCEP* 20 (Dec. 1959):361-65.

Schulberg, Herbert C. "The Mental Hospital in the Era of Human Services." *Hosp Comm Psych* 24 (July 1973):467-72.

Schulberg, Herbert C., and Frank Baker. "The Changing Mental Hospital: A Progress Report." *Hosp & Comm Psych* 20 (June 1969):159-65.

_____, *The Mental Hospital and Human Services.* New York: Behavioral Publications, 1975.

Schulberg, Herbert C., Ralph Notman, and Edward Bookin. "Treatment Services at a Mental Hospital in Transition." *AJP* 124 (1967):506-13.

Schwartz, M. S., and C. G. Schwartz. *Social Approaches to Mental Patient Care.* New York: Columbia University, 1964.

Schwartz, R. A. "Psychiatry's Drift Away from Medicine." *AJP* 131 (1974): 129-33.

"Scrutinizing Community Mental Health." *Science News* 109 (Apr. 10, 1976): 232.

Segal, Steven, and Uri Aviram. *The Mentally Ill in Community-Based Sheltered Care.* New York: John Wiley and Sons, 1978.

Seigler, Miriam, and Humphry Osmond. *Models of Madness, Models of Medicine.* New York: Macmillan, 1974.

Slovenko, Ralph. *Psychiatry and Law.* Boston: Little, Brown, 1973.

Smith, Harvey L. "Mental Hospital Organization: Challenge and Response." *MH* 15 (Feb. 1964):67-71.

Smith, W. G., and D. W. Hart. "Community Mental Health: A Noble Failure?" *Hosp & Comm Psych* 26 (Sept. 1975):581-83.

Smith, W. G., J. Kaplan, and D. Sicker. "Community Mental Health and the Severely Disturbed Patient: First Admission Outcomes." *Archives of General Psychiatry* 30 (May 1974):693-96.

Sobey, Francine. *The Nonprofessional Revolution in Mental Health.* New York: Columbia University Press, 1970.

Solomon, Harry C. "Some Historical Perspectives." *Ment H* 9 (Feb. 1958):5-7.

_____, "Half a Century of Hospital Psychiatry." *Hosp & Comm Psych* 19 (Dec. 1968):367-71.

Sommer, R., and H. Osmond. "Symptoms of Institutional Care." *Social Problems* 8 (1961):254-63.

Spiro, Herzl R. "On Beyond Mental Health Centers." *Archives of General Psychiatry* 21 (Dec. 1969):646-54.

Srole, Leo, Thomas S. Langer, Stanley T. Michael, Marvin K. Opler, and Thomas A. C. Rennie. *Mental Health in the Metropolis.* New York: McGraw-Hill, 1962. An important epidemiological study.

Stein, Leonard, and Mary Ann Test. *Alternatives to Mental Hospital Treatment.* New York: Plenum Press, 1978. A good study of recent innovative community projects.

Stewart, Alex, H. G. LaFave, F. Grunberg, and M. Herjanic. "Problems in Phasing out a Large Public Psychiatric Hospital." *AJP* 125 (1968):82-88.

Stotland, E., and A. L. Kobler. *Life and Death of a Mental Hospital* Seattle:

University of Washington Press, 1965.

Stuart, Richard B. *Trick or Treatment: How and When Psychotherapy Fails.* Champaign, Ill: Research Press, 1970.

Susser, M. *Community Psychiatry: Epidemiologic and Social Themes.* New York: Random House, 1968.

Tallman, Frank F. "The State Mental Hospital in Transition." *AJP* 116 (1960): 818-24.

Tancredi, L., J. Lieb, and A. Slaby. *Legal Issues in Psychiatric Care.* New York: Harper and Row, 1975.

Tarumianz, M. A. "State Mental Health Programming for the 1960's." *Ment H* 13 (Mar. 1962):176-78.

"Ticklish Treatment." *Newsweek.* July 30, 1973, pp. 74-75.

Tischler, G. L. "The Effects of Consumer Control on the Delivery of Services." *American Journal of Orthopsychiatry* 41 (Apr. 1971):501-05.

Townsend, John Marshall. *Cultural Conceptions and Mental Illness.* Chicago: University of Chicago Press, 1978.

Trotter, Robert J. "Preventing Psychopathology." *Science News* 108 (Aug. 9, 1975):90-91.

_____. "Schizophrenia: A Cruel Chain of Events." *Science News* 111 (June 18, 1977):394-95.

Ullmann, L. P. *Institution and Outcome: A Comparative Study of Psychiatric Hospitals.* New York: Pergamon Press, 1967.

Vail, D. J. *Dehumanization and the Institutional Career.* Springfield, Ill.: Charles C. Thomas, 1966.

Wanklin, J. M., D. F. Fleming, C. Buck, and G. E. Hobbs. "Discharge and Readmissions Among Mental Hospital Patients." *AMA Archives of Neurology and Psychiatry* 76 (1956):660-69.

Wayne, George J. "An Evaluation of New Trends in Psychiatric Hospitals." *Ment H* 13 (Jan. 1962):10-15.

_____. "The Special Contribution of a Halfway House." *Ment H* 14 (Aug. 1963):440-42.

Wechsler, Henry. "The Self-Help Organization in the Mental Health Field." *JNMD* 130 (1960):297-314.

Weisman, G., A. Feirstein, and C. Thomas. "Three Day Hospitalization: A Model for Intensive Intervention." *Archives of General Psychiatry* 21 (Nov. 1969):620-29.

"Where Is my Home? The Closing of State Mental Hospitals." *Hosp & Comm Psych* 25 (June 1974):393-401.

Whittington, H. G. "Social and Community Psychiatry: Some Hard Questions Face Us." *AJP* 126 (1970):1487-88.

Yolles, Stanley F. "The Right to Treatment." *Psychiatry Digest* 27 (Oct. 1967):7-13.

_____. "Social Policy and the Mentally Ill." *Hosp & Comm Psych* 20 (Feb. 1969):37-42.

INDEX

ABOUT THE AUTHOR

LELAND V. BELL earned his undergraduate degree at Wayne State University, his master's at Pennsylvania State University, and his doctorate at West Virginia University. He also studied at New York University and the University of Michigan. He has had extensive experience as both college teacher and researcher.

Dr. Bell's interests and publications embrace the history of psychiatry, political extremism, art, old age and death, and labor. He has conducted seminars and taught courses on the history of mental health care at many universities and colleges, and is currently professor of history at Central State University in Ohio.